P9-CQE-066

The WEALTH CREATORS

GERALD GUNDERSON

The WEALTH CREATORS

AN ENTREPRENEURIAL HISTORY
OF THE UNITED STATES

T·T

TRUMAN TALLEY BOOKS / E. P. DUTTON

NEW YORK

Published in the United States by Truman Talley Books • E. P. Dutton,
a division of NAL Penguin Inc.,
2 Park Avenue, New York, N.Y. 10016.

Published simultaneously in Canada by
Fitzhenry and Whiteside, Limited, Toronto.

Library of Congress Cataloging-in-Publication Data

Gunderson, Gerald.
The wealth creators.
"Truman Talley books."
Bibliography: p.
Includes index.
1. Entrepreneurship—United States—History.
2. Wealth—United States—History.   3. United States—
Economic conditions.   I. Title.
HB615.G86   1989   338'.04'0973   88-30963
ISBN: 0-525-24729-7

DESIGNED BY EARL TIDWELL

1 3 5 7 9 10 8 6 4 2

First Edition

This book is dedicated to Douglass C. North,
Luce Professor, Law and Liberty,
Washington University in St. Louis—
entrepreneur, scholar, and mentor.

Contents

Contents

The WEALTH CREATORS

1

Founding the Colonies

Three hundred years ago nothing suggested the American Colonies could ever become a major world power. There were fewer than 200,000 Americans, about as many as are now living in Dayton, Ohio, or Fresno, California. Dispersal along more than 1,000 miles of the Atlantic Coast further reduced their influence. The typical colonist could not afford goods and services worth $1,000 per year in today's prices. And the total purchasing power of all colonists in the late seventeenth century was less than that of a middling community of 20,000 Americans today.

Obviously the economy has undergone an enormous transformation since the late 1600s. Population alone has increased more than a thousand times, far outpacing that of any other major economy. Also the supply of goods and services an average American

commands is at least ten times greater now. Today's economy, therefore, is the union of these two forces, more than 10,000 times larger
than its seventeenth-century predecessor. In other words, an entire
year's output in Colonial America could be turned out in the first
fifteen minutes of a contemporary workday.

An expansion that goes on this long, compounding to such huge
dimensions, cannot be explained as a run of good luck. Profoundly
powerful—and tenacious—forces had to be working. But all the
standard explanations suggested for this astounding expansion fail to
portray anywhere near the sustained power necessary. They invariably exhaust their influence within a decade or so, leaving most of
the three centuries unanswered. They usually are a variant of the
abundant-resource school; that is, the huge increase in gross national
product (GNP) is explained by a large supply of land, labor, or
capital, one of the basic inputs in the economy. One popular variant
attributes America's growth to unusually rich natural resources.
Such an explanation begs the question, however, by neglecting to
explain what caused the (equally perplexing) expansion in that input.
Most natural resources were useless—and thus ignored—for thousands of years previous to Columbus and, even then, were only
gradually put to work. Likewise, although America benefited from
one of the largest immigrations in human history, most arrived after
growth was obviously creating the opportunities to attract the new-
comers.

The most common explanation of modern growth, as well as an
example of the abundant-resource school, is the Protestant ethic.
This approach was articulated by Max Weber about a century ago,
but the concept has such instinctive appeal that most apply it without
realizing its pedigree. The Protestant ethic looks to such qualities as
hard work and thrift to explain growth. There's no doubt that, other
things being equal, such qualities yield greater output. Economists
would say that these traits increase the supply of labor and capital,
respectively, and thus support more production. It is also true that
many individuals pursuing this strategy provided comfort for their
family and security for old age.

Our suspicions that the Protestant ethic or similar models are
only a branch line of the main track of economic growth have been

confirmed by modern scholarship. Most growth results from improved knowledge creating new forms of resources rather than from working and saving expanding the existing categories. This distinction is evident in the huge gap between contemporary opportunities and the types of resources employed in Colonial America.[1]

Suppose that the American colonists had worked sixteen hours a day and reinvested 50 percent of their earnings—in other words, practiced the Protestant ethic with a vengeance. Within decades, let alone three centuries, such unusual behavior would have increased the stock of labor and capital relative to natural resources and current institutional and technological opportunities. This would have forced the return to working and saving into diminishing returns. It would also have made the other elements of the productive process correspondingly more scarce. Thus, carried very far, the Protestant ethic implies a Malthusian world. It would drag a society down into the same dismal cul-de-sac as an intensifying shortage of natural resources. It may be a good guide for individuals to teach their children, but it is a poor device to explain the history of developed economies.

Toward Growth

Life soon teaches us that individuals cannot expect a free lunch. Economic growth, however, provides an economy with free lunches by expanding resources and opportunities. When that immense impact is appreciated, our portrayal of history will be drastically changed. For the most part historical accounts have been built on the premise that there is no free lunch. Assuming that the central question is how to parcel out a fixed supply, historians have focused on each society's tactics for coping with allocation.[2] To continue the lunch analogy, one asks who gets the largest salad and whether the sandwiches are roast beef or peanut butter. But if, as the American experience illustrates, the supply of lunches can expand manyfold, it is appropriate to focus attention on the forces prompting that cornucopia rather than to compare alternative table arrangements.

Americans have been aware that their political system departed

—— 3 ——

dramatically from traditional European governments and offered a promising model to newer societies. Yet over the long term, the quiet evolution in the American economy has clearly outdistanced the effect of the Revolution and the adoption of constitutional government on American society. Contrast the extent to which the American economy would have developed under continuing British rule with that of another hypothetical American society, which won independence from the Revolution but ceased growing. An appropriate comparison might be between the present United States at the living standards of contemporary Canada—which remained in the British Empire after 1776—and those prevailing in the United States about 1790 after independence and the Constitution were consummated. This contrast shows that economic growth expanded opportunities much more than independence, almost to the point of making the latter insignificant by comparison.

Economists have traditionally apportioned economic resources into three basic categories: land, labor, and capital. The taxonomy was devised centuries ago when each category was closely identified with a particular social class—land with landowners, for example. Economic growth, by mixing the three resources in new applications, has eroded much of the distinction. But the ossified specification of labor is causing particularly damaging mischief. Labor is treated as a direct counterpart to land and capital, even though it is distinguished as being governed by its own interests and emotions. Supervisors quickly learn that while machinery and raw materials can be shoved around to try out new layouts, employees must be approached more judiciously. Workers respond to respect and consultation. Motivation becomes increasingly important as employees such as copywriters and teachers assume greater responsibility in shaping the service. This effect of participation reaches its peak when an entire economy is shaped by such motives, which is to say one organized by markets and private enterprise. Individuals not only create and renew the organizations of the economy, but, as consumers, compel its existence.

About a generation ago some economics textbooks introduced a remedy to the trivialization of human efforts by the old classification of labor. They added a fourth resource, entrepreneurship, which

measured the impact of individuals' creative activities in the economy. Unfortunately, this approach wilted in the lingering shadow of
the Great Depression. Economists, like most of their contemporaries, were preoccupied with the problem of stimulating employment.
Putting people back to work promised more output than raising the
productivity of those already employed.

Recently such public concerns as the competition from foreign
producers have rekindled interest in growth and increasing productivity. This reversed the marketing of public programs. A decade or
two ago promoters of a program played up every possible angle that
might spur some part of the economy. Such demand for employment
effects were believed worthwhile even at the sacrifice of some efficiency. Today, in contrast, the benefits in growth, productivity, innovation, and competitiveness are emphasized; in other words, objectives that frequently use fewer resources.

Leaving entrepreneurship out of the textbooks is pernicious
because students must comprehend economic systems with a vital
part missing. Without an entrepreneurial element an economy would
cease adapting to new circumstances and soon disintegrate. Every
economy, no matter how traditional or tightly regulated, relies on
entrepreneurs for survival. Resourceful plant managers and innovative repairmen, for example, stop the Soviet economy from slipping
into total bureaucratic gridlock.

Denying the entrepreneurial element is akin to a physician's
trying to treat people while denying the existence of a heart. He
might suffice in treating such minor ailments as cuts or sprains or
performing such mechanical procedures as setting broken bones. But
suppose he undertook major surgery assuming that the heart and the
associated circulatory system were insignificant, so that bleeding was
considered a messy but inconsequential side effect. No doubt word
of mouth would drive such a surgeon from practice before the medical board could decertify him.

Thus it is understandable that many otherwise perceptive people have been misled into thinking of an economic system as a
mechanical contraption. If the human element, which imparts initiative or ingenuity in an economic system, is neglected, individuals
would be expected doggedly to pursue their habits, even when they

become self-defeating. One could take advantage of people's failure to respond to incentives to impose public goals. For example, an imposition of minimum wages could compel employers to pay workers more because the employers might not reduce their use of labor even in the face of higher costs. Or if factories in a state were required to give advance notice of layoffs, local employment might rise because other employers considering locating there would not be dissuaded by the prospective cost.

This expectation about behavior contradicts that which is employed in economics, which assumes that raising or lowering the reward for any activity prompts a corresponding increase or decrease in its supply. "Supply-side economics," then, is really just ordinary economics except that its proponents emphasize the power of such incentives. Thus, it is not surprising that "supply-siders" typically believe that entrepreneurship is important. They share with students of entrepreneurship the belief that the information and incentives embodied in prices are crucial in directing effort toward society's most productive ends. They are also leery that public programs might misdirect the creativity and energy that those signals evoke.

Disappointments with public policies have caused increasing doubt that the economy can be managed while neglecting the effects of entrepreneurial behavior. Even those not sympathizing with such implications are more sensitive to the pervasive role that self-interest plays in shaping society. While public programs may nudge individuals in intended directions, they seldom can control them, and frequently misjudge and misdirect their responses. The entrepreneurial instinct seems irrepressible. The heightened appreciation of its importance makes individuals more inclined to trust its unpredictable creativity.

Spotting Entrepreneurs

We can spot entrepreneurs by detecting their primary activity: the creation of additional human opportunities. They devise new technologies and organizations that permit activities which previously were infeasible. Clearly, the automobile is an example of an entrepreneurial creation in that it extended opportunities in shopping, travel, and the choice of a residence. Henry Ford (among others) combined such materials as steel, rubber, and glass into a novel form that yielded more human satisfaction. This demonstrates another symptom of entrepreneurship: the addition of wealth and value to society. The entrepreneur's creation expands the effective reach of others' resources.

Portraying entrepreneurship in this manner extends it well beyond the domain of business, with which it is often associated. It may sound incongruous to speak of entrepreneurship in the arts or government or nonprofit organizations, but to do so only consistently applies the definition. A new charity such as We Are the Children or even a catchy expression such as "Are we having fun yet?" fulfills the prime function of adding value by expanding human opportunities. Much activity that people term *creative* is also entrepreneurial and could be facilitated if it were treated as such.

Another quality alerting us to the operation of entrepreneurship is someone developing an opportunity that others overlook. Most people encountering a frustration write it off as a bad experience and shy away from repetitions. But entrepreneurs are prone to ask, "Can something be made of this?" They find suggestive insights in malfunctions and incongruities. Some entrepreneurs are labeled odd because they see the world so differently. But this novelty can be crucial, suggesting better approaches.

While entrepreneurs dream, they don't just daydream. A third identifying characteristic is that they work persistently to carry out their ideas. No doubt many people have visions that would improve the world—if implemented. But most don't have the energy or the gumption to see them to fruition. Entrepreneurs have a bias for action. They endure the drudgery in anticipation of the rewards. But many also obviously enjoy the challenge for its own sake. They love their work. What others consider as workaholic behavior they treat as recreation, enjoying the challenge more than nearly anything. Entrepreneurship is part of the human trait of identifying oneself by one's own work, along with wanting to do a good job and to make a difference in the world.

Entrepreneurs also can be located by searching beyond the restricted domains within which many people assume they are confined. They are commonly associated with high tech, such as computers and genetic engineering. All careful surveys of contemporary activity, however, report that productive entrepreneurial ventures are spread widely across the economy, with at least as many in declining or mature sectors as there are in the fashionable growth sectors.[3] The media have focused on the latter so much that they have become shorthand for innovation and enterprise. This stereotyping conditions people to misconceived expectations, which inevitably are shattered. Too many have inferred that timely entry into a growth industry, producing a product in intense demand, guarantees success. But very quickly competitors assert themselves and a shakeout occurs. Then those investors who naïvely expected to cash in on growth lose out to those whose products incorporate innovations providing a competitive edge.

Entrepreneurs detect and pursue opportunities throughout the economy, which is to say, wherever the previous limits of human ingenuity can be extended by further innovations. Even well-established commodities such as steel, chickens, and tire recapping undergo changes in costs or substitutes, which prompt entrepreneurs to improve their services. New technology also widens possibilities in established products as, for example, when electronics was recently incorporated into such old standards as sewing machines, wrist watches, and library catalogues. While public attention is attracted by flashy new technologies, a market economy quickly makes them subservient to human wants. Opportunities draw entrepreneurs to innovate across the full spectrum supplying human desires.

A major misconception is that entrepreneurs assume particularly large risks. The bulk of studies show that many shun risky actions and, indeed, often take issue when someone suggests that such behavior is central to their function. The risks in creating a venture seldom occur as a huge, make-or-break decision; rather, a development usually unfolds as continuing, small problems, where mismanagement of an individual opportunity often can be corrected and then recouped by persistence. Many entrepreneurs do not think of themselves as risk takers because they don't recall facing momentous decisions along the way (with the typical exception of their agonizing deliberation to begin the venture). They expect new problems each day and understand that many of the attempts to solve them will misfire numerous times before something works. They also recognize that if they stopped attacking them, the problems would soon compound and the venture would unravel. But they intend to keep working, so they do not consider this a risk.

When evaluating the tactics of entrepreneurs, it is essential to consider that everyone must cope with risk. Even occupations and investments that are considered safe can be ambushed by life's surprises. Government employees, once thought to have career tenure, have been furloughed during budget cuts, and physicians, who earlier turned away patients, have returned to making house calls. While entrepreneurs deliberately identify uncertainties in order to clear away barriers to better service, they simultaneously outrun many of the problems that afflict established organizations. Entrepreneurs have the enormous advantage of initiative. When they create new products, technologies, and industries, others are compelled to adjust to their handiwork. In effect, entrepreneurs operate from the least vulnerable and risky position, controlling the uncertainty of the future by shaping it to their own design.

Entrepreneurs are also not one-shot promoters. To someone observing from a distance, new products often appear to have been created in one, huge breakthrough. But the appearance of sudden genius is illusionary. Most enterprises take form through small, uncertain steps. Moreover, though entrepreneurs must have a sound personal conception to build from, they can't go far without the aid of an effective team of managers. Entrepreneurs who cling to the lone-wolf style, which sometimes suffices early in the venture, are one of the most common entrepreneurial failures. A managerial team may be less nimble taking initiatives, but it is also more likely that one of its members will spot an opportunity or a looming mistake.

As an entrepreneurial venture grows, its members learn a lot about the niche that the product serves. Frequently the firm becomes recognized as the best source of such expertise in the world. Accordingly, an entrepreneur is discouraged from acquiring ventures outside his field where he cannot use his hard-won skills. Entrepreneurs seldom form conglomerates (that is, attempt to meld collections of unrelated businesses), but like most well-managed firms, stick to their knitting. They build on the advantage of their specific areas of knowledge, acquiring only those firms whose technology or marketing structures extend their own strengths. Their internal expansion follows the same strategy, edging into areas that draw upon their expertise and the orientation of the firm.

Entrepreneurs are also noted for knowing what they really do not know. Most people do not question the operation of most things, and by not doing so, overlook the anomalies that events suggest. Unconventional occurrences, such as sales to unlikely customers, trigger the curiosity of entrepreneurs. Rather than simply being thankful for good luck, they seek the specific factor that prompted the surprise. In fact, entrepreneurs constantly ask questions, if only of themselves. And their curiosity is productive. Rather than dissipate their energy on whatever crosses their path, they allow their attention to be shaped by clear, long-term goals. This tactic for sifting clues also benefits from detecting insights that most would neglect as irrelevant.

Entrepreneurs take seriously the signals coming from markets. When customers show an interest in a lower-priced version, they work to develop one. They do not doggedly insist that the expensive model is much better, and standards certainly should not be sacrificed for a shoddy item. They are also honest enough to modify a product that is not selling rather than stubbornly wait for buyers to come to their senses and realize how great the creation was after all.

Finally, ancestry and childhood do not predestine an individual to be an entrepreneur. There has been far too much emphasis— indeed, considerable nonsense—that one's course in life is largely shaped early in life. Perhaps a determined mother can implant seeds that later blossom into a persistent, creative entrepreneur, but there have also been more than enough successful children of permissive mothers to lend much credence to such arguments.

Entrepreneurs, like pianists and bricklayers, are at least as much made as born. The above rules of thumb exemplify major parts of a body of guidance that can be consciously learned. But, reciting such principles does not guarantee success any more than memorizing the *Red Cross Handbook* on swimming guarantees one will not drown.

The principles are only relevant as they are worked out in what are always novel circumstances. Entrepreneurship is a practice, something like medicine or law, where the utility of the theory depends on the quality of its application. And as a practice, it can be learned. This is why we should discount reasoning that alleges that certain individuals are strongly predisposed to becoming entrepreneurs. Much depends on the individual's willingness to work and learn.

To learn a practice, one begins working through the relevant textbooks, but to develop proficiency one soon must incorporate practicums such as internships. Doctors take residencies, and many law graduates serve as clerks while studying for the bar. Likewise, the intensity and style of entrepreneurs can really be conveyed only by examining their performance in particular settings. The American experience is fortunately rich in illustrations. Not surprisingly, the greatest economic expansion in world history also supplied the widest array of examples of entrepreneurial achievements.

The Founding Entrepreneurs

The American economy got started late. A full century elapsed after Columbus before Europeans began seriously to consider developing the eastern seaboard of the United States. They had explored along the coast enough to estimate what the region could yield, but expensive transportation to the area smothered all ventures.

About 1600, European entrepreneurs took a second look at America. English trading ventures in India and Russia were yielding extraordinary returns, in excess of 200 percent per annum on invested capital. Understandably merchants searched for comparable opportunities, hoping to replicate those successes. In this optimistic perspective, America warranted a second effort.

But to create a colony in America, the aspiring entrepreneur had to overcome two separate hurdles, each formidable in itself. First, he had to win a charter from the empire claiming that locale, which usually meant England. Aspiring proprietors exceeded available colonies, so the Crown's agents pitted candidates against one another in order to squeeze out the best terms for the government.

The entrepreneur also had to create a viable operation out of local resources, which had yet to yield anywhere near a competitive return. Success required the formidable combination of redeploying resources in accord with local costs rather than those of Europe, creating exports that were competitive in international trade, and devising organizations that encouraged participants to harness their personal interests toward those of the colony.

English officials passed each serious proposal for a charter through several bureaus seeking to further the government's goals. Understandably, the administrators favored those whose proposals promised to maintain the English flag in that part of the world by building successful settlements. It also helped if one could show promise of developing exports that would pay taxes and complement England's pattern of foreign trade. Much like contemporary firms, aspiring companies quickly discovered that it was necessary to employ an experienced agent at government headquarters—London, in this case—to assemble a convincing prospectus and guide it through the bureaucratic channels.

A charter was necessary, but by no means sufficient, for success. The company had to raise an unusually large quantity of capital with less than promising prospects. The expectation of quick returns fostered by India soon proved excessively optimistic. Investors would have to be very patient; indeed, they must accept a sizable risk that their entire commitment could be lost.

Each company also had to develop a team of managers that could find salable local products. A strong, creative leader on the site proved essential. The governor had to be willing to live in primitive isolation for extended periods, mollifying community problems, which not infrequently threatened to destroy the colony while he was coaxing products into commercial supply. Clearly, the manager had to be granted sufficient discretion to cope with unanticipated conditions and yet somehow be held accountable for all the assets the shareholders were allowing so far beyond their reach.

Companies screened candidates for governor carefully, recognizing the stakes. They hired managers experienced in exploring and colonizing North America. For example, Captain John Smith, of Pocahontas fame, was consulted frequently by organizers of later colonies after his accounts of his American exploits became circulated. (We might call this an early example of overblown celebrity publishing.) Or, companies hired experienced English landowners or merchants such as John Winthrop, a Puritan farmer, who was selected to head the Colony of Massachusetts Bay. They also sought to devise incentives to encourage those selected abilities. Managers, and sometimes important subordinates, were given stock to align their energies with the interests of the chartered company.

Even the best manager misfires when his organization is structured for the wrong environment. The founders fashioned the chartered companies to cope with the influences that appeared most important, but often other concerns proved critical in practice. Accordingly the products, means of organization, and even the styles of managers often had to be adjusted once the colony was under way. The Virginia Company, for example, allowed its colonists to elect their own manager upon arrival in America, but instructed them precisely about what should be their (three) specific objectives.[4] These explicit charges—planting crops, building a fort, and exploring the environs in detail—seemed appropriate to protect the colony and prepare for further undertakings. But they were shaped by experiences with trading outposts. Jamestown never developed any significant trade with the natives, even to the degree of obtaining badly needed corn. Small wonder that the Jamestown settlers soon challenged the company's directives and dismissed several managers as they sought remedies. The company trustees (far) back in London completely lost their influence until the structure was realigned.

The company's initial venture was a failure by anyone's standard. Fewer than 100 of the first 650 colonists survived the first three years, and nothing resulted from initiatives in local manufacturing. The company began revising both its structure and goals in its second year. Jamestown's inspiration was the East India Company, which dispatched manufactured goods to Asia to exchange for local products. This was a relatively simple, inexpensive operation requiring only organizing voyages and maintaining trading outposts. In North America, however, tradable indigenous products did not exist, and for decades Europeans sought to develop substitutes.

The first reorganization of the company marked the search for new arrangements that could profit from the (as of yet only partially understood) American environment. Sir Thomas Smythe, a London merchant who had played an important role in establishing several colonies, and the East India Company, took the lead. His leadership renewed the company's direction, which had drifted while the founders were confounded.

Smythe strengthened the colony's administration in Virginia by making the governor accountable directly to the company in London. He also expanded the colony's paid-in capital, recognizing that creating a viable colony was taking much longer than expected. He sought more investors by extending voting on company affairs to all shareholders and allowing them to purchase shares in installments. They also were allowed to redeem their shares in land in the colony. This last option symbolized a strategy the venture was crafting. As the company abandoned hope of employing a trading post, it shifted toward creating a settlement large enough to produce its own exports. Ownership of the land, therefore, became a means for sharing in the gains of the venture. Moreover, it stretched the company's increasingly scarce capital.

Smythe also nudged the colonists to seek commercial exports. His first candidate, industrial products, proved unsuitable in Virginia. Labor and capital, major inputs, were expensive because most had to be imported. Only techniques that emphasized cheap, local supplies, such as the production of pig iron, proved suitable, and even those required a long period of adaptation.

Thomas Smythe was not able to push the Jamestown settlement far enough to reach viability. But the qualities that made him one of England's most successful Colonial merchants were, nevertheless, evident in his American effort. Clearly he took the initiative, attempting tactics that appeared promising even when he lacked a good sense of the form an overall solution might assume. In common with those of most entrepreneurs, many of his experiments failed in earlier trials, but also in common with others he learned from experience about the environment he was attempting to serve. While others contributed what proved to be critical elements to Jamestown's success, the social learning his leadership fostered went a long way toward preparing the appropriate conditions for success.

During the revised efforts, thousands of settlers were sent to reinforce Jamestown. Food supplies improved, and the Indians retreated out of threatening proximity. The company constructed ironworks, sawmills, and shipyards and sent over artisans skilled in silk and glass. But none of these efforts proved self-sustaining, and they were quickly discarded when the ultimate solution, tobacco, appeared in 1614.

The price of tobacco had risen as smoking had continued to gain popularity after its introduction into Europe in the late 1500s. Thus when the cross of a Caribbean and a local variety yielded a vigorous, productive plant, Jamestown residents inferred the obvious and rushed to grow profits. This was good news for them—as well as the English government, which was concerned about nailing down its claim to the region—but, ironically, bad news for the founding company. The residents abandoned the company's enterprises to clear their own land and grow tobacco.

We now recognize that the problem that bankrupted the Jamestown Company—as distinguished from the settlement—is common. Entrepreneurs who are not able to complete a solution to a problem end up assisting those competitors who are. The structure of a chartered company was not suited to encourage the appropriate form of innovations, nor could it recoup much of the gains that emerged from the settlement. As is often the case, key innovations developed outside the structure and grasp of organizations specially created to that end.

The success of the neighboring tobacco colony of Maryland, founded in 1630, demonstrated how far Virginia's experience had advanced useful knowledge since 1607. Maryland escaped the initial seven years' "starving time" by recognizing that the American Colonies would have to assure their food supplies while earning a living from tobacco. Furthermore, Maryland drew immigrants by dropping Virginia's religious test for residents. An important motive for founding Maryland was to provide a refuge for Catholics then being persecuted in England. But as other American colonies discovered—such as Rhode Island and Pennsylvania, which became havens for dissenters—there were not enough of that group to make the colony viable. Consequently, the founders extended freedom to other religions in order to assure it for their church. This attracted a motley, but sizable, increment of settlers chafing at varied restrictions in Europe.

The proprietors of Maryland also improved on Virginia's administration, especially in the volatile function of relations with the parent English government. Several times the Virginia Company had been nearly destroyed by shifts in the royal administration in London. Maryland's existence was soon put to a similar test, but the colony adopted a dual structure to fend off threats. Lord Calvert kept tabs on maneuvers within the royal government in London so his brother in Maryland, Calvin Calvert, could apply his full energy to promoting the colony's growth.

Many of Maryland's problems with London grew out of a dilemma generic to intra-imperial relations. The imperial government very much wanted to get a successful colony established. Once a solid claim on the locality was assured and the colony began contributing to imperial trade, however, London had much less vested interest in the specific owner or proprietor. In other words, the government had less incentive to uphold its agreement with the founder, especially when parties to the original understanding changed. It is no wonder that, much like modern American groups maintaining lobbyists in Washington, D.C., proprietors such as Lord Calvert permanently maintained representatives at the seat of government discretion to safeguard their ventures.

The major alternative to the "Virginia Model" in creating settlements was the Massachusetts Bay Colony. Its later start, in 1630, was both good news and bad news. Massachusetts was warned away from some of the mistakes of earlier colonies. By the mid-1620s more was understood about the best means to organize a colony. There was also keen appreciation of how intense the colonists' appetite for capital was.

By 1630 New England had also become encumbered by the overlapping claims of proposed colonies. Some of the claimants were never defeated but had to be endured until finally death removed them. As long as Massachusetts developed successfully, however, England would jeopardize the colony's claim to the region by threatening to impose another proprietor. Thus, much like Maryland,

Massachusetts had to maintain vigilant representatives in London to protect its interests.

Even before the settlement began, the rationale behind Massachusetts Bay's design evolved. At first it was expected to be a seasonal outpost supplying Europeans who visited the nearby fishing banks each year. Then the Plymouth Colony, south of the proposed site, demonstrated that trade with the Indians could support at least a small settlement year-round.

The most likely supporters of the colony were the English merchants in the overseas trade, sizable numbers of whom dissented from the Church of England. Their support could be increased by providing for the enterprise to serve as a refuge for Puritans. But to contribute much toward that end the settlement would have to be much larger, well beyond the size that a trading post implied. The promoters began considering other activities for the settlement, such as agriculture and lumber products, that might employ more residents. They decided to open the way with an advance party of several hundred in 1629 before sending more than a thousand settlers in seventeen ships the next year.

Massachusetts hit upon another innovation in colony building that, while seeming minor—even petty—at the moment, ultimately helped it a long way toward success. Governmental authority over a chartered company had to be applied where the directors met. The leaders of the colony surreptitiously took the charter document with them when they departed England in 1630. Moving control to Boston was a deft move, making imperial control much slower and more cumbersome. Americans thoroughly absorbed the implications of this tactic. They repeatedly sought to shift the focus of control, particularly into their legislatures, to reduce British control throughout the Colonial period.

The Massachusetts colonists quickly set about administering themselves, creating their own structure complete with the equivalent of governor, Senate, House of Representatives, judicial system, and town officials. During the first two decades a comprehensive legal code was assembled. The colonists felt sufficiently secure to deny the king's directives several times—and their judgment proved correct. For a while, the expanse of the Atlantic stifled the imperial government, and later, the English Civil War diverted its attention.

It was not until 1680—fifty years after the founding of the colony—
that a royal governor was dispatched to Boston! By then the growth
of the local economy and the inroads of local practices had considerably reduced susceptibility to imperial influence. The colonists appeared to understand that the force of the new reality created by
taking the initiative can be a powerful entrepreneurial tool.

Spurred by religious zeal and shielded from royal meddling,
about twenty thousand immigrants were drawn to Massachusetts in
the first twelve years. The arrival of the new residents, along with
their assets, fueled a local economic boom. For more than a decade
all available hands were kept busy putting up homes, shops, and
public buildings; clearing fields; roughing out roads; and constructing boats, wharves, and fishing equipment. When the influx slowed,
however, the economic stimulus did also, so the colony slipped into
a recession, complete with falling prices and widespread unemploy-
ment. The colonists were now compelled to find a permanent basis
for their economy. The limited local market necessitated that exports
had to be developed in order to pay for imports. At first they attempted to use the resources near at hand: fish, wood products, grain,
and salted beef. But such commodities couldn't yield much on net
because the cost of delivering them to available markets was several
times their local price.

No doubt aspiring exporters in Massachusetts found paying so
much to shippers disheartening. But rather than retreat into cyni-
cism, they turned to the entrepreneurial tactic of asking how this
might be turned to their own advantage. They noticed that other
American colonists also faced high shipping costs and reasoned that
costs might be reduced by consolidating such services for all colonies. Of course hindsight makes the logic behind the creation of this
market appear much more obvious and straightforward than it was
for those who grappled to formulate it. It is easy to overlook the false
starts, the plodding frustration, and the continuing uncertainty that
preceded the success.

Boston merchants created an entrepôt for Colonial America
where cargoes to and from Europe were exchanged. They gathered
up smaller shipments destined for export from along the coast, consolidating them for shipment across the Atlantic. Likewise they
began importing larger orders, selling some to other colonies. The

savings in freight from using larger, more efficient vessels on the cross-Atlantic leg of the trade compensated for the added handling in Boston. After incorporating some of their own innovations, the Massachusetts Bay colonists could underprice most competitors. Given the dominance of freight costs at that time, they were developing a service whose revenue exceeded every sector in the Colonies, including tobacco. Moreover, it was free from a restriction to a particular combination of soil, climate, and rainfall, which set a ceiling on other products, tying them to a particular region.

Creating new markets is one of the entrepreneurs' most important, as well as most demanding and risky, functions.[5] The time, creative energy, and resources required to forge a new market are irreversibly lost if the effort fails. Had the Boston merchants failed to find American customers for the particular goods they purchased in quantity, they would have had to absorb the losses as well as write off the time spent in prospecting for outlets for the goods. Of course, they did not fail, as is evidenced by their portrayal here—a good example of entrepreneurial behavior.

As did Virginia's, Massachusetts' experience became a model for nearby colonies facing similar environments. While the Massachusetts Bay colonists were fashioning an economy, sizable numbers of immigrants moved on, searching for a locale that suited them better. A large fraction of the early immigrants came because they had strong and—by contemporary English standards—radical views of how an ideal society was constituted. Not infrequently this led to bitter disputes about church and society in Massachusetts, resulting in some preferring to attempt their own versions of utopia elsewhere rather than compromising their vision.

The dispersal was not completely driven by religious considerations. Tillable acreage around Boston Harbor quickly filled up. Thus, early on there was an incentive to consider more distant cultivatable areas. The meadowlands along the lower Connecticut River, for example, attracted those who wanted to become graziers.

Within a few decades after 1630, settlers had established beachheads along the entire New England coast from Connecticut to Maine and inland along water routes allowing transportation to the coast. Many of these smaller settlements were vulnerable to larger powers, however. Therefore, they sought to bolster their security by forging alliances with other colonies. Plymouth and the settlements in Maine joined Massachusetts. The groups in Rhode Island put aside their differences sufficiently to form a confederation. And the colonists of New Haven, after attempting to retain independence by merging with the adjacent communities on the Connecticut shore, decided that it would be best to join the larger colony of Connecticut after all.

The pressures pushing the smaller settlements toward consolidation probably were similar to those that had shaped early Massachusetts. Residents of that colony experimented with many ways of specializing in production and commerce, both within America and with the outside world. But during the early years, the degree of demand for many goods and services was not large enough to capture the full gains of larger-scale production. Many products such as shoes, hardware, and clothing were bespoken—individually crafted—for consumers because imported models were usually too expensive. Even when standardized goods were available, high transportation costs tilted Massachusetts' organization toward local self-sufficiency. This rewarded growth because, for example, as immigration increased the number of residents, local producers could specialize further, thus making a widening array of goods and services cheaper. Local production not only saved on transportation and handling costs but also matched the product more closely to local requirements. Such increasing returns to scale raised the expected earnings of immigrants and new enterprises in the colony. Even before settlement began, for example, the founders of Massachusetts Bay sensed the venture would have to be large to be successful. Virginia's early efforts, which appeared to have been frittered away in repeated, undersize commitments, were fresh in their minds.

No doubt the gains from larger economic operations encouraged the smaller New England settlements to bond together. But political considerations also were quite important. Both Virginia and Massachusetts had major disputes with the royal government. Smaller settlements could expect even less leverage and could be correspondingly more vulnerable. The smallest independent settlements, such as those at New Haven, Connecticut, and York, Maine, were the most vulnerable of all. Leaders of such colonies recognized the threat and considered ways to meet it. As the safety afforded by larger principalities became apparent, the entrepreneurial instincts of local leaders began seeking beneficial mergers.

Pennsylvania: Creating Freedom

Elements of the two basic American models of a colony, Virginia and Massachusetts, were combined with refinements into the greatest success of the late Colonial period: Pennsylvania. It, of course, began as the entrepreneurial vision of William Penn. Like the founders of the New England colonies, Penn sought more than economic goals. He became a Quaker as a young man, which prompted numerous scrapes with the English establishment, including being jailed four times. To complicate matters, Penn came from a prominent family. His father, Admiral William Penn, contributed to the English defeat of the Dutch Navy in the early 1650s. This drew even more attention to the errant son but, at the same time, offered him an opportunity to create a permanent escape from his predicament. Despite his beliefs, Penn was allowed to participate in the national government, where he earned considerable respect. The Crown owed his father £ 16,000 when he died in 1670, but lacked anything near that amount of cash. Thus, when Penn petitioned for the charter to Pennsylvania, that obligation of the Crown no doubt contributed to its approval.

By Pennsylvania's founding in 1680, the economic promise of the American colonies had been raised by improved transportation and the advantages of larger settlements. But Penn was most interested in creating a sanctuary for his fellow Quakers. While he reasonably expected to attract sufficient settlers for economic reasons, all the Quakers in the world were not sufficient to ensure that they would rule Pennsylvania. He drew upon his entrepreneurial instincts to devise the solution of guaranteeing all residents personal and religious freedom. This was a drastic step in an era when even the most enlightened governments felt duty bound to suppress heretics. But it underlined the irony of freedom. Unless one is willing to tolerate others spouting abrasive, even wrongheaded, views, one can't be assured of being allowed to speak out unhindered oneself. Penn demonstrated his commitment to this open, tolerant colony by relinquishing some of his rightful powers as proprietor.

Penn's key contribution was to implement freedom by ensuring its indivisibility, recognizing that in order to assure it to one group, such as the Quakers, it must extend to all others within the colony. Accordingly, he developed the Charter of Pennsylvania, which guaranteed all Pennsylvania citizens religious freedom as well as other freedoms that were often infringed at that time. Pennsylvania was settled quickly and became very prosperous because, in addition to Quakers, it attracted other groups escaping hostile environments in Europe, such as the Amish and the Mennonites who are now called the Pennsylvania Dutch. The basic structure and rules of Pennsylvania assured each group that it would be free to practice its own beliefs.

Pennsylvania not only extended social freedoms but also imposed fewer restrictions on economic activity than almost anywhere. This combination of advantages helped Pennsylvania become the most successful colony in the 1700s. It grew fastest, and Philadelphia became the largest American city. Given the appropriate incentives the colonists put their energies as well as their beliefs to work. Thus an unprecedented combination of political, religious, and economic incentives spurred the Colonial showcase.

William Penn functioned as an entrepreneur by creating new opportunities for people. He created something that they wanted but that had not existed. Penn wanted freedom for his fellow Quakers but hardly anyone would undertake the effort to move to Pennsylvania just to help provide freedom for Quakers. What was necessary was an environment that attracted immigrants for more universal reasons, accomplishing what Penn wanted as a by-product. It had to be a mutually beneficial arrangement. One of the most misleading concepts about economic affairs is that they require exploitation. Voluntary exchange between two parties cannot be exploitation. One has to offer the other party something that is believed to be a gain. Penn did not exploit anyone or force anyone to provide freedom for Quakers; he offered better conditions so that colonists would join him. Creating value must be the entrepreneur's basic tactic because he lacks any other means of compelling people to provide him with something.

2

Innovating Within the Colonial Environment

Colonial enterprises faced a basic, almost intimidating constraint. Most of the demand for the types of goods they produced was thousands of miles away in Europe, and transportation raised the price of delivering them severalfold over the distance. (Ironically, the lavish supplies of raw materials the Americans possessed would have been a bonanza in densely settled Europe, but the separation made most of them worthless.) The advantage of having sufficient customers to support the efficient production of common products, which established economies came to take for granted, was not possible. Consequently, only specialty items such as furs, which were valuable relative to the cost of their freight, were profitable to produce in America for European markets. Most early sixteenth-century investors in Europe examined the prospects of the American Colonies and dismissed them as dismal candidates for growth.

Nevertheless, alert colonists sought techniques that could bypass the stringencies of their environment. Those enterprises that succeeded usually emphasized using raw materials that were locally abundant. Even by the time of the Revolution, after a century and a half of vigorous growth, the American Colonies remained sparsely settled. There were still fewer than three million Americans, only a small fraction of the inhabitants in the developed area of Europe, and fewer than now live in Connecticut, one of the smallest states. Consequently there were abundant trees, minerals, fisheries, and farmland available to each resident. Supplies were so abundant, compared with those in contemporary Europe, that they produced culture shock in immigrants. They were aghast to see Americans "abusing" land and materials, "squandering" them without heed to cost. Experience had conditioned Europeans to expect that such abundance was inconceivable.[1] Nevertheless, there were so many natural resources that even after huge amounts had been consumed, no opportunities were foreclosed. Any entrepreneur who could devise a productive way to employ natural resources garnered huge supplies for his own use. The critical skill was transforming local abundance into products that were profitable in distant markets. While raw materials were almost free for the taking, they were also usually cheap relative to their bulk and thus prohibitively expensive to transport. The trick was to extract concentrated value out of cheap volume.

Pig iron illustrates how a successful transformation might be achieved. It built on the contemporary backwardness of metallurgy, which required large amounts of charcoal to smelt iron. Growing the basic raw material, trees, ties up land for a long time and thus was very costly in densely settled Europe. American producers using local wood could undersell producers in Europe, even after absorbing the freight across the Atlantic. In the early 1700s, the Americans became the world's largest exporters of pig iron. Potash, a distilled form of wood ashes used in soap and glass, benefited from similar economics. And barrel staves, which served the function of today's cardboard cartons, also converted cheap raw materials into concentrated value.

A transformation developed offshore that was clearly American, as well as quite possibly the most important Colonial example of converting natural resources into economic output. Even before the American Colonies were founded, the Dutch and English were already harvesting whales above the Arctic Circle. By later standards these were amateurish operations—waiting for the prey to venture inshore and dragging the catches up on the beach. The early American colonists adopted these tactics, particularly along eastern Long Island and southeastern New England where whales migrated closest to shore.

Whaling technology began a major advance when a sloop, blown far off Nantucket by a severe storm, encountered a large number of sperm whales. These were much larger than the right whales, which were pursued close to shore. Mariners had sighted them off and on for thousands of years, but the critical difference was that the Nantucketites had been sensitized to their commercial possibilities. Whalers readily entered the newly discovered grounds, but it quickly proved impractical to tow each whale back to shore for processing. The improvisation of cutting up the carcasses and sending the blubber back to Nantucket in barrels for rendering also proved expensive. So the whaling ships were enlarged in order to accommodate the boilers, cutting areas, and barrels necessary to render oil at sea.

The focus of innovation shifted to shore with Joseph Starbuck, the leading merchant of Nantucket, assuming a central role.[2] The key to developing the new trade proved to be providing ships and equipment to minimize the cost of oil. Enlarging ships to equip them to stay on the whaling ground longer between provisioning in port became important. Vessels grew from about 20 tons in the early 1700s to more than 100 tons by the Revolution. Starbuck also organized longer voyages, finding several additional areas that attracted sperm whales along the edge of the Gulf Stream.

The payoff to these innovations could be gauged when a whaler located a school of prey on the high seas. He could pursue them for weeks at a time, if necessary, killing them and then circling back to work through the backlog of carcasses. The ultimate test of this organization occurred in the first half of the nineteenth century, when a run-up in oil prices sent whalers—literally—to the ends of the earth. It became standard procedure to undertake voyages of

10,000 to 15,000 miles, often lasting several years. Outside of stops for water and fresh food, the ships could remain at sea for years until they had accumulated a cargo of oil.

Local Tactics

Small Colonial markets meant that most enterprises took on certain characteristics. Managers had to act as generalists. Organizations had to shift offerings of services frequently in order to survive; one product in spotty demand could languish a long while. Proprietors dealt in sundry goods, adjusting among them as demands and supplies dictated. Managers had to be jacks-of-all-trades, moving, for example, from merchandising to lending to manufacturing handicrafts and back to merchandising again. Storms on the Atlantic frequently delayed imports, compelling them to improvise. Merchants also moved into local political offices naturally. The modern concern about keeping private and public affairs strictly separated did not exist; indeed, it would have foundered when faced with local governments too small to support full-time officials.

Another challenge of this entrepreneurial environment was devising organizations to make the most of small markets. Most colonists lived in rural areas, conducting much of their trade through small villages. Until the eve of the Revolution, the largest towns in Colonial America had fewer than twenty thousand people; in other words, they were no larger than a middling-size suburb of a modern city. Most settlements were much smaller, not much more than what would be termed a crossroads: a couple of stores and shops and a few homes for the shopkeepers.

Such commercial "centers" were the focal point for gathering up the agricultural produce to be shipped out of the area as well as distributing incoming goods. Because the market for both was usually small, most merchants assumed both functions; that is, they acted as commodity dealers collecting local products in addition to merchandising products. This arrangement confounds our modern expectations about retailing. We take for granted that supermarkets only *sell* goods. Hardly anyone would contemplate bringing in a bag of produce expecting to barter for groceries. Specialized agricultural agencies now collect crops in agricultural areas and move them on to processors. But most Colonial merchant operations had to perform both functions to survive.

Merchants had to assume other major activities as well, including providing credit to customers. Americans borrowed to augment their capital wherever possible, particularly from Europe, the cheapest source. But a separate medium for transferring funds was not feasible yet, so lending was tacked on to mercantile connections. Farmers and tradesmen purchased goods on credit from a local merchant who, in turn, obtained stock on credit from others further back in the network. The retail merchant was compelled to serve as a part-time lending officer, judging which customers could be entrusted with credit. While not formally trained for his role, he was probably better placed than most to assess the creditworthiness of the locals. By assuming responsibility for arranging loans and payments, merchants also adopted the role of an early-day American Express office, transmitting payments and settling notes drawn at distant locales. Especially in larger cities, merchants also initiated local manufacturing, often out of frustration with the delays and expense of foreign sources. Sometimes this meant underwriting major new enterprises, such as mills or foundries, whereas at other times it was as simple as contracting with local artisans for a batch of products.

Colonial merchants were compelled to be generalists. Only in the largest port cities could they afford to restrict themselves to particular lines of goods, telling customers, "Sorry. We only deal in. . . ." Generalists draw extensively on a special set of skills. A specialist spends considerable time developing expertise and then keeping track of developments within that specialty. A generalist, in contrast, must be able to move among disparate tasks, seldom developing specific skills in depth. He seldom goes much beyond the basics before he is drawn into other concerns. Most Colonial merchants provided an array of services, learning a decent amount about each but seldom developing depth in limited areas. This orientation contrasts with the managerial style we associate with American executives, which began in the second half of the nineteenth century when large integrated steel mills, oil refineries, and similar complex businesses emerged. Directing such enterprises required considerable familiarity with the technology shaping the product. Their top managers spent long apprenticeships working in specialties before they assumed broader responsibilities within a company.

As individuals rise within a large modern company, their decisions necessarily incorporate a broadening array of issues and influences. Top managers must weigh influences from production, marketing, finance, research and development, and external relations, such as stockholders, regulatory bodies, and lobbyists. Thus they become today's generalists. In other words, a successful chief executive officer (CEO) or company chairman today exercises skills similar to those required of Colonial merchants.

Of course, Colonial merchants operated on a much smaller scale. In addition, they remained specialists in the sense that while they handled varied products and services they became intimately familiar with conditions in their locality. But overall, they were generalists, dealing with disparate concerns, shifting back and forth with demand. The merchant had to be adaptable: when ships didn't arrive as expected, he had to devise new outlets for the commodities collected for export. No-shows also meant devising substitutes to fill gaps on the store shelves.

Ship captains faced challenges similar to those placed on the merchants and thus succeeded by mastering similar skills. Each port offered unforeseen problems—or opportunities—to entrepreneurs. Anticipated supplies were sold out, or there wasn't much demand for the ship's cargo. The captain constantly had to judge how best to adjust to changes. It is understandable that merchants and ship captains had similar characteristics. The qualities that promoted success at sea also made for an effective, established merchant. Oftentimes the former acted as a stepping-stone to the latter. It was common, for instance, for a young man to expect a career composed of a sequence of assignments aboard ship to culminate in the rank of captain. And a successful captain could expect to return to home port to become a partner with a local merchant, eventually earning a senior partnership and assuming control of the firm. Thus there was an understood, informal track for developing merchants, even though formal educational certification such as an M.B.A. was far in the future.

Had specific formal schooling existed, however, it still could not have replaced the function of experience in evaluating how a young man might perform as a merchant. Experience provided relevant training as well as identified those who could assume additional responsibility. (This, of course, is another example of the timeless maxim that there is no substitute for experience or, more trenchantly, good judgment comes from experience and experience comes from bad judgment.)

Thus within the network of merchants, shipowners, and associated occupations was a hierarchy of positions building upward from what today we would term entry-level positions. Today's college graduates often begin as trainees, such as in sales. After a short orientation the new employees are sent out knocking on doors to explain the product and convince customers that the services are worthwhile. This is an important dimension of experience not provided in college as well as a tough test demonstrating whether participants are suited for such an environment. Every business hierarchy must incorporate this function, providing a filter through which the capable can learn and demonstrate their suitability for promotion. Thus while Colonial business didn't employ formal systems of training, it necessarily devised a sequence of steps to accomplish the function.

Workers typically began young. It wasn't unusual for fourteen- and fifteen-year-olds to hold positions that filled the role of the entry level for merchants. In retailing they could deliver goods or messages, sweep the floor, and tend the fire. Later they could be entrusted with handling stock. For continued good performance, they could be moved up to clerk, a critical role. Previous to the typewriter and the Xerox machine, each piece of correspondence had to be hand-copied several times. Ocean shipping offered a comparable progression from cabin boy up through first mate. Whatever the hierarchy, employees had an opportunity to develop expertise while employers could assess the promise of their work. Business still finds that recruiting and developing good employees is one of its largest and most critical tasks. Even though products and organizations have changed drastically, providing a dependable supply of employees still remains a common, central concern.

The Landed Entrepreneurs

America's abundant land presented another major opportunity to entrepreneurs. The economics of operation limited most real estate holdings to a size the owner could manage himself. However, with so much acreage being acquired, developed, and exchanged, it was inevitable that opportunities for major entrepreneurial creations would appear. One of the most noticeable, prompting several of the largest personal fortunes during the Colonial period, occurred in South Carolina in the mid-1700s. The rapid growth of cotton textiles getting under way in England increased the demand for dyes to color the natural gray cloth. The colony's up-country land proved ideal for raising indigo plants, which yielded the color we now associate with blue jeans. Local rice planters, such as Henry Middleton, quickly set about developing indigo farms. But even more suggestive was the response of the resident Charleston merchants who scaled back their trade and shifted resources into agriculture. The two wealthiest merchants, Henry Laurens and Gabriel Manigault, were in the forefront. (Their stature is indicated by Laurens's becoming president of the Continental Congress, and Manigault is commonly believed to have been the richest American of his day.) Both purchased established rice plantations and large tracts of undeveloped frontier land as well as indigo acreage. That they combined the different types of land—duplicating the tactic of Middleton—suggests that they had discovered gains in integrating the disparate operations, probably by fully utilizing slaves, because the peak activity of the crops on the three types of land occurred at different seasons. Together, Middleton, Laurens, and Manigault owned more than 100,000 acres—150 square miles—on the eve of the Revolution.

The Growth of Interior Markets

Settlers moved westward, hoping to replicate the advantages of a developed, commercial society by getting in on the ground floor. The migration continued throughout the Colonial period because those expectations were generally fulfilled. Most migrants improved their property and tapped into the gains of their neighborhood's specialization. But as so often happens, growth set off other far-reaching consequences that could only be vaguely anticipated. In the mid-eighteenth century, developing interior markets began drawing apart from the established networks anchored on the Atlantic coast. This was an early indicator of the trend for the next two hundred years. One of the best examples of this effect occurred in southern New England, where it had profound repercussions on the port of Boston.

Massachusetts Bay had grown rapidly in the first half of the Colonial period by developing as an entrepôt. That strategy worked superbly from 1640 into the early 1700s, creating considerable employment and wealth in Boston. But about 1710, the demand for the entrepôt's handling services peaked and began to slip. By 1740 the trend was clearly down. This ran counter to the overall pattern of trade among the American Colonies and that with other nations, both of which continued growing very rapidly.

Boston's advantage had been built upon the condition that traffic into most Colonial ports was insufficient to capture the full economies of scale in direct foreign trade. The port consolidated such smaller-than-optimum shipments in order to reap those efficiencies. But by the early 1700s the volume of commerce of other major ports was approaching levels where direct trade across the Atlantic became competitive. Philadelphia, for example, grew to be America's largest city in the late Colonial period. Moreover, its hinterland, which augmented its trade, surpassed Boston's. By the early 1700s a large area in southeastern Pennsylvania was producing wheat for the export market. The port opened trade directly to England and the Caribbean, bypassing Boston, whose role as a middleman began to dissolve.

Thomas Hancock, whose surname developed a larger legacy than his entrepreneurial contribution, appeared at this juncture.[3] (Nephew John, who assumed the business, immortalized the name when he signed the Declaration of Independence.) Thomas was a younger son of a minister, so by the time he began his career, his family could not provide much help. He pursued the common path of middle-class youths of that day, learning a skilled trade by being apprenticed to a tradesman. Hancock became a journeyman book-binder, but that milestone soon was forgotten as he aggressively pursued goals well beyond it. Even by the time he became a journey-man, he had already prepared much ground, as is evidenced by his being able to make an extraordinary move. Today it is commonplace for young Americans to travel to Europe. But the expense of such a trip in the early 1700s restricted travel mostly to the rich. Hancock didn't announce his reasons for going to Europe, but subsequent events suggest he wished to develop connections with English export-ers.

Colonial merchants depended on the trust of European export-ers to supply goods on credit. A carefully cultivated connection with a merchant house in London or Bristol was a major asset. American merchants commonly gained access to foreign suppliers as junior partners in a firm when a senior partner wrote a letter to the effect that "Mr. X has proven himself, so now we will allow him to transact business matters with you on behalf of our firm."

On returning to Boston, Hancock opened his own store. He carried European products financed with credit advanced by the suppliers, in addition to his own crafts. In effect, he bypassed much of the incremental approach that young men usually followed to become Colonial merchants. Within a few years, when he turned twenty-five, he had several other craftsmen working for him. He imported goods, wholesaling some to other merchants in America, bought American products for export, extended credit, contracted for batches of manufactured products and, in general, provided the full range of services that a port merchant found necessary to be competitive. But he was also beginning to develop the special form of relations that were his particular entrepreneurial contribution to the New England economy.

The year 1740 seemed a bad time to start a business in Boston. Another aspiring local, Ben Franklin, took one look around and left for Philadelphia, the obvious growth center of the time. Franklin had a "high-tech mentality." Thomas Hancock must have believed he could improve some part of the Boston economy. (Of course, it is harder for an established merchant to pull up stakes because he depends on carefully cultivated connections. Such relationships are a location-specific investment that cannot be transferred.)

Hancock made the very best of the changing conditions. He understood that while Boston was losing its function as an entrepôt, expansion was still brisk in interior New England. Whereas earlier settlements had been near the coast or rivers that provided access to it, pioneers were now moving inland in sizable numbers. Communities and social organizations were being formed there, so while their remoteness precluded them from becoming wealthy yet, their aggregate income—and spending—was becoming substantial. That market became Thomas Hancock's focus of expansion. He shifted emphasis from the entrepôt activities of importing and exporting goods in foreign trade to servicing local markets and merchants. He probably reasoned something like this: There are numerous customers out there and although few will become wealthy, they will make a decent living, implying a significant amount of commerce in each of those rural crossroads. So look to the secondary towns, inland beyond Providence, Hartford, and the like. There will be aspiring merchants back there looking to get started. If I help them along, they're going to patronize me.

Thomas Hancock's niche was serving those smaller markets— in effect, a "Wal-Mart" strategy. Today Wal-Mart is one of the most prosperous retail chains in the United States. It prides itself on providing careful service in small towns. It builds relationships by recruiting local residents to manage stores, cultivating customers with elements of the atmosphere of an old general store. The key is to achieve this while retaining the advantages of a larger business: buying goods in quantity and offering the low prices that such volume allows.

Hancock reached into the countryside to create contacts with small merchants. It requires a careful sensitivity to deal with small buyers who expect attention and yet individually don't buy much. It may take ten transactions from them to equal the purchases of one port merchant. Hancock built long-term connections with these shopkeepers, developing the types of products and services they required. For instance, they needed someone who could handle the farm produce that the local farmers were exchanging for goods. So he spent considerable energy organizing this service. They also needed financing and expertise and, in some cases, something as simple as someone to deliver their mail. Hancock could produce such services because he developed a trading network specifically structured for them. Hancock demonstrated that one can prosper in what is commonly written off as a declining industry. The key is to devise services suitable for the changing environment, not to be disheartened by conditions in general. As long as a sector continues to produce economic output, improvements in employing its resources will be socially valuable and rewarded.

The Colonial Record

By the eighteenth century, North Atlantic contemporaries regarded the American Colonies as the growth sector of their time. Immigrants and aspiring investors instinctively turned to them. The strongest tangible measure of American prosperity was population. Americans established a record seldom equaled in human history. The colonists grew from the few thousand who founded the first colonies to almost three million on the eve of the Revolution. The significant aspect was that most of the increase resulted from the natural growth of residents rather than from further immigration. The growth of domestic population was 3 percent per year, one of the highest sustained increases known. Observers of today's lesser developed economies express concern over growth rates of around 2 percent per year, believing that sufficiently high to dissipate hard-won increases in economic output. But the colonists had no such concerns; indeed, just the opposite. They understood that every additional hand contributed to the public welfare.

A few scholars have suggested that this surge of population growth was only a powerful form of Malthusian economics at work, with the population growing especially fast to absorb discoveries of land. But this seems unlikely. Population growth approaching the American rate has almost invariably occurred in conjunction with improvements in human well-being.[4] Usually this has meant rising per capita incomes, but it also includes the post–World War II phenomenon of modern health technology drastically increasing life spans in lesser developed countries. Moreover, the specific indicators that would point to a Malthusian climate were missing—in fact, moved in the opposite direction. Land did not become scarcer and labor cheaper; rather, development continued to expand usable land faster than the colonists could absorb it.

A second major indicator, per capita income, reinforces this anti-Malthusian conclusion. There are more uncertainties about reconstructing per capita incomes at that time than reconstructing population estimates, but most experts agree the trend was up.[5] A median value of conjectures is about one-half percent annually. This is small compared with more recent performances but is significant, indeed, revolutionary, when compared with most previous history. One-half percent per year leads to a doubling of personal income in 140 years, which was about the time span of the Colonial period. An increase that large prompts consumers to make major shifts in their spending patterns and, therefore, to cause corresponding shifts among the producing sectors of the economy. No doubt the rise in personal incomes caused the noticeable improvements in housing and clothing that observers reported in the latter Colonial years.

The implication of this rise of incomes for longer spans of history is even more striking. Had that rate of growth prevailed from the official end of the Western Roman Empire in A.D. 456, per capita incomes would have increased by more than 200 times by the founding of the American Colonies! Obviously that did not occur, and the enormous amount that incomes fell below the level that such a sustained rate would have achieved underlines how sharp a break with previous human experience the Colonial period represented. Historians usually assign the onset of modern growth to the Industrial Revolution and conclude, accordingly, that manufacturing and capital were the critical components energizing growth. The experience of the American Colonies clearly challenges that view. Growth can get a good start in predominantly agricultural societies, but markets and entrepreneurs appear critical.

What made the American Colonies so successful? How did a small, isolated corner of the world develop to be such a standout? No doubt the explanation begins with the Colonies' particular European heritage. The most prosperous and innovative economy in Europe when the American Colonies began was Holland. As the seventeenth century progressed and more colonies were established along the

Atlantic coast, England assumed leadership in Europe. Both these economies had substantial markets and a respect for personal property. This was an important departure from most previous European history, where regimented commerce and arbitrary impositions of governments had frequently dampened incentives to improve.[6] The American colonists carried this approach into North America, and given its initial success, it is not surprising it became deeply embedded. But while necessary, the foregoing were not sufficient conditions. Ultimately the success of Americans depended on what they could do for themselves.[7]

The American success was a culmination of many small improvements, but the total impact on the Colonies can be gauged by the sectors it turned into showcases. The productivity of each major American export was improved dramatically during the Colonial period. Introducing crops into a new environment allowed refinements, especially as American entrepreneurs understood that reducing costs was crucial to competing in world markets. Some of the gains were huge, even by modern standards. From 1620 to the middle of the eighteenth century, the cost of producing tobacco fell by a factor of more than ten. Even after 1630, when most obvious adjustments had been completed, costs still fell by a factor of more than five. Even though records in the pivotal early years of other major exports such as rice and whale products are missing, they also appear to have greatly reduced costs. Such sectors were large enough relative to the entire Colonial economy that their contribution to the aggregate was substantial. Of course, learning and innovation also occurred in the remainder of the economy, but these records are harder to reconstruct.[8]

The Americans were also helped by participating in a sector that was growing rapidly throughout the North Atlantic—ocean shipping. Its earliest gains had permitted the Colonies to get under way by allowing Europeans to begin to settle on the western side of the Atlantic Ocean. These gains continued during the Colonial period at a relatively rapid rate of .8 percent per year according to the most comprehensive calculations.[9] This increased shipping productivity by more than three times in the course of the Colonial period, reducing the cost of the service by more than two thirds, and explains why the colonists kept extending the limits of settlement and introducing new, previously unfeasible, products. But the Americans went further, advancing from being passive beneficiaries to contributing participants in shipping. New Englanders led in developing intracolonial commerce and then expanded into trading with other countries. By the Revolution, Americans were serving commerce as large as their own and had become net suppliers of both ships and shipping services to the other North Atlantic economies as well.

Falling freight rates made it worthwhile to produce for more distant markets, reducing self-sufficiency. This furthered another characteristic of growth: specialization. A sizable share of economic activity could gain from economies of scale in which increasing output reduces the average cost of production. High freight costs had condemned the earliest settlements to a debilitating degree of self-sufficiency. As this barrier was lowered, the colonists shifted toward products in which their locality had a particular advantage and, therefore, could sell competitively elsewhere. This created—what is now widely recognized as—gains from trade that raised the incomes of all participants.

Such a reorganization was evident in the tobacco trade, where specialized brokers, called factors, assumed the intermediate steps of gathering up tobacco from Tidewater farms and preparing it for the transatlantic trip. A similar specialization occurred among merchants in the major ports when the volume of trade increased. But it is likely that much of its impact occurred within agriculture, in subtle forms that have eluded most chroniclers.

Most farmers had their primary specialization, such as tobacco or wheat, firmly in mind when they began developing a farm. But while one export was worthwhile—in large part because the region was organized to deliver it—everything other than expensive imports was provided locally. The distance of interior farms from water transportation accentuated this secondary local sufficiency.

Falling transportation costs prompted farmers to add supplementary crops and, in turn, purchase a growing portion of their consumables such as furniture, clothing, kitchenware, tools, and hardware. They replaced local items, ranging in quality from the creations of proud craftsmen down to crude, household improvisations. This commercialization became evident in the organization of coastal farms as well as the upsurge in improvements to rural roads before the Revolution.

Each improvement in transportation and communications enlarged the feasible area of settlement and enticed Americans farther into the interior. This westward march was so pervasive that even disruptions as large as the Revolution could not stall it. Behind the advancing fringe of pioneers, however, was a far more significant effect—the increases in the price of previously settled land. Reductions in transportation costs increased the net margin on farm produce, thereby raising the value of the land producing it. This increase became so predictable that Americans began incorporating its effect into their planning. Settlers spent years converting a section of wilderness into a working farm, confident that the land market would reward their diligence. Investors purchased both undeveloped acreage and working farms, expecting appreciation. In fact, for the colonists land became the stock market of its day. It was the most widely held and traded asset, the principal form of acquiring and holding wealth.

American land was also contradicting Parson Malthus, who would be cited so widely in the twentieth century, even at the time he was formulating his famous theory of inevitable population pressure. Had he examined the American experience more closely he would have been much more optimistic about long-term prospects. Land did not become scarcer in America as population expanded. Its rising value reflected rising productivity rather than a looming scarcity. As a result, most Americans could, and did, share in its ownership and appreciation, far removed from the dismal Malthusian prediction that looming scarcity would concentrate its control in a few hands while the bulk of the population eked out subsistence wages.

3

Entrepreneuring Permanent Opportunities During Revolutionary Times

The American Revolution was not a surprise to those following Britain's relations with the Americans. Tensions had been building for a long time, at least as far back as 1740. The diverging interests of the two societies made it harder and harder to fashion policies that benefited both sides.

Of those forces restructuring Colonial relations, the expansion of the American economy had to be one of the strongest. America grew from a few isolated outposts requiring protection against hostile forces to a regionally dominant, self-reliant power with distinct interests in international politics. During the French and Indian War from 1754 to 1763, for example, the Americans weren't convinced that they should help the British expel the French from Canada. They didn't feel threatened by the French presence; indeed, the French served as a counterweight to British influence over them.

The Americans' temptation to go their own way was encouraged by the existing technology of defense. Initially they relied on the British Empire to provide their naval protection because of the British Navy's advantage in size. Ships could be concentrated to apply considerable pressure on a particular locality. This put small settlements, such as the early colonies, at a severe disadvantage in providing their own protection. But as their economy and population grew, Americans were progressively less vulnerable to naval intimidation. Expansion inland made more of their commerce internal, buffered from maritime intrusions. The Americans came to believe that they could get along without the British and thus were less willing to pay any implicit costs of remaining in the empire. Britain's efforts to enforce her formal rights spurred escalating conflicts that erupted into warfare in 1775. When the Declaration of Independence was signed in 1776, it simply confirmed the de facto independence that had already developed.

The Revolution was America's longest declared war, with the fighting dragging on for eight years. Much of the conflict occurred on home turf, thus having a major impact on the Colonial economy and its businesses. But most accounts of the Revolution neglect the techniques that shaped the warfare and thus fail to explain how its conduct affected Colonial business.

British officials understood that subduing the Americans would not be easy. As the most experienced maritime power they recognized the difficulties of extending power across the Atlantic. The state of ocean transportation still made it very difficult to deliver and supply a large army over that distance. The British elected to make a preemptive strike, hoping to quash the Americans before other powers, particularly the French, could come to their aid. In retrospect this still appears to have been their most promising tactic. But they underestimated the strength and determination of the Americans to absorb that thrust. The British never had enough resources completely to blockade the American coast and thereby throttle America's maritime commerce and nascent navy.

British attempts to destroy the centers of Colonial resistance by striking into the interior became extraordinarily expensive and fell short of subduing any major region. Armies were tied to a cumbersome supply train in which everything was transported in horse-drawn wagons. They could outrun their supply lines in three or four days, and so had to stop for supplies to catch up. Typically, while the British were able to capture Colonial ports and coastal areas, the American army retreated into the interior, regrouped, and although not victorious, persisted as a provocative representative of a sovereign power. As the war continued, it became obvious that the British could not win a complete victory. France, and later Spain, joined the Americans, dropping their earlier clandestine approach to giving aid. During the latter part of the Revolution the British were pulled into a war among the major colonial powers such that they could spare only a fraction of their resources to fight the Americans. They recognized that they would have to reach a settlement that incorporated American independence.[1]

In essence the British were defeated by the size of the American economy, accentuated by its distance from Europe. In other words, the British did not lose to American generals as much as they lost to American entrepreneurs, who had created an entirely new economy in this seemingly unlikely locale. One hundred years earlier the American Colonies would have been fortunate to have been noted on most military maps, but now they had stymied one of the world's greatest powers. It is a fitting example of how entrepreneurs can provide new options and, thus, alter the course of world events.

The Business of War

When the fighting began, American business had to learn to operate in a very different environment. Shippers and merchants lost British protection for their trade, as well as legal access to the British Empire, the largest market of the day. Indeed, now they were hounded by the strongest maritime power in the world. Direct trade between England and the self-proclaimed United States was obviously out of the question, but there were still large gains from trade with the developed nations of Europe. The same incentives applied to businesses within England, prompting them to create subterfuges to continue trade with the Americans. The main way of accomplishing such exchanges was creating entrepôts in neutral ports to shield them from hostile parties. The Dutch island of St. Eustatius in the Caribbean was so busy that when the British declared war on Holland in 1781 and attacked the port, they captured 2,000 American merchants and sailors along with $5 million worth of ships and cargo. These are about as many maritime resources as could be found in Philadelphia, America's largest port, when peace resumed. At such locales goods were transferred, relabeled, and generally disguised to create the appearance of neutrality. Of course, the extra steps raised the costs of the trade. Also, belligerents were not so naïve as to miss what was going on, so they harassed the traders on minor pretexts. But the gains from the exchange were sufficiently large to make such costs appear tolerable nuisances in comparison. Recent disclosures of American products being shipped clandestinely to Russia and Iran remind us how strong the incentives to devise roundabout exchanges can be.

Wartime expedients raised the cost of imports, lowered the return on exports, and shifted domestic incentives toward greater self-sufficiency. Thus, there was a sharp increase in efforts by domestic merchants, craftsmen, and farmers to create replacements for imports. Special attention was given to raising local output of linen and woolen cloth, paper, salt, gunpowder, and iron products. Symptomatic of the environment was the construction of a farm workshop in rural Massachusetts turning out nails and knife blades. The driving force behind the enterprise was a fourteen-year-old, Eli Whitney, whose contributions to American manufacturing would soon become celebrated in the 1790s.

The war prompted other special efforts by American business. Prevailing practice allowed civilians to capture the enemy's merchant vessels. Given the Americans' extensive involvement in shipping, this could have proved to be important, either as a handicap or an advantage. American merchantmen had powerful reasons to make the most of the opportunity: they sold their prizes and divided the proceeds among officers, crew, and owners. Understandably many more Americans signed on for that service than for the army, which paid a pitifully small wage. At the peak more than five hundred American vessels scoured the North Atlantic and Caribbean for

British merchantmen. (The British Navy lacked sufficient resources to bottle up the entire American coast until the last year of the war.) They captured more than two thousand prizes, which—including their cargo—cost the British upward of one hundred million dollars. This was probably the strongest factor pressuring the British to negotiate an end to the conflict.[2]

Another special business effort spurred by the war was not nearly so successful. Americans had little experience organizing and supplying militia operations of more than a few months' duration. Furthermore, they had never before been denied the use of water transportation along the coast, by far the cheapest means of mobilizing supplies. Moreover, for the first time the financial authority of the army supply officers was seriously doubted.

The largest challenge in keeping the American army combat ready was supplying adequate food and—in the era before the internal combustion engine—fodder for its horses. The problem was not a general shortage of food, but rather moving it punctually to where the army was operating. In the early years of the conflict when the main army operated in New England, it was well fed. Indeed, the Continental Congress stipulated standard daily rations to prevent the quartermasters from overspending. But once Washington moved to the Middle Atlantic colonies operating west of New York City and around Philadelphia, conditions deteriorated. Local provisions proved inadequate in large part because both sides swept through the countryside seizing supplies. The locals quickly learned to conceal their stocks.

With the British Navy interdicting sea routes the Americans had to resort to wagons to bring in supplies. This made them dependent on crude, back-country roads, particularly the amalgamation spliced together in a long arc around New York City, to tap the supplies of southern New England. Ironically, the Americans now battled the same conditions that prevented the British armies from striking very far into the interior, but with the added penalty that their supply lines were even longer.

Keeping Washington's army operational became an enormous task. With supply wagons seldom traveling more than ten miles in a day and the weather not infrequently stopping them for weeks, supplies had to be put on their way to the army long before their expected use. The length of the routes multiplied the task because the supply teams consumed several tons of food and fodder for every ton they delivered. Operating this leaky, disjointed pipeline proved to be one of the most difficult management tasks of the Revolution, as is suggested by how seldom it worked adequately.

The entrepreneur who proved most up to the challenge was Jeremiah Wadsworth, who earned the nickname of "quartermaster of the Revolution." He was a very successful young merchant in Hartford, Connecticut, having completed the advance from cabin boy to ship captain in ten years. The skills Wadsworth had honed as a merchant, particularly purchasing farm produce and trading bills of credit, were put to their utmost test. He had to coax an unusually large amount of food, hay, horses, wagons, and teamsters from the southern New England countryside, even by peacetime standards. To compound the difficulties, he couldn't offer much more than depreciating government bills of credit in payment. His record in delivering supplies in 1778 and 1779 earned him the lucrative contract for the French armies, which paid costs plus a commission in gold coin. Wadsworth's creativity in fashioning a supply line probably contributed more to the American cause than most of its generals and statesmen. Without his particular entrepreneurial achievements, neither would have had much to defend or represent.

The American war effort was nearly destroyed away from the battlefield. The Colonies never became formally unified during the war. At first they cooperated unofficially through the Continental Congress. Even the Confederation, which superseded it in 1781, depended upon widespread consensus. Both forms lacked the traditional power of government to tax or otherwise control resources. They had to convince most of the states that it was in their self-interest to join each proposed initiative. Early military operations were financed through a combination of loans, new paper money, and *commissary receipts* (these functioned as loans because they were redeemable with interest from the Continental treasury). The arrangement worked for the first years of the war because it was expected that the fighting would be short-lived, and then Americans would fulfill the obligations of this quasi-central government. By

1779, however, it became clear that the war had gone well beyond the limits of temporary sources of financing. Each winter the lack of suitable quarters, food, and clothing greatly shrank the American army to a small core. In 1779 and 1780 it threatened to disband entirely. Parts of the army were ready to mutiny because they had not been paid, even in badly depreciated Continental currency.

This crisis threatened America's national credibility. Thus the British, having been unable to destroy American independence by force of arms, might still have expected to subdue them by persisting with the war. The English leaders would not have neglected this eventuality. Having employed a large professional army for some time, they understood that adequate food and shelter were necessary costs of maintaining its effectiveness. Any army was a long-term asset. Shortchanging its supplies reduced its future as well as immediate effectiveness.

One of the wealthiest merchants of the late Colonial period stepped forward to stave off the financial crisis. Robert Morris had developed a prosperous store in Philadelphia, which extended to the usual activities of bills of credit, manufacturing, and land.[3] His location prepared him for his next role because during most of the war the Continental Congress met in or near Philadelphia. Morris served in the Continental Congress during the early part of the war from 1775 to 1778, putting a considerable amount of his enormous energy into procuring supplies for the army. He left government service in 1778 in order to devote full time to his private operations. But in 1780 Congress desperately appealed to Morris to return to stem the collapse of its purchasing power and preserve the war effort. He assumed the newly created position of superintendent of finance in May 1781, along with the expanded fiscal powers the title implied. Morris's basic task was to use the substantial strength of the private economy to support what the majority of Americans viewed as a worthwhile project but one that lacked a credible mechanism to implement.

Morris's bold initiatives included chartering the Bank of North America to provide a reliable currency in the economy, issuing "Morris notes"—backed by his personal collateral—to facilitate government payments, and lobbying for a 5 percent tariff to fund the accumulated debt. He also made fiscal operations more businesslike by creating a separate revenue-collection agency reaching into each state and energetically sought to settle the backlog of government bills.

Morris stopped American finances from spiraling into destruction, but even his energy and innovations failed to narrow the huge gap between spending and revenues, so another fiscal crisis erupted in 1783. This time foreign loans and the winding down of the fighting after Yorktown allowed the patriots to survive. But Morris's individual role should not be slighted. His initiative certainly bought Americans time. Most entrepreneurs are soon surpassed by others who begin farther down the road so that, ultimately, an entrepreneurial contribution is providing a benefit sooner, or, as in this case, postponing a cost. Even holding back a disaster for as little as a few weeks is a very large contribution for one individual to make to three million countrymen.

Setting New Ground Rules

When the Americans evicted the local British officials in 1776, they had to reconstruct a part of their political system they had come to take for granted. The departing imperial officers not only vacated the executive function of Colonial governments, but also undercut the authority and legitimacy of the entire institutional structure of the Colonies. Replacing the governor and his staff was relatively simple. After all, the Americans had spent a good part of the previous century working to limit and direct the influence of the royal governors. But the break also necessitated a fundamental appraisal of the foundations of government, an area in which the Americans had developed ideas that departed significantly from the British model.

The changes in government had to be addressed at a dangerous time, when the urgent problems of coping with a war could have warped the structure that would shape the long-term development of the society. The common law, private property, and other elements of the English tradition had clearly been central contributors to the rapid progress of the Colonies. And the future promised additional development if the Americans could reestablish a balance between social order and innovation in their new institutions.

The citizens of the newly independent states shared several strong concerns that shaped the reorganization of their governments. They recognized that governments had to be granted powers in order to carry out their responsibilities, and yet their recent clashes with the British had instilled a deep distrust of such authority. Thus in each state enormous energy was invested in seeking arrangements to maintain resistance to unwarranted governmental expansions. One tactic, which spread from Virginia to the other states, was the division of governmental powers into distinct, separate branches. This created permanent checks within government by forcing the legislative, executive, and judiciary branches to be watchdogs on one another. Furthermore, the legislative branch, which was seen to be most powerful, was divided into two houses by upgrading the old governor's council into a full-fledged senate. In addition, states specified preambles and intentions in their new constitutions. The most influential was clearly that of Virginia, whose bill of rights specifically prohibited the government from interfering with a wide array of personal freedoms.

The efforts of the states demonstrated an important virtue of the American federal system, which has been evident since. The states provided many productive experiments about shared concerns. All of the eleven new constitutions—Connecticut's and Rhode Island's governments required only minor changes—emerged as similar documents in response to common concerns. Yet, together they had confronted a wider array of concerns and discoveries than any individual state. One indicator of the volume of this collective form of learning is that many of the features adopted in the national constitution were borrowed from state discoveries.

Creating a National Government

Even before the state governments began to be reformulated, Americans felt it necessary to coordinate their resistance to the common British threat. The first Continental Congresses, in 1774 and 1775, developed bargaining positions vis-à-vis England, but gave little thought to assuming the function of a sovereign nation. However, independence thrust many such functions upon them, even though officially they remained a gathering of advisory delegates from their respective states. As independence continued to look more permanent, rather than merely a bargaining stance aimed at the British, the Continental Congress began drafting a plan for confederating the states in 1777.

While the necessity of conducting the Revolution compelled the Continental Congress to act as if the Articles of Confederation had been approved, that formal step did not come for another four years. The lag is instructive, showing the respective advantages and disadvantages of voluntary collaboration to conduct collective affairs. The Articles of Confederation specified unanimous approval by the states for both adoption and amendment. In addition, it imposed a stringent three-quarters majority rule for adopting legislation. This appeared to be an invitation to gridlock whereby a few states could hold the programs of the majority hostage to their own selfish ends. But it also encouraged all parties to spend much more effort working out arrangements that benefited all participants. In other words, the majority couldn't run roughshod over the interests of the minority, but had to craft a program that persuaded them it was in their own interest as well.

The influence of this procedure became evident in the deliberations on western land, the largest issue blocking approval of the Articles of Confederation. Four states, Virginia, New York, Connecticut, and Massachusetts, claimed overlapping sections of western land north of the Ohio River. The claims were clouded by conflicting precedents of discoveries and settlements, so that a clear-cut judicial resolution seemed unlikely. Moreover, states without claims felt threatened by the additional area and influence that might be added to their neighbors. The final accommodation was to cede all claims over western lands to the Confederation, allowing every state to benefit through national sale of the land.

The acquiescence of the four claim-holding states to national distribution was sufficient to win final approval of the Confederation. But the deliberations about the distribution of land continued constructively with the decision to create new states from the western land rather than create colonies or expand existing states. They also created a uniform system of survey and sale. The Northwest Ordinance of 1787 capped this process by spelling out the steps whereby new states could be admitted to equal status in the Confederation. Ironically it came at the end of the Confederation's existence, proving a fitting tribute to its encouragement of long-term, peaceful accommodations to social issues.[4]

Whatever the Confederation's advantages for the long term, it was America's perceptions of its liabilities, especially for short-term actions, that caused it to be supplanted. One obvious weakness was the absence of an executive branch. During the Revolution, for example, committees of the Continental Congress had supervised such functions as military operations, revenue, and foreign affairs. Nearly everyone, including the participating committee members, expressed doubts about the effectiveness of this arrangement. The lack of the power to tax was another sore point. For a long war, such as the Revolution, raising resources by borrowing was bound to degrade the public credit and lead to inflation. (Although it is suggestive that when spending for the war was totaled up afterward, 80 percent of the expense had been shouldered by the individual states in proportions that coincided with reasonable estimates of their respective shares.)

A third complaint of Americans about the Confederation was its weakness in dealing with foreign powers. Its organization, which functioned something like a beefed-up alliance among sovereign nations, left considerable leeway to individual states in foreign economic affairs. The Confederation negotiated commercial treaties with major trading powers during the 1780s, but there was still an important range of terms that had to be worked out between each state and foreign power. Thirteen states added up to hundreds of negotiations. No doubt, had the situation persisted much longer, states would have found ways to simplify relations by forming regional associations to standardize procedures and pursue negotiations.

What really rankled the Americans was the hard-nosed pressures other nations applied during trade negotiations. Particularly grating was the tactic of playing neighboring states off against one another to hammer trade concessions from them. Again, some of the American discomfort might have been erased by experience. Nothing prevented the states from forming coalitions to present a unified front. Ironically, these humiliating experiences may have worked to the Americans' advantage. The foreign negotiators mostly worked at breaking down barriers to their own goods, particularly tariffs. The latter, of course, protect domestic producers but, as we now recognize, at a more-than-offsetting cost to local consumers. Thus rough handling by foreigners may have been like childhood's cod-liver oil: we abhorred it, but it was good for us.

When the Constitution consolidated authority over foreign trade in the federal government, therefore, the primary beneficiary was American pride. Over the long haul its economic effects have been, on net, damaging. It bolstered the power of organized producers to restrict competition, paving the way for such monstrosities as the Morrill Tariff, enacted during the Civil War, and the Smoot-Hawley Tariff of the Great Depression.

The Constitution

Whatever the actual merits and demerits of the Confederation, a sufficient number of Americans perceived its shortcomings to start a movement to replace it. This concern prompted the convention in Philadelphia in 1787, whose instructions were to consider modifications to the Confederation. But the changes the delegates concluded were necessary were so fundamental that they soon focused on drafting an entirely new government. Their handiwork has had a profound impact on American business and entrepreneurs because it fixed so many of the basic tenets that would channel their activities. During its first century of operation, the Constitution allowed Americans to do much as they wished. In its second century, however, its effect moved the other way, as it implemented the emerging public view that government should assume a more comprehensive and directive role.

Every nation beatifies its founders along with the specific locations and documents they immortalized. Thus it is hardly surprising that the Constitution has acquired layers of uncritical adoration. Yet viewed objectively, it is surprising how successful and enduring it has proved. Few attempts at a new form of government have escaped failure within a century, while the survivors have often undergone major revisions. There have been surprisingly few substantive changes to the Constitution. The first ten amendments, the Bill of Rights, stem from a general understanding worked out in the process of approval. Of the remaining fifteen amendments, only five were passed in the first one hundred years. The three most important dealt with the enormous conflict of the nineteenth century, slavery. Ten amendments have been added in the twentieth century, but four were procedural changes and two, the Eighteenth and Twenty-first, instituted and then repealed Prohibition, canceling out each other. The four substantial amendments, clearly reflecting the times, allowed an income tax, granted women the vote, limited the presidency to two terms, and prohibited the poll tax.

Almost certainly a major reason that the Constitution has weathered so well is that it is structured to encourage compromise and consultation in its operations. The major participants in the convention clearly had thought seriously about how people are wont to behave and thus the type of institutional arrangements that would encourage the best from them. This approach is best exemplified in the person of George Mason, who can lay serious claim to being the entrepreneur of American government.[5]

Mason spent almost all of his life managing Gunston Hall, his family estate in northern Virginia. He was a reticent individual, possibly because when he did venture out he found most participants in public affairs to be shallow and selfish. Nevertheless, he devoted considerable energy and thought to public offices and became an informal senior adviser to the leading Virginian revolutionaries, including Washington, Jefferson, and Henry.

Mason was pulled into active public service as a member of the Virginia Committee of Safety, which assumed the state's executive functions when the royal governor was expelled. He drafted much of the new state constitution, as well as the Virginia Declaration of Rights. Both of these documents were widely emulated by other states in crafting their own counterparts. It is not surprising, there-fore, that Virginia sent Mason as a delegate to the Constitutional Convention in Philadelphia and that he became one of its most effective participants.

The achievements of George Mason are an excellent demonstra-tion that ideas can have powerful consequences; man is not totally governed by his physical environment or the goods that he has learned to extract from it. Rather, he can also devise institutions that enhance the value of social interactions. An entrepreneur fashioning worthwhile innovations, therefore, can contribute as much to human welfare and fulfillment as can a tangible mechanical invention. When Mason worked out such principles as the division of government into offsetting branches and the explicit recognition of individual rights, he freed Americans—and many others who later borrowed their discoveries—from much of the arbitrary coercion to which govern-ments are wont to resort. He understood that governments are oper-ated by humans and, thus, should incorporate mechanisms to guard against well-intended but ill-acting efforts to wield their powers.

4

Building Value as Ground Rules Shift

Americans barely had their new government under way when their independence was given its first full-fledged workout. In 1792 England and France became embroiled in the Napoleonic Wars, whose name was obviously taken from the exceptional leader who gave France such a bright moment in international affairs. Had the Americans not just won freedom from Britain, they would have been compelled to support her campaigns in the Western Hemisphere. Instead independence enhanced their leverage with the major powers. They assumed the role of a neutral intermediary trader, much like the one certain Caribbean islands had played during the Revolution.

During the fifteen years after 1792, large quantities of goods were diverted through the United States in order to disguise their source. Sometimes they were repackaged, but they were invariably given new shipping papers in order to make them appear to be products of neutral America and, thus, exempt from the ravages of the warring powers. These re-exports provided a major boost to income and employment in the United States during this period. Of course both England and France recognized that this maneuver was undercutting their tactic of economic warfare, so they harassed those American shipments suspected of aiding their opponent. These tactics led to periodic confrontations with both belligerents, but nevertheless, on net, Americans gained considerable wealth.

The war in Europe also stimulated the demand for domestically produced goods such as food and ships. European food supplies were disrupted by the fighting, and many European commercial ships were pressed into military uses. The sum of these stimuli prompted prosperity throughout the American economy. Contemporary observers noted exceptional levels of construction both in major ports and in the countryside. New shipyards and wharves appeared in virtually every northern port. Adjacent to them were new warehouses, shops, and homes. These homes provided some of the best monuments to the period. The ones along Chestnut Street in Salem, Massachusetts, and the Battery in Charleston, South Carolina, are tangible artifacts of the exceptional prosperity of the era.

Expansion reached to the limits of the economy. Finding the demand for food intensified, farmers shifted their efforts toward marketable crops. To move the produce to the port cities and bring back the merchandise purchased with the proceeds, roads and bridges were improved. Common seamen were probably the most spectacular beneficiaries. Their wages jumped from $8 to $30 per month, meaning that a year at sea could earn enough to start a fair-size farm. It also explains why in every foreign port locals clamored to join up, particularly deserters from British ships who had been impressed into service for a tiny fraction of that rate. Of course, this gave the British Navy all that much more reason to search American merchantmen for contraband.

While America gained from the Napoleonic Wars, she could not expect foreign conflicts to provide recurring help. The economy evolved such that the next occurrence in Europe—World War I, which proved to be a full century later—was less beneficial. But certain features of the experience did portend developing trends, helping American entrepreneurs anticipate future conditions. Foreign trade had grown little from 1775 to 1790, but then rocketed upward, increasing about six times by 1808. Thus the limits to specialization that small markets had imposed since the Colonial period quickly receded. The major port merchants began to carve out distinctive niches. This adjustment was most evident in the fastest-growing segment, re-exports, which was particularly inviting to specialized procedures. By the time such goods arrived in American ports, the slowest, most tedious task of assembling them into shiploads for export had already been accomplished. The crucial function now became dispatching ships to minimize the cost of freight and damage by hostile powers. It was fertile ground for a creative specialist as well as a helpful warm-up for the larger mercantile environment about to develop in America.[1]

The merchants of the port of Salem, Massachusetts, made the most of Napoleonic prosperity, and among them Joseph Peabody stood out.[2] He had just reached thirty when the conflict began, having already demonstrated exceptional talent and resolve in advancing to where he could make the most of the maritime opportunity. He had begun without advantages, being the ninth child of a small farmer. During the Revolution he served on a series of privateers, rising to captain. He became a minicelebrity one night when loyalists attacked his ship while it was anchored in the Potomac River. Wounded, and still in his nightshirt, he led the badly outnumbered crew in a spirited defense that cowed the attackers into retreat.

Successful commercial voyages in the 1780s earned Peabody the position of merchant in Salem in 1791, just as the wars in Europe got under way. He was soon dispatching ships to the Baltic, the Mediterranean, and the West Indies, taking advantage of the depletion of British and French merchantmen. He also initiated voyages to China, India, and the East Indies, where the cutback in European voyages also raised the returns on cargoes. Plowing back his substantial profits into ships, cargoes, and port facilities, Peabody developed a sizable maritime enterprise by the end of the conflict.

No doubt the Napoleonic Wars helped his progress, but Peabody would likely have been an outstanding entrepreneur at almost any time. He understood the implications about enlightened leadership and company culture that have become recognized recently. Rather than bargaining aggressively with each customer, he encouraged his employees to develop their skills by rewarding their improvements. More than thirty-five cabin boys rose to captain in his enterprises, no doubt partly encouraged by the example of the owner himself. The care he showed for his crews demonstrated itself in exceptionally small losses to ships, only one—and that to military action—in the fifteen-year period. Peabody presaged the modern view that quality, by reducing losses, is often the most effective way to reduce costs. He also demonstrated the timeless business principle that unquestioned honesty is a major advantage in negotiating. By 1810 his promise was accepted on par with that of the federal government.

Turning Inward

While American merchant ships led North Atlantic commerce at the turn of the nineteenth century, their eminence fell surprisingly quickly. By the 1820s they had given up a good share of these markets and by the Civil War had been driven out of all but a few specialty trades. The standard explanation for this reversal has been based on changes in technology, such as the appearance of iron steamships. But this is suspect because Americans proved capable of using both steam engines and iron when it suited their purposes. The shift likely reflected more fundamental economic changes. When businesses provide similar products, competition turns on their respective costs. Technology obviously affects these costs, but so does the local supply of inputs. A farm located in downtown Manhattan may use farming methods every bit as advanced as those in Iowa, but the cost of land in the former ensures that no farms survive there. Likewise American merchantmen did not lose out to such competitors as the British after 1820 because they were less technically proficient. Rather, they found their costs for labor, materials, and services in home ports creeping above levels they could afford to pay.

Ironically, it was America's success that did in its own shipping. Emerging opportunities elsewhere in the economy, especially the development of western land, were bidding for the country's resources and raising their prices. When an American could go west with a reasonable prospect of acquiring his own farm, it took more to persuade him to keep working on the wharf or enlist aboard ship. Thus, ultimately, it was the economy's progress vis-à-vis other nations that caused it to withdraw from the international shipping market, much as the erection of a large factory near a small town these days raises the cost of clerks for local shopkeepers.

The American withdrawal set off wide-ranging adjustments in the Atlantic ports. Imports into every major port except New York shrank. In marked contrast, that city became a new entrepôt, taking advantage of the gains from specializing in foreign trade. While services for shipping, such as finance and stevedoring, boomed in lower Manhattan, suppliers in other ports sought new opportunities. Stephen Girard in Philadelphia was an early example.[3]

Girard was born to a well-connected family in France but, because of mishaps including the death of his mother, had to begin his career at the bottom. He became a cabin boy at fourteen, working his way up the typical mercantile ladder from there. By age twenty-three he had reached captain, but then, because of a major business loss in the Caribbean, diverted to New York to attempt to recoup. Three years later, he owned half the ship he commanded. Girard clearly sought the fast track, overcame severe obstacles, and advanced through his own initiative.

The British capture of his home port of New York in 1776 forced Girard to put into Philadelphia. The temporary refuge developed into his permanent base of operations, so much so that his name became part of the city's continuing legacy. When Philadelphia also was occupied by the British, he turned to merchandising in the countryside. Both these occurrences might appear to be bad luck but, like many successful people, Girard made the most of seeming chance. He used unpredictable events to advance his goals, relocating to the then-largest market in America.

Girard took full advantage of maritime opportunities in the

twenty years following the Revolution to extend his operations, owning up to six ships in addition to the wide scope of his mercantile efforts. He also broadened his base through major investments in real estate, insurance, and bills of exchange. Thus when foreign trade slowed, he understood the operations and needs of other sectors and shifted smartly to take advantage of them. As a merchant he had seen how valuable a reliable means of exchange and a mechanism to mobilize capital were. When Congress refused to renew the federal charter of the first Bank of the United States in 1810, he converted it to his private operation. By the War of 1812 he was able to underwrite a good portion of the government's loans, demonstrating how quickly he put his resources and skills to work in internal markets in the economy.

Another famous merchant, John Jacob Astor, also illustrated the American shift toward domestic concerns.[4] Astor came to the United States from Germany in 1784. His apprenticeship and training had been in musical instruments, but he quickly grasped that greater opportunities were developing in the fur trade. He extended his operations in turn into Canada, the Louisiana Territory, the Northwest, and China, as barriers to American operations in each area were dropped. The breadth of his operations drew him into developing the merchandising and shipping systems that delivered furs.

But fur trading in America was decreasing in each region because settlements destroyed the natural habitat of fur-bearing animals. Astor judged that opportunities in the sector were declining, or at least were not as attractive as another opportunity he discovered under his nose in New York City. He noticed that the returns on the property around his headquarters in New York exceeded those in fur trading. Thus he shifted his efforts increasingly toward real estate. He was much more than a passive investor who held property, waiting for it to appreciate. He had a keen eye for developing sites to provide the particular services that would become advantageous as the city developed. Astor followed what we now recognize to be a good entrepreneurial rule of thumb: rather than spread his creative energies thinly, he stuck to his knitting. He began to close out his fur trading in the 1820s, transferring the resources to New

York, He spent the remainder of his rather long lifetime—he died in 1848 at eighty-four—as a major landlord and real estate developer in New York City.

MAKING SOMETHING OUT OF THE EMPTY WEST

The attention of Americans was being directed inland by a huge, yet unfulfilled potential. They had been consistently moving westward since the Colonies were founded as improvements in transportation and the expanding market kept pulling frontier areas into profitability. When Britain acceded to independence for the Americans, she yielded them all the territory out to the Mississippi River, most of which was unsettled. Moreover, in the following sixty years, that area was more than tripled as Americans possessed all the land to the Pacific Ocean.

The British assumed all this vacant territory would keep the Americans safely preoccupied for a long, long time. Extrapolating from the rate of settlement in the Colonial period, it would take them three hundred years to reach the Mississippi River, and a minimum of six hundred more to reach the Pacific! But they—and most Americans for that matter—failed to appreciate the revolutionary impact that economic incentives would have in accelerating the timetable.

At the beginning of the nineteenth century most land west of the Appalachian Mountains was unsettled because it was inaccessible, not because it lacked intrinsic value. On the contrary, much of it surpassed the land the colonists had learned to employ along the Atlantic Coast. There were substantial supplies of copper, iron ore, and timber. Most of the arable land would produce more per acre than the land then in cultivation. In particular, the huge expanse of midwestern topsoil piled up by the last Ice Age, which has since come to be known as the cornbelt, was the best large section of nonalluvial farmland in the world.

In the first years of independence these resources might as well have been on the moon. The cost of packtrains, wagons, and flatboats bringing the produce out to a market would have consumed its selling price several times over. This area, along with most of western America, continued to be noneconomic and unsettled until appropriate technologies and institutions tied it into existing markets.

Harbingers of these conditions appeared at least as early as the Revolution. Even during the disruption of the war, Americans kept moving farther into the interior, seeking a better life. They carved out roads to connect themselves back into the productive exchange of coastal markets. As settlement proceeded and the volume of such trade increased, traffic on the roads grew, making it worthwhile to upgrade them. Rural Americans invested considerable resources in their roads: removing obstructions, leveling the roadbed, and building bridges. The roadways were still well below modern standards, becoming quagmires in the spring or after a heavy rain, and choking dust during dry periods. Despite their shortcomings, they served their purpose of enhancing specialization and trade within the economy. Indeed, the importance of that function increased even faster than the economy because commerce continued growing within a locality for decades after initial settlement. Farms underwent further development and were also frquently subdivided into additional homesteads. Villages and commercial facilities expanded. Each locality worked through an extended learning process whereby its best crops and techniques of production were established.

The immediate payoff of better roads in settled areas in the late eighteenth century caused Americans to look westward, visualizing additional, enormous potential for their services. A rule of thumb at that time was that it cost as much to transport goods thirty miles overland as it did to send them clear across the Atlantic Ocean. The differential explains why the Colonial economy was organized around a maritime base. It was much more promising to work with parties along the coast or across the ocean than to develop new enterprises in the interior. But the reverse side of the lopsided transportation ratio was the huge reward if costs of land transportation could be reduced. The enormous supply of fertile acres and natural resources would expand the base of the economy many times over. It also came to dominate the basic orientation of the economy, shifting interest away from maritime activities toward a domestic, introspective approach to economic affairs.

Thus by the end of the eighteenth century all the prerequisites for domestic transportation becoming a growth sector were in place. Its widespread recognition ensured that aspiring entrepreneurs would mount a broad, persistent assault on the problem. We now recognize that such widespread and persistent efforts are necessary to produce the new technology that propels a growth sector. The requisite new techniques can never be created suddenly and full blown in a "eureka" breakthrough. Rather they require numerous refinements and the interaction of many minor innovations to build up the necessary skills. This is why it is essential to have an environment that prompts entrepreneurs to keep chipping away at the problem for an extended period. This is also why all major growth sectors have required a minimum of a half century to reach full fruition.

Like other emerging growth sectors, domestic transportation began by squeezing the most out of the existing technology at hand.[5] Intensified incentives can invariably stretch current methods further than believed possible. The basic requirements of serviceable, all-weather roads had been known for thousands of years. Roman artifacts testified to that. But American ingenuity, assisted by recent English experiences, squeezed a surprisingly large amount of services from the mundane medium.

The key to improving roads proved to be not so much developing technology as creating social institutions that elicited the appropriate incentives. Most roads had been the responsibility of the local town. As traffic increased, however, an increasing portion also traveled longer distances, which meant passing through more of such local jurisdictions. Not only was traffic costly to local communities but this structure encouraged travelers to abuse the roadway. It was recognized, for example, that the wider the area of the road's surface on which a given load is dispersed the less damaging it is to that surface. (This explains modern-day load limits and weigh stations for trucks.) A teamster could reduce wear on a road by carrying lighter loads or using wider wheels on the wagon, but such steps cost more, running counter to his self-interest.

The English had hit on a solution to the perversity of this arrangement by instituting turnpikes. These were private roads, charging each traveler a toll scaled to its usage and wear, and expecting to earn a competitive return on its investment. It was also an early-day example of what we have come to call *privatization,* turning public services over to private suppliers. As do current initiatives, the intention was to increase productivity and improve the use of resources by creating property rights that aligned incentives with social returns.

The first American turnpike of note was completed between Philadelphia and Lancaster, Pennsylvania, in 1794, ending widespread dissatisfaction with the conditions of that route, which extended all the way back before the Revolution. The project was organized by a private corporation whose offering of shares to the public was quickly subscribed. This allowed most of the sixty-one-mile project to be completed in two years. Nine tollgates were spotted along the route, collecting fares by a schedule that carefully discriminated among users by employing forty-six classifications.

The Lancaster Turnpike quickly attracted many more travelers, including some who had abandoned the previous route in frustration over its wretched condition. Reports of its success spread rapidly because Americans thought its example might be the solution to their frustrations with their own local roads. In the next three decades more than ten thousand miles of turnpikes were built in America. The majority were in southern New England and the Middle Atlantic states, where their density reached the equivalent of twenty through roads running completely across the region. Coverage was particularly great in Connecticut, where more than five hundred miles of turnpikes were completed in a state averaging only ninety miles wide and sixty miles north to south. In other words, on average there was one mile of turnpike with each square of land slightly longer than three miles on a side. The significance of these measurements is underscored by recognizing that turnpikes served heavily traveled, primary routes. They connected many times their own mileage of the lesser traveled, local farm-to-market roads.

The turnpikes dramatically improved the convenience and speed of travel between towns. Twisting, rutted roadways littered with stumps and large rocks were replaced by all-weather roads. Grades were smoothed out, streams bridged, and crushed stone applied to the roadbed in the form of a rounded crown to shed water. New turnpikes were almost always hailed as an improvement. When they opened, a surge in wagon and stage travel followed as farmers, merchants, and teamsters grasped expanded opportunities. Even though travelers predictably resorted to *shunpiking*—using local routes to bypass toll stations—they generally agreed that the gains in time, the increased cargo, and reduced bruises more than compensated for the tolls.

The value of the turnpike organization was emphasized by state legislatures frequently turning *existing routes* over to private companies in order to improve their condition. Thus, it didn't require the construction of new facilities to warrant imposing tolls; the improved use of existing resources justified shifting to private management. Turnpikes not only encouraged timely maintenance but, by imposing charges according to individual usage, encouraged travelers to make road investments last longer. The rate structure penalized such destructive practices as overloaded wagons and narrow wheels. Thus, the creation of tollroads illustrates how the creation of appropriate property rights can remedy perverse, external effects in an economy. Americans observing the situation then probably did not size up the situation so formally, but their instincts correctly guided them toward the solution.

The enthusiastic reception of turnpikes contrasts with the sustained failure to win federal funding for internal transportation. Proponents of government subsidies never gained much assistance for national roads and waterways in the nineteenth century. No doubt, much of the explanation lies in the reluctance of voters, such as those in the Northeast, to pay for projects that would disproportionately benefit others, particularly those in the West and the South. Another contributing factor was that proposed projects often did not promise sufficient returns to elicit much support. Residents in areas requesting aid had the opportunity to build their own tollroads but, relative to area and population, they undertook far fewer, and, of those, the majority required supplemental state funding to compensate for the lack of local revenues. When the locals judged that their own projects didn't warrant their support, it became that much more difficult to convince taxpayers elsewhere to pick up the tab.

Americans seeking to improve transportation also experimented with canals, another English technology. There was reason to expect that they might solve America's transportation problems, pulling new areas into the national economy. Because shipping goods by water cost only one hundredth of what it cost to send them overland, building waterways might yield huge gains. Initial canal projects seemed to confirm this logic. Before 1815, small projects bypassed natural obstructions, tying together natural water routes such as Albemarle Sound with Chesapeake Bay to complete an inland water connection from Maryland south to North Carolina. These emboldened New York State to undertake the Erie Canal in 1817, a project more than ten times longer and much more technically demanding than the preceding ventures. It proved to be both the high point and the downfall of American canals.

Upstate New York, between Albany and Buffalo, was the most promising east-west route along the Atlantic seaboard for a major canal. Not only was the terrain relatively flat, with access to dependable supplies of water, but it traversed good agricultural land that would be spurred into production by access to cheap transportation. Commerce developed along the first sections of the project so rapidly that the New York legislature elected to use toll revenues to add an extensive system of feeder canals. Other states, notably Pennsylvania, Ohio, and Indiana, sought to emulate this success by commissioning systems of their own. But their experiences ranged from poor to—in the case of Pennsylvania—disastrous because they tried to deny American topography. Canals are capital-intensive, a resource particularly scarce in the United States. Moreover, this expense was intensified by the distances between the major markets that the projects sought to serve. In addition, many routes were ill-conceived, running dry for long periods or, in the absurd case in Pennsylvania, built as a jury-rigged system over the Allegheny Mountains. It took some states decades to rebuild their credit and credibility after such fiascoes. These failures also explain why few private groups undertook canal projects, focusing their search for the solution to overland transportation elsewhere.

The Steamboat: Learning to Walk on Water

Although canals failed to provide the sought-after breakthrough, the presumption underlying them, that water could provide cheap transportation, was still sound. But more productive tactics had to be devised. Rather than incurring the substantial capital expense of building new water routes to ideal specifications, the trick was devising a means to use the free ones that nature provided. In other words, it required far fewer resources to propel a boat than to remodel river systems. Though the solution might have seemed obvious, the necessary technology proved exceedingly difficult to implement, largely because it required solving three interlocking problems.

The first element was provided by Oliver Evans, a prolific Philadelphia inventor, who was developing steam engines for stationary applications. His refinements upped their power relative to their weight, also making them more advantageous in providing a source of mobile power. The second major problem, transmitting the power into effective propulsion, was solved by one of the most inventive minds in American history.

The entrepreneur who is commonly credited with developing the American steamboat spent the majority of his adult years in Europe.[6] Robert Fulton was born in Pennsylvania in 1765, but left for England in 1786 to study painting under another American expatriate, Benjamin West. The aspiring artist seemed to be making good progress, placing works in exhibitions and being accepted in artistic circles, but in 1793 he turned to designing canal systems. Most likely Fulton saw quicker returns there and, given his usual initiative, immediately followed that logic.

Canals were a growth industry in England at that time, and the natural center for their planning and construction was Manchester in the Midlands. Fulton moved there, soon winning several contracts. He also gained the respect of the local engineering and scientific community, which included such emissaries as Robert Owen, the utopian industrialist, and John Dalton, the chemist. In 1796 he published a book advocating a nationwide system of small, uniform canals, which demonstrated his broad entrepreneurial perspective as well as a technical command of the field. He was, for example, far ahead of most in recognizing the incremental nature of important innovations. He also was remarkably discerning about the specific effects through which improved transportation would benefit society.

But as was to be the usual case, Fulton's vision outran local opportunities, so in 1797 he went to France. He stayed on well beyond the short visit he planned, developing, among other devices, submarines and torpedoes to attack warships, as well as a promising prototype of a steamboat. Ever impatient, he returned to England when the French Navy cooled to his military proposals, and struck up a partnership with Robert Livingston, the American envoy negotiating the Louisiana Purchase. In 1806 he returned to the United States, bringing along a steam engine to complement his considerable experience in building an American steamboat.

Fulton quickly directed his creativity toward a steamboat designed for local conditions. But his tremendous energy also kept drawing him into other major projects such as canals, gunboats, and torpedoes—a practice that persisted for the remainder of his life. To spur service on the route between New York and Albany, the state of New York had promised a monopoly to the first shipper to complete the route satisfactorily. Within a year, Fulton's *North River Steam Boat*—unofficially called the *"Clermont"* after his home— had earned this monopoly.

This exclusive franchise proved to be much less valuable than might have been supposed. Rivals soon attacked its legitimacy in the courts and brazenly launched direct competitors. Well after any of its practical value was dissipated, the Supreme Court invalidated it in a landmark case prohibiting states from restricting commerce. Fulton had similar difficulties enforcing his steamboat patents. Challengers claimed that they lacked novel features; they were merely a new arrangement of established techniques. Fulton countered that this was a valuable form of novelty in itself. Today we understand that he was correct, that economic contributions should not be measured by technical inventiveness alone. Of course, patents must be based on tangible techniques, so his position constantly forced him onto the defensive. It is now clear that Fulton's primary advantage had to be that of most any successful firm in a rapidly developing industry: that of sustained, productive innovation, directed toward consumer desires.

In just five years beginning in 1810, Fulton built and operated steamboats on Long Island Sound, the Ohio River, and south along the Atlantic Coast, and expanded service up the Hudson River and around the New York harbor. Each boat incorporated engineering improvements and additional conveniences for passengers. But on each route competitors quickly appeared countering with their own innovations in boats and services. The pressures on Fulton grew, particularly because he made a classic mistake for entrepreneurs, failing to develop a management staff to assume some of the expanding responsibilities. His health suffered from the frantic pace, so that when he fell into the Hudson River in the winter of 1815, his vulnerable condition degenerated into pneumonia, which killed him three days later. Though his early demise was not totally surprising given his history, it was a tragic loss of one of America's greatest inventors and entrepreneurs.

Fulton never saw the steamboats his enterprise built and operated on the Ohio and Mississippi rivers. This was ironic because that region soon proved their most important application and yielded their most distinctive design. Eastern steamboats, such as those developed for the Hudson River, were crafted to serve passengers and express freight. In other words, they sought the luxury market, leaving bulk cargoes to the cheaper, coastal sailing vessels. To this end, the steamboats were designed long and narrow to achieve speed and were handsomely decorated. But when the new technology began to be applied to western rivers, the tactics underwent a complete about-face. This proved to be the third, pivotal link transforming the steamboat into a national asset.

Western rivers were frequently too shallow to accommodate the V-shaped keel of ocean and coastal vessels. Shallow water was most often found in upper tributaries and during the fall. Thus shipbuilders began to flatten out the hull of the western boats. This also aided the loading and storage of bulky cargo. Another of the steamboats' picturesque features was dictated by the lack of loading facilities along rivers. Shipbuilders moved the paddle wheels from the sides to the back, where they could keep the boat pressed snug against the shore during loading. To reduce draft in order to slip up to the bank, the engines were moved up to the deck.

As western steamboats approached their ultimate form, they took on a cumbersome, distinctly "unnautical" appearance, which provoked derision from blue-water sailors. But the structure proved remarkably effective—indeed, one of the most important inventions in American history. The boats could reach into areas where commerce had not been remotely feasible previously, opening up huge regions of the middle of the United States to development. By 1860 steamboats could deliver goods to most river locales for less than a cent per ton/mile. That was one twentieth of the cost of wagons—in the limited circumstances where the latter had access to passable roads. Steamboats had a comparable advantage in upstream transportation over other forms, such as flatboats and keelboats. No wonder then that Americans quickly filled so much of the interior when only decades before it had been considered incorrigibly inhospitable. By a conservative measure, useful land in the economy had been tripled.

Railroads: Capping the Transportation Revolution

Just as steamboats were assuming their major role in the economy yet another major innovation in transportation appeared. The railroad also was imported from England, and required considerable adaptation to serve American conditions. Its advantage over steamboats was that it could go where rivers did not; but at the same time this was also its disadvantage, because it had to provide its own, expensive right-of-way. Consequently, railroads were never able to reduce their costs enough to compete with water transport for the cheap, bulky commodities that the majority of interregional trade comprised. But their advantage in speed and safety made the extra expense worthwhile by allowing them to capture the premium markets for passengers and express freight. Of course, railroads also came to dominate transportation between towns where natural waterways were unavailable or unsuitable. This included areas such as the Northeast, where waterfalls and rapids made rivers impractical, as well as the High Plains, where rainfall was too meager for a comprehensive river system.

It was the latter region that was settled after the Civil War and where the transcontinental railroads made their most dramatic appearance. But by that time much of the benefit of cheaper transportation to the economy had already been incorporated in the more densely settled East. Thus, the railroads were the capstone of a dramatic—indeed, revolutionary—transformation in the economy, but they did not cause most of it. This distinction has been overlooked all too often in historical accounts so that the "Iron Horse" has become almost venerated.

Developing the railroads was a huge task, which will warrant a separate examination later. But, it is important to identify causal relations precisely. It is the entrepreneurs' skill in phrasing such questions that allows them to specify improvements that most overlook. By the end of the nineteenth century railroads had assumed most of the transportation of passengers among cities. But had Americans suspended other efforts to innovate until railroad technology matured, they would have wasted enormous opportunities. They would have forfeited using America's free water highways to reduce costs and, therefore, the specialization and exchange that has raised American material welfare so much. Entrepreneurs are too perceptive to overlook such a large opportunity and too impatient to allow it to slide.

Finding Out at a Distance

The dramatic improvements in transportation allowed Americans to begin trading regularly over an extended area. Though in 1830 their full effects still had a long way to go to completion, it was obvious then that these gains were transforming American economic life. The expansion of feasible horizons was breaking down local insularity and self-sufficiency. Individuals and localities were discovering advantageous niches from which they could serve a good portion of the economy. As usual, change was traumatic for those who shunned uncertainty and adjustment, but overall Americans benefited from the huge increase in incomes and choices.

Given the massive improvements in transportation, it is hardly surprising that other sectors in the economy had to adapt. But the full extent of the impact is suggested by the development of entirely new sectors strictly to serve the remodeled economy. For example, a huge gap was opened between the greatly enlarged possibilities of trading and the traditional slowness of acquiring information about trading opportunities at a distance. Predictably this sparked an intense search to improve the latter.

In the Colonial period, most trade took place within neighborhoods. Individuals knew many of their trading partners and had a good idea about what prices should be. The limited portion of goods that came—or was sent—a longer distance was subject to considerable uncertainty concerning price, quality, availability, and delivery. After 1800 trade increasingly occurred among people who lived far apart and didn't know one another personally. Such transactions were best conducted in abstract, generally recognized market procedures. This meant carefully specifying quantities, prices, and delivery arrangements much more than had been necessary in local transactions.

It was costly for merchants to wait for news of distant market conditions that arrived at the speed of existing transportation. The value of market information depreciates because conditions begin to change as soon as they are reported. A merchant in New York, for example, who sent an order to Chicago to buy flour might have received a reply two weeks later that it had not been available at the requested price or had been purchased, but at a significantly higher price than' expected. Thus, while the cost of shipping goods had fallen, decisions about transactions with distant parties remained frustratingly uncertain. Indeed, for many merchants this risk virtually blocked participation in distant trade.

The problem met the solution in the person of an unlikely entrepreneur.[7] Samuel Morse, like Robert Fulton, was a talented painter who found that society valued his skills much more when applied to mechanical inventions. While returning from England he spoke with a shipmate who was familiar with Michael Faraday's recent discoveries about electromagnetism. Morse inferred that electric current might be employed to send "instantaneous" messages over long distances. By 1836 he had developed a working model of the telegraph, but its inability to transmit more than a thousand feet made it impractical.

In 1844 Morse won a $30,000 grant from the federal government to build a demonstration line from Washington, D.C., to Baltimore. The project was a technical success, most notably scooping other means of communications about the Democratic party's presidential convention, but the government refused to underwrite a larger system. Morse turned to licensing private companies. By 1850, they had erected a comprehensive network between major commercial centers.

The regional companies undertook numerous, independent experiments with apparatus and new means of organization. They learned from one another's successes and drove costs down dramatically. For example, by 1860 the cost of building a mile of telegraph line had been reduced to about one tenth of Morse's demonstration project. In the 1860s the companies improved coordination by forming a national network and being assumed by Western Union. They also extended their lines to California and (underwater) to Europe. It marked a major milestone in human affairs when people six thousand miles apart could communicate almost instantaneously.

The results were predictable. Merchants extended their operations over a much wider area as the delays and uncertainty of working in distant markets fell. The telegraph took Americans a long way toward creating a national market by eliminating much of the disadvantage of distance. It became so much a part of life in the 1860s that the general populace could receive daily updates on the Civil War in newspapers. This contrasts with the month-long delay of Americans in the southern colonies learning of the battles of Lexington and Concord.

Toward Literacy and Communication

A parallel, but more subtle improvement in information was reflected in the widespread increase in literacy and reading. In the Colonial period most Americans received only a few, short years of schooling. It was, for instance, considered essential to learn to read the Bible because much public discourse employed its terms. But most colonists, as one can soon notice by reading diaries from the era, didn't become very proficient. (Even George Washington's writing was filled with errors. If he were to enroll in college today, he would be sent directly to remedial writing.) Today with cheap paperbacks and so much printed material we consider "junk mail," it is hard to visualize a time when owning a few books denoted wealth, and donating a thousand volumes was sufficient to have colleges such as Harvard or Yale named for you.

During the first part of the nineteenth century the cost of printed materials went down drastically. The development of the rotary press, which replaced the process of printing sheets individually on a flat press, reduced the cost of newspapers and led to a dramatic increase in newspaper circulation. Almost everyone could afford such publications regularly. In addition there was more information in newspapers to entice readers. The telegraph began to provide a steady supply of up-to-date material, very much in contrast to the warmed-over dispatches of earlier publications.

Improvements in mail service also encouraged literacy through quicker delivery of periodicals. These had little resemblance to modern magazines, looking more like a booklet of mimeographed sheets; but nevertheless, they were regular sources of information—and education. Magazines soon began to be directed toward particular groups: farmers subscribed to those concerning agriculture; households to those concerning ideas in home economics; and bankers to those concerning financial reports. As Americans read more, they became more knowledgeable about the makeup of the economy. Periodicals provided continuing information and commentary about markets, products, transportation, insurance, and credit.

Trade was also aided by developing special languages that eased communication at a distance. Many common products are homogeneous—what today we might call generic products or commodities—because a buyer can't distinguish which supplier produced a given lot. This is characteristic of those agricultural products that were produced in the largest volume, including wheat, cotton, corn, and tobacco, which can be graded by uniform standards of quality. The market provides prices appropriate to each grade, so that once the grade of a product is known the appropriate price is understood, even at a distance.

Participants began to devise commodity grading systems spontaneously. Once it is known, for example, that the item is No. 2 Wheat or Grade-A Cotton or Rough Cotton Sheeting, the respective quality becomes clear to buyers nearly everywhere. This eliminated the necessity of inspecting each batch of goods and, therefore, of actually being present. In the Colonial period the contents of most barrels had to be examined because universally understood grading systems had not yet been adopted. An important advantage of grading systems is that commodities can be fully described over the telegraph. A dealer could say, "The price of No. 2 Hard Red Wheat in Chicago today is $1.14 a bushel," and buyers would know exactly what was available and whether that was attractive to them. Grading standards extended to homogeneous industrial products such as cotton textiles. Indeed every product that shared common qualities was soon graded accordingly, so that people could employ that shorthand to economize on information.

Once participants agreed to a common set of product standards, contracts could be struck for transactions in the future. Futures markets developed in both New York and Chicago, allowing participants to assure either future sales or purchases. This can be very advantageous. For instance, consider the advantage for a farmer who has wheat growing in his field but needs to borrow money. He can use his wheat for security against a loan by selling it for delivery at harvest. Or a flour mill can guarantee production supplies by purchasing deliveries at future dates. Each such arrangement helps markets operate more efficiently. Futures markets allow individuals to achieve a better distribution of resources into the future by adding a means to plan, invest, and reduce risks. But they depend upon good communications unifying a developed national market.

5

Exploiting the New National Market

The major advances in transportation and communications drastically enlarged and improved the economy, but full adaptation waited until entrepreneurs could develop large, allied sectors. Each new area required its own extended period of creation, which was usually as difficult to develop as the initial improvements in transportation. Each also had to be sustained by the intense, persistent consumer demand similar to that which had sustained the search for appropriate technical advances in transportation.

Several important sectors emerged out of the process of national specialization and reorganization, but the one that has received the most attention is manufacturing. Many commentators have gone so far as to contend that it initiated modern growth. A common term, now going back a century, describes the comparable English experience as an "industrial revolution." This expression has often been employed to depict what is believed to be central to the transformation to a modern economy, but it is very misleading. Industrialization seldom becomes the largest sector during modernization in an economy; rather, it is only part of the broader commercial sector that is invigorated by modernization. It is the exchange of goods and services—as distinguished from unspecialized self-sufficiency—that underlies the search for better methods. Furthermore, the second word in *industrial revolution* is equally misleading. The transition required a good part of a century, so it had to be a *very* deliberate "revolution."[1]

Entrepreneurs instinctively search for a demand that has yet to be satisfied. Developing one that is large enough to energize an emerging sector is an exceptional accomplishment because it must be sufficiently strong to pull sizable resources away from goods and/or services that are already being purchased. Thus the fundamental explanation for industrialization must be that it provides services that people find even more valuable. A shift so dramatic cannot occur unless major changes in the economy open the way. Consumers may shift from one good to another when there are close substitutes, such as different brands of frozen foods, but only major new opportunities will prompt them to support an entirely new sector.

In the late eighteenth and early nineteenth centuries per capita incomes were increasing in America and Western Europe. This allowed consumers to purchase more and better items. Given the average person's meager wardrobe, it is hardly surprising that consumers spent so much of their gains in income on clothes. Much of the populace could afford only one outfit, which was carefully patched and mended in order to last years. Only wealthy individuals could afford large wardrobes, a contrast which was so obvious that one's dress became a clear symbol of social standing. Thus, for most of the populace, which spent a large part of the year in one shirt or dress, it is understandable that a second would be attractive.

Rising incomes in the 1700s boosted the per capita demand for clothing and, therefore, cloth. But it was obvious that making clothes less expensive would release a further surge of eager buyers, especially for cotton goods. England began importing cotton cloth from India in the 1500s. Because it was laboriously handmade it was expensive, but its comfort and washability surpassed local materials. Most eighteenth-century residents of Western Europe and North America wore wool, which became uncomfortable in warm weather.

When entrepreneurs examined the clothing market they noted that the largest cost component by far, about 90 percent, was labor. First the fiber had to be hand-spun into yarn. The next step, weaving the thread into cloth, was also very labor-intensive. Then it took considerable time to sew the material into finished clothing and even more to add decoration or dye to it to make it attractive.

An entrepreneur pondering this sequence instinctively suspects that inputs of labor could have been reduced somehow. Thus in England, the largest market for cotton textiles in the 1700s, aspiring inventors kept working on promising mechanical contraptions. The interest became so profound that Parliament offered prizes to the successful mechanizers of the central steps of spinning and weaving. By 1770 economical machines were beginning to appear. They first spun fiber into threads or yarn, the simplest of the processes. Their adoption reduced the cost of cloth substantially because the labor requirement in spinning was reduced by a factor of sixty. Meanwhile, inventors continued to improve the more complicated step of mechanical weaving such that by 1810 some fabrics had become competitive with hand weaving.

Between 1820 and 1850 mechanization was extended to woolens, specialty fabrics, and lace and ribbons. In the 1840s the first sewing machines appeared, which reduced the labor required to assemble clothes. Improvements in related cotton growing, shipping, and marketing contributed to reducing the price of finished cloth by a factor of ten compared with the beginning of the process in the mid-1700s. Thus over the course of about one hundred years entrepreneurs worked out a comprehensive technology that drastically cheapened the cost of the product and converted it from a luxury good into a mass-market commodity. One symptom of the gains in production efficiency was that midway in the transition English producers stopped buying cotton cloth and began purchasing cotton fiber from India. Despite the cost of both shipping the material halfway around the world—and back—and the meager wages earned by hand-loom weavers in India, English textiles drove most such locals out of business.

In England, the manufacture of cotton cloth developed in the Midlands, which was one of the least-developed areas and was removed from London, the commercial center. It seemed one of the least-promising sites, lacking most specialists that innovating sectors draw on. The most likely explanation is simply that costs were lower. Plenty of cheap labor and adequate water power made manufacturing most competitive in that locale. When the industry was trans- · planted to the United States, a similar pattern developed. Manufacturing moved into declining farming areas to the north of Boston on the Merrimack River and to Rhode Island and eastern Connecticut. These were sites where water power was available but had been bypassed by the previous commercial expansion, which kept the prices of local resources lower. The textile mills, for example, are known for having recruited young women off local farms. Many of them soon left for other interests, but they provided a pool of productive labor before moving on.

The United States lagged behind Britain in adopting such technologies because the resources that the new sector used most intensively were more expensive in America. In general, manufacturing was capital-intensive. Also, although it required less labor per unit than the handicraft methods it superseded, it still ran up large wage bills. Thus Americans tended to adopt the new techniques more slowly, even though their higher incomes, by themselves, would have caused them to buy cotton textiles sooner than the English. As with many new technologies at that time, local conditions caused American business to wait for refinements from Europe.

Americans were importing sizable amounts of textiles from England when the Revolution began. By disrupting that trade the fighting caused Americans to begin creating domestic substitutes, but they were not competitive once trade resumed. The obvious means of catching up was to acquire English expertise. The English, however, clearly wishing to protect their advantage in textile technology, prohibited anyone knowledgeable about recent textile techniques from leaving the country. Americans began placing subtly worded ads in publications in England to the effect that they would pay handsomely for a *mechanic,* what today we would call an engineer. While the textile trade could never be mentioned, a perceptive reader could infer what was really at stake.

Thus tension developed between the Americans attempting to acquire the technology to improve production at home and the English attempting to monopolize the fruits of their entrepreneurial successes. Today Americans disdain "industrial espionage," such as when the Japanese poke around seeking to learn how to make better transistors in Silicon Valley. But countries always have an incentive to appropriate better technology. However, the shoe was on the other foot in those days. It was more promising for Americans to borrow successful techniques from England than to create them for themselves.

Samuel Slater became very proficient in building textile machinery while completing an apprenticeship with a partner of Richard Arkwright, the pioneer of mechanical spinning.[2] He recognized that there was an intense demand for skills such as his in the United States. After carefully reviewing the details of current machines, he sauntered down to the docks and inquired about ships going to America. He actually hid in a barrel until one was safely at sea. On arrival in New York he advertised his expertise. He soon received an invitation from the Brown family in Providence, Rhode Island, who had experienced continuing difficulty creating their own spinning operation. They offered Slater a very attractive position: a partnership with considerable equity in the firm in exchange for his technical and managerial skills. Thus began the successful manufacturing of cotton yarn in the United States.

Slater's hopes of getting off to a fast start were quickly dashed. The machines that Moses Brown had collected to spin yarn were hopelessly amateurish and obsolete. Slater had to start from scratch, designing new equipment from memory. But this proved to be slow because of a dearth of skilled craftsmen to translate blueprints into working equipment. Once machines were operating, Slater spent considerable time streamlining the flow of material and organizing the factory.

Solving the production bottlenecks identified other obstacles. When American production was a part-time, household operation, each neighborhood pretty much used its own output. But the output of Slater's mill swamped the local market, forcing him to develop outlets in larger markets, particularly Boston and New York. In effect, Slater was bumping into the wide range of drawbacks that an entrepreneur starting a major industry is likely to uncover. America had little experience with factory organizations and, consequently, markets, such as those for labor, capital goods, and merchandising, had not developed to serve them. Slater had to create wide-ranging, supportive services in order to achieve his original mission. Eventually Slater became very wealthy, with interests in more than a dozen mills as well as other enterprises. But a good indicator of his difficulties in getting under way in America is that it was a full decade after his arrival before he could begin his second yarn mill.

In 1810 American transatlantic snooping paid off again. Francis Cabot Lowell was a Boston merchant whose vantage point would certainly have alerted him to Slater's success and the burgeoning demand for cotton textiles.[3] He announced he was not well. Doctors were generally not much help at that time, so the standard treatment for the minority who could afford it was to visit a climate believed to be more salutary. But Lowell went to England—in particular, to the west Midlands of England, which are often damp and cold. This raised doubts that health was his primary consideration. And what seemed to make him feel better?—strolling through cotton mills. They were intensely noisy places with cotton fibers—the source of brown lung disease—flying around greatly in excess of modern pollution standards! He reported feeling much better on his arrival back at Boston.

Lowell hired Paul Moody, a first-rate engineer, and worked with him to develop the sketches of textile machinery he had made furtively in England. The twosome proved a dynamite combination, making numerous improvements on the British designs as they developed complete drawings. One gain was to automate the flow of materials, using machines to substitute for expensive American labor wherever possible. Another notable improvement was adding mechanical weaving at the end of the production sequence. This was the first time that a fully integrated mill had been achieved anywhere in the world—indicating that Lowell had leapfrogged England's long-standing lead in textile technology.

The resulting factory, constructed west of Boston in Waltham, was a huge project turning out yardage that replaced the output of hundreds of thousands of households. As such, it required an exceptionally large quantity of capital, well beyond what financial markets were prepared to provide at that time. But funds quickly were raised through the Boston Associates, an informal partnership of some of the richest merchants in Boston. Within a few years, the organization was earning such a high return on its investment that its problem reversed to that of turning eager investors away.

The operations at Waltham were soon expanded so much that all possible water power for the mills was squeezed from the site. The Associates then began to develop an even larger source on the Merrimack River, northwest of Boston. They named the site Lowell after the founding entrepreneur, who died in 1817, just three years after the Waltham mill began production. (One can hear him on his deathbed saying, "Tell the English. See, I really was sick.") But perhaps an even larger tribute to Lowell was that his organization, the Associates, kept expanding for another decade as the largest and most innovative firm in the rapidly growing industry. Beyond bringing the technology from England, he assembled a management team that continued to improve it as well as profitably coordinate its application at numerous, disparate locations.

In poetic justice, those who built success with technology borrowed from across the Atlantic soon found others copying them. Other manufacturers, seeking to share in the hefty profits, expanded the textile industry. It grew much faster than the economy from 1815 to 1840, as mills were shoehorned into almost every feasible water-power site in the Northeast. Waterfalls, rapids, and other breaks in river elevations that formerly were viewed as liabilities because they blocked river navigation became usable assets. What was once a regional disadvantage became an important ingredient in building a product attractive enough to be sold throughout the economy.

Utilizing water power was one of several challenges entrepreneurs had to surmount to provide cotton textiles. Ultimately they had to mobilize resources and fashion organizations as well as match their product to consumer wants. The payoff came in a drastic transformation of household time that is hard to appreciate today, when the adjustments have been fully absorbed. Factory production of cloth required only one one-hundredth of the time it had taken to do the same work at home. Previous to mechanized production the typical household probably averaged two to three hours per day at that task. This meant upward of a thousand hours per year were saved in each household. A week or two's income purchased the comparable product at the store. Since the bulk of this work had been done by women and girls, it represented one of the larger gains for women's liberation in human history.

Textiles became the largest manufacturing sector in the pre–Civil War economy. Not surprisingly, its influence and connections extended well out into that economy. For example, the industry employed machinery extensively throughout its operations. It was one of the largest purchasers of industrial machinery and, in important ways, the initiator of the machine-tool industry in America. It also created a huge demand for machinery to further process all the resulting textiles. In particular, the sewing machine saved hundreds of millions of hours of hand-sewing each year after 1850. Thus the industry's demand for machinery became an important contributor to a parallel industrial development, machinery made from interchangeable parts.

Seizing the Lead in Innovation

Eli Whitney became one of America's most famous entrepreneurs.[4] He was a fascinating individual who suffered defeats as well as achieved fame, but his efforts certainly pushed the economy along toward some of its distinctive strengths. Whitney was born in 1765, about a decade before the Revolution, in Westboro, Massachusetts. At that time, ambitious residents were thinking of leaving; local agriculture had peaked well below the prospects of newer, western sectors. (Ironically two hundred years later highly skilled people returned to the area to work for such high-tech companies as Data General.)

The first indication of the depth of Whitney's purpose was the effort he put into obtaining a college degree at Yale College, a benchmark that only a tiny fraction of the population achieved. Whitney had neither the funds nor the preparation for Yale. In addition to starting late, he also had to proceed at a reduced rate while working his way through college. He was one of America's first "nontraditional" students. Moreover, Yale wasn't structured to serve someone with Whitney's interests, so he had to take extra steps to reach his goals. He was essentially an inventor and an engineer. Yale was a liberal arts school in the very strict meaning of the times, not having any of the professional programs offered today. The majority of students intended to become ministers. So Whitney was an unlikely student—late, poor, and ill-suited to the school's program. Most contemporaries expecting to develop interests like Whitney's typically apprenticed with a practicing professional: another engineer, for example. The logic of such an influence became tangible when Whitney was unable to find a job after graduation. No one advertised for someone with his credentials. He reluctantly took a position much beneath his training, as tutor to a planter's children in Georgia. Today we would say that he was overqualified. At that time, schoolteachers were not required to have more than a few years of schooling beyond that of their pupils.

Whitney did not teach when he arrived in Georgia—there was a dispute about the salary he had been promised—but became caught up in a big problem on the plantation, one preoccupying much of the South. By 1790 it was clear that the demand for cotton was growing enormously and that the American South was the world's most favorable locale in which to grow it. But the growers' hopes faced a major barrier. The productive, short staple variety of cotton was filled with seeds. Since Whitney's time, ways have been developed to use cotton seeds in cooking oil, cattle feed, and margarine. But at that time they were an expensive nuisance. Southerners were experimenting with mechanical devices, such as crushing the seeds by passing the cotton bolls through a series of rollers in order to sift them out more easily. Although all previous experiments had proved disappointing, potential returns remained so high that considerable creative energy was still focused on the problem.

This was an ideal environment for Whitney, whose mechanical instincts went right to the heart of such a challenge. He set to work in the plantation shop and soon produced the basic solution: the cotton gin. It employed rollers whose teeth rotated in opposite directions to tear the fiber apart, freeing the seeds. The principle was soon applied to larger, more sophisticated machines that used auxiliary power to process large quantities of cotton. Thus, there was an obvious, rapid payoff to Whitney's inventive genius. This was good news for the economy as a whole—indeed, for the developed world.

But the next phase of development proved costly for Whitney, bringing the type of problem that would bedevil him again. He was much less effective in fashioning a means to deliver his innovation's services. He formed a partnership to manufacture cotton gins, expecting to command a premium price and return large profits. No doubt this strategy would have worked up to a point. But the partnership was so slow to build machines that at least 99 percent of the demand remained unsatisfied. This made it virtually irresistible for others to circumvent Whitney's arrangements to supply them with machines. The principles of the technology were so simple that someone with reasonable mechanical skills could translate them into a working model. Thus by attempting to monopolize the market for cotton gins, Whitney compelled massive illegal copying of his invention. He overlooked the obvious implication that the cotton gin could not deliver its rewards unless it was put to productive uses. Some buyers may be patient for a while, but when the vast majority of potential users clearly suffers from its absence, others will create new means of supply.

Whitney should have created something along the lines of a licensing or franchise system. That is, he should have made the patent available so that producers could have provided adequate machines in a timely manner. The amount charged for such a license would have returned far more on net than selling a few of his own machines. It was a deadly mistake in marketing.

Most of the benefits of the invention of the cotton gin were captured by growers in the South. Later Whitney initiated lawsuits and won some compensation from individual state legislatures. But this process dragged on so long and the cost of the legal fees was so high that the net gain was small. This is not an uncommon problem for entrepreneurs. As Peter Drucker observes, entrepreneurs who fail to develop a process to success primarily create competitors, not profits. Whitney obviously developed a good concept. But he didn't develop it into a form where most could benefit from it. This illustrates the important distinction between inventors and entrepreneurs. Whereas inventors provide inventions, typically mechanical devices, entrepreneurs develop systems to deliver usable services into customers' hands. In other words, the entrepreneur's function extends over a wider domain, significantly larger than mere invention. Occasionally inventors reap large rewards, but much more often it is the entrepreneurs who accumulate significant wealth. Inventions in isolation seldom solve social problems. A comprehensive, entrepreneurial system is required to translate the services of the invention into a useful format for consumers. Entrepreneurs reap the rewards for bridging that scarce, critical step.

The experience with the cotton gin didn't stop Whitney from further efforts at invention, however. Indeed, like many good entrepreneurs, Whitney seems to have been inspired by the possibilities of success he could envision if he went through the process again, avoiding initial errors. Not surprisingly, the second time around he did much better at marketing, but this time had trouble delivering on the technology.

After the Revolution the newly independent United States had to establish its position among world powers, not infrequently reaching the threshold of warfare with rivals. But the nation was not prepared for armed conflict. Just as the United States had had a pickup military force in the Revolution, it had to scrape together an ad hoc force for each new crisis.

The prime weapon of armies during Whitney's era was the musket, which required months for skilled artisans to fashion into a working weapon. This meant that existing armorers took decades to accumulate the firearms required for a major army. It also required an equally large effort to keep them operating because each broken part had to be returned to the artisans for recasting. At the time of the American Revolution, the British Army—which was considered one of the best managed—had a backlog of ten years of repairs for muskets (imagine taking your gun into a shop for repairs and hearing the proprietor say to come back in a decade, it should be ready then)! This frustrating state of affairs resulted because each gun was handmade by forging and filing each part until it worked. And an individually crafted part could not replace its counterpart in another weapon. Sometimes sellers tout the virtues of their goods bring handmade, but for this purpose, being handmade appeared to be entirely disadvantageous. Standardized muskets would have beaten handcrafted models in every dimension.

The American government wanted a large stock of firearms, and fast, but such quantities were not available in any market. So when Whitney offered to supply ten thousand rifles to the War Department at half the going price within the astonishingly short time of two years, they readily accepted, even though they remained skeptical that he could do it. Whitney was willing to try it because he believed he could create a new technology that would bypass the existing problems.

The system he had in mind used what are now called *interchangeable parts.* It grew to be a very important technique of manufacturing in the United States by the Civil War, but in 1798, when Whitney made his proposal to the War Department, it was largely visionary. And he began to appreciate just how visionary his concept was after he began developing such a system. It proved to be a very long, frustrating struggle from principle to practice. He began determinedly, setting up a factory in Connecticut, but problems, which he was never able to overcome in the course of twenty years of sustained effort, soon appeared. The roadblocks were primary shortcomings in machine tools; that is, machines that cut metal parts. To make his system work, they had to be able to cut, punch, bend, and shape metal pieces to much finer tolerances. Moreover, they had to work quickly in order to be cost-effective. Thus the key to interchangeable parts was developing a new breed of machines. This proved to require a demanding, novel technology in itself.

The problem Whitney faced is similar to the major challenge that the electronics industry, where most gains have come through miniaturization, has faced since World War II. In the 1950s vacuum tubes were replaced by the transistor. Then ways were found to combine transistors together in chips, and finally integrate groups of them into a miniature computer on a chip. This was accomplished by improving techniques, continually making components smaller, thereby speeding up calculations as electronic signals traveled smaller distances to complete calculations. It also reduced material and power requirements as progressively more computer power was squeezed from a given unit.

Interchangeable parts were essentially the technology of shrinkage of their day. The problem was to produce finer tolerances in machinery so that parts meshed more closely, until the threshold was passed where parts could be interchanged without further shaping. Whitney achieved only partial success with this goal, so the remainder of his life was a study in frustration as he traveled to Washington, D.C., to beg the War Department to hold on, promising that success would be coming soon, and then returning to his shop north of New Haven, where he kept refining his machines. He made progress, including important contributions to the milling machine, but had not crossed through the threshold of general interchangeability when he died in 1825.

Whitney added one other contribution in his frustrated quest for interchangeable parts. He understood that the best location in which to attack the problem was Connecticut. Possibly his ties with Yale were helpful, but more likely he understood that the technology necessary to solve these problems might be more forthcoming in southwestern New England. The techniques necessary to create interchangeable parts ultimately came from Connecticut, in conjunction with a few outposts in Rhode Island and up the Connecticut River in Massachusetts and southern Vermont. Interchangeable parts were developed within a regional concentration much like Silicon Valley, which we have come to use as shorthand for a synergetic, localized concentration of electronic firms. Such enterprises gain from one another's proximity as they borrow and lend innovations while working out a common technology.

Alas, much like his recognition of the potential payoff to interchangeable parts, Whitney's vision of locating in Connecticut outraced the payoff. Specialized producers of machine tools were just forming when he died. The cotton textile manufacturers, for example, had to build their own machines. Some of these internal operations then split off to become independent suppliers for other manufacturers. But even in the 1840s, when railroads became important, organizations did not yet exist that could meet their demands for specialized machinery. One indicator of the breadth of the gap was that textile machinery shops at Lowell, Massachusets, and Paterson, New Jersey, were among the first to produce locomotives. Whitney was gone by the time specialized producers could begin to apply generalized expertise to the broad array of machines necessary in a sector such as firearms.

The nature of the problem is illustrated by the Blanchard stocking lathe, which was invented by Thomas Blanchard in 1818 to cut musket stocks. When its application was perfected, it was subdivided into sixteen separate machines, which, in combination, made only one part of the weapon! But while the investment made to develop all that machinery was enormous, the payoff of its applications was potentially even larger. In principle, the lathe could be adapted to reproduce many irregularly shaped wooden objects. In due course, it was applied to produce hat blocks, ax handles, ox yokes, wheel spokes, oars, and shoe lasts.

Interchangeable parts required a dramatically new technology, so there is no question that the major inventions in machine technology were indispensable. But the "American system of manufactures," as the English called it, also required a large market in order to absorb the output of all those specialized machines. The market and the technology were symbiotic. Thus the growth in the national economy encouraged the invention of technology for interchangeable parts. This becomes evident in the achievements of a little-known American entrepreneur whose life and interests paralleled, and then surpassed, those of Eli Whitney.

Simeon North was born in 1765, the same year as Whitney.[5] Like Whitney he grew up on a farm but began working with mechanical projects in the farm shop as soon as possible. North made scythes for local farmers, but appears also to have undertaken other lines, since in 1799—a year after Whitney's first government contract—he obtained a federal contract for cavalry pistols. In contrast to Whitney he delivered his product on time, establishing a reputation he doggedly sought to uphold for the next fifty years.

North proved more successful than Whitney, probably for two reasons. First, pistols were less complex to manufacture than muskets and the history of interchangeable parts showed that its application generally succeeded in order of increasing complexity. Suggestively, North entered the larger market for muskets in 1823, just before Whitney died. Second, North appears to have been a better manager. He was more realistic than Whitney in promising deliveries and more meticulous in refining his production line. By way of example, North guaranteed interchangeability among his pistols before 1810, and possibly before Whitney. North kept refining his production methods right until his death in 1852 at the age of eighty-seven.

But by that time his contributions were overshadowed by another well-publicized entrepreneur, Samuel Colt.[6] Colt built a huge armory in Hartford in 1847, about twenty miles from North's factory in Middletown (which, in turn, was about the same distance north of Whitney's location outside of New Haven). Colt carried through the ultimate logic of interchangeable parts and mass production, using specialized machines to turn out hundreds of thousands of revolvers each year. During the Civil War annual output was pushed into the millions. That is a good illustration of how far the technology of interchangeable parts had been advanced since 1800, when the War Department had to cajole producers for a good part of a decade to raise ten thousand weapons.

The obvious improvements in the production of firearms had widespread counterparts in American manufacturing. As engineers in the machine tool industry solved a problem in one sector, they turned their expertise to similar problems elsewhere. Interchangeable parts became central to the production of clocks, cutlery, tools, hardware, sewing machines, printing equipment, and agricultural implements. After the Civil War typewriters, bicycles, electrical and office equipment, conveyors and elevators, and automobiles were also made using interchangeable parts. The reduction in cost that turned each product from a luxury available only to a few into a common commodity followed the usual pattern. In the 1700s, for example, clocks were so large and expensive that only those who lived in mansions could afford them. A village typically helped its residents keep time by placing a communal model high on the town hall or church. In the nineteenth century, improving technology made "shelf clocks" feasible for most households, followed by pocket watches, giving individuals the gift of time.

6

Building Late-Nineteenth-Century Complex Enterprises

Until 1830, American businesses were almost always small and directed by a simple managerial structure. They were largely proprietorships, owned by one person, or partnerships of a few owners working together. Managers and owners were largely synonymous, except in limited cases where passive investors, called sleeping partners, supplemented capital. Managers seldom had anything like the leverage that modern corporations obtain by drawing capital from thousands of stockholders. Companies in industries in which the technology dictated large operations, such as turnpikes, canals, and railroads, were broadening their base of ownership to raise more capital, but most others remained small and simple. The growth of the economy was about to alter that pattern, however. Widening markets and rising personal incomes were opening the way for much larger and more sophisticated organizations.[1]

Cyrus McCormick's reaper company pioneered the transition to the new environment.[2] McCormick began his enterprise as markets started to become oriented to serve the national economy. Falling transportation costs prompted each area of the economy to begin to specialize in particular crops and products. In the 1820s Virginia and New York had been the largest wheat producers in the United States. But when in the 1830s McCormick began working on his reaper, wheat production was moving west as more productive land became accessible. By the 1850s the major wheat-producing states were Wisconsin and Illinois. Of course, this westward trend continued after the Civil War.

The regional specialization of agriculture rewarded growers producing local specialties, even though the unique qualities of a crop increased their risks. With wheat, for example, the harvest had to be completed within about two weeks because the weight of the maturing grain collapsed the stalks, making them matted and nearly impossible to reap.

In the 1830s wheat was harvested by mobilizing every appropriable laborer into the fields with a scythe. The cut grain was bound into shocks that could be threshed later at a less frantic pace. Thus a farmer had to restrict his annual production to the amount that could be cut in this short period. Moreover, relying on temporary harvest labor was becoming increasingly frustrating. As long as crops were diversified, reapers usually could be found in the locality, often by farmers helping one another. But when every farm required extra help at the same season, workers had to be imported. Independently, American labor was becoming more expensive irrespective of its supply in any locality. Thus farmers understandably sought new means of performing this function. In particular, they hoped that some form of mechanical innovation could speed harvesting. During the 1830s numerous inventors worked on prototypes of reapers, among them Cyrus McCormick.

McCormick came from a prosperous family in western Virginia and shared many of the interests of his father, Robert McCormick. History memorializes Cyrus, but Robert experimented with improving reapers in his farm shop for a long time. Cyrus's experience argues against a common presumption that the ideal entrepreneurial background is hardship, a form of a tempering-through-fire view.

Childhood environments do not dictate success later, because entrepreneurs, to a large degree, develop critical skills through practice, particularly the effort they put into their work. Cyrus could have forgotten his father's groundwork, allowing it to disappear into obscurity but, instead, he made a commitment to carry the project forward as a major, personal mission. Robert McCormick's version of a reaper was not very effective, but neither were competing models in the early 1830s. Cyrus took over its basic features, adding improvements, and by the mid-1830s felt ready to offer it for sale among neighboring farmers. Cyrus McCormick proved paradoxical, however. Although he demonstrated desirable entrepreneurial qualities, including staying with a task and worrying about details until everything worked, he also had a latent rash streak. Several times he went off on a tangent, completely neglecting his primary business. In 1839 he went into the iron business, idling the reaper project and losing the momentum he had built. The iron industry was growing rapidly at the time, so the switch was not pure caprice. But in 1840 he returned to developing the reaper, particularly emphasizing the effort to develop marketing.

By the mid-1840s McCormick had learned much about what was necessary to make reapers profitable. The reaper was a large, cumbersome piece of equipment, hence very expensive and fragile to ship. McCormick attempted to bypass this drawback by franchising his design to manufacturers in other parts of the country. This reduced transportation costs but created new, unexpected complications in quality and service. Farmers only valued reapers when they could depend on them for harvest. The regional manufacturers did not give nearly as much attention to service after the sale as farmers demanded. Reapers were probably the most complex equipment widely employed on American farms. They required careful assembly, frequent adjustments and maintenance, and an experienced operator in order to deliver dependable service. The franchised manufacturers did not devote enough attention to the machines, which frustrated buyers and prompted a general perception that reapers were not worth their price. Farmers commonly joked that anybody could make a reaper work, all that was necessary was four mechanics, one stationed at each corner of the field as the machine made its circuit.

While McCormick grappled with the dilemma of service, he also suffered increasing isolation as wheat farming continued shifting west. He decided it was essential both to assume manufacturing and move to the market. So in 1847 Cyrus McCormick picked up his operations, with as many skilled employees as he could persuade to go with him, and moved to Chicago.

His decision was serendipitous. McCormick was there to reduce transportation costs and position his operations in the largest market for reapers, but he probably had not realized just how important direct contact with consumers would be to improving his product. Each operating reaper was, in effect, an experiment that could suggest improvements to a discerning observer. The area around Chicago provided McCormick's engineers with steady, accessible feedback on innovations and features. They were, to employ modern jargon, close to the customer, a quality that is believed crucial to business success today.

By the 1850s the Chicago plant was producing reapers by the thousands annually, rather than the former dozen or so from each workshop. The McCormick operation was one of the first to employ interchangeable parts on an assembly line, drastically reducing that component of costs. Thus in the 1850s attractive costs and reliable service began to be joined. The interaction between the engineers and customers improved the reapers' reliability, making them profitable for farmers. The scuttlebutt on the farms now began to work *for* McCormick, reporting that the reaper was a good deal because it could cut fifteen or twenty acres per day where a man with a scythe could do two or, at most, two and a half. Once farmers could rely upon the reaper, harvest productivity went up markedly and each farmer could commit to larger acreages in grain.

Much of this advance became possible because McCormick created an organization whose services extended well beyond the stage of production, what we now recognize as a *vertically integrated* firm. He discovered that he could not confine his efforts to building reapers, no matter how good the product. He had to ensure that operators were trained, the machine was made ready at the customers' farms, and repairs were readily available; even financing was provided. The last function came about because the reaper was an expensive machine, selling for $125 to $150, which, in the 1850s, represented a good share of a farmer's yearly income. Most didn't have such cash in hand so, lacking other lending agencies, McCormick had to extend credit in order to make his machines salable. McCormick's franchise system was shaping up by the onset of the Civil War. While other companies adopted some of its features, McCormick led in building a comprehensive organization.

These efforts evolved toward today's franchised dealerships, which are common in such sectors as automobiles and industrial equipment. They are advantageous for products that are expensive, require specialized service, or benefit from financing, installation, and instruction in operation. The franchise dealer is designated as the exclusive seller of that brand in an area, giving him a spatial monopoly. (Of course, competing franchise lines prevent him from acting as an absolute monopolist.) While it sounds risky to restrict customers to one dealer, the dealer is also obligated to provide repairs, financing, and whatever other services are necessary to make the product useful. Typically, the manufacturer maintains regular contact with the franchisee through visiting agents. In addition to checking up on franchisees, they update them on new models, service instructions, training, financial arrangements, and advertising. Thus the relationship between the franchised dealer and the manufacturer is structured to be mutually beneficial, enhancing the service of the product in an area.

Since McCormick's time a wide range of products, for both consumers and manufacturers, have adopted this structure to assure optimal services. Some products, such as elevators, pumps, conveyors, and electrical equipment, require special installation expertise. The company mechanic might have a tough time getting one running. Some products require specialized repair or maintenance. An untutored local mechanic often will do more damage than good. Other products benefit from special financing, as was the case with the reaper. Still others, such as electronic equipment, require frequent updating as the embodied technology is improved. A good share of the products in America have at least one such characteristic, so variations on the system of franchised dealers pioneered by McCormick have become commonplace.

Ultimately all products are valued for the services they provide, so vertical integration is an attempt to satisfy a particular type of demand. McCormick's reaper was the tangible evidence of his efforts, but in isolation that physical form was nothing more than a nuisance. It was an awkward, ugly object sitting in a farmer's shed and of little value parked on the lawn, supporting flowerpots. Farmers wanted some arrangement that cut a lot of grain reliably during a certain, short period each year. This distinction between a product and the services it renders became increasingly important after the Civil War. As American consumers become wealthier, they could afford more commodities but were particularly concerned about obtaining services that improved their lives, including those enhancing the use of the goods they purchased.

McCormick's continuing adaptations to his market yielded the prototype vertically integrated firm, which represents a watershed in American institutions. Previously American businesses operated at only one stage of production. When manufacturers sold their product to merchants, their responsibility and involvement ended. For instance, when the textile mills began producing, independent brokers called commission merchants developed. They arranged for the sale, shipment, and insurance of textile products to merchants, receiving a commission as compensation. They obviously had a vested interest in the health of the industry, but they were not employees of any of its firms. McCormick's enterprise, which incorporated such elements of distribution within one firm, thus represented a major restructuring.

The Imperative of Vertical Integration

It is very unlikely that when Cyrus McCormick resumed building reapers in the early 1840s he could have envisioned the large, complicated structure his company would eventually assume. Few entrepreneurs begin with such an all-encompassing vision, and fewer yet develop it as anticipated—that is basic to the discovery process. Moreover, some entrepreneurs set out to create a comfortable position by virtue of confining their vision to what they imagine to be a manageable size. But in a significant number of markets, the logic of the product's technology and demand carries it well beyond such original designs.

Enterprises in such environments discover that the pull to extend their services is powerful, indeed compelling. Customers seem much more responsive to more comprehensive offerings. In undergoing such an expansion, moreover, a company invariably changes its operating structure. Companies move away from environments such as those that predominated in early nineteenth-century America, where coordination among different levels of production was organized by markets with prices synchronizing each producer's sale of its product to the next level. In the last half of the nineteenth century some large companies began to internalize some of this coordination rather than rely on other firms. In other words, allocation decisions were being shifted into the firm rather than being achieved through exchanges in markets.

Companies supplying goods strongly subject to demands for broadened services found themselves being pulled inexorably toward expansion and greater complexity.[3] John D. Rockefeller, for instance, was an astute observer, but it is unlikely that he envisioned his firm integrating all stages of production, including buying crude oil, transporting it to the refinery, distilling it into a series of useful products, shipping those products out to markets worldwide, developing a marketing arm, and meshing everything administratively. No one can be so clairvoyant during the early years of an industry. It is much more likely that initially he simply expected to make money operating a refinery. But later he added other functions as he discovered the saving and profit of each.

One or more of three forces were invariably important when firms integrated during the late nineteenth century. First, high-volume production, employing some form of a continual process, such as a production line or processing of materials, was present. A second characteristic was the production of perishable products where the mode of delivery could significantly affect quality. A third occurred when the product required a specialized auxiliary service, such as installation, operator training, maintenance, or financing. At least one of these characteristics was present whenever a firm integrated successfully. Oftentimes the first two conditions overlapped; that is, high-volume production and perishability coincided because the techniques to keep consumer goods, particularly food products, palatable in the late nineteenth century were limited. Cigarettes, for instance, tended to dry out because packaging materials in the 1880s could not provide an airtight seal. American Tobacco had to monitor the condition of the product carefully until it reached the consumer. For bananas and fresh meat, perishability was the central consideration in structuring distribution.

New technologies developing in continual production allowed enterprises to turn out enormous quantities of homogeneous goods. In the era before electric ranges or pilot lights on furnaces, for example, matches were a household staple. Tens of millions of American households added up to a demand of a hundred million or so daily. By 1900 Diamond Match could supply the entire national market in one factory. Automatic machinery prepared matchsticks, dipped them in ignitable material, formed paper boxes, and packaged them into cartons. The improvements in labor productivity were remarkable, increasing several hundredfold as tedious hand labor was taken over by machines.

Production in other industries such as breakfast cereal and flour was similarly revolutionized. Large, integrated mills that could process thousands of tons of flour and package it in ten- to twenty-pound bags replaced the numerous, local flour mills characteristic of the early nineteenth century. As with matches, a single mill became a significant portion of the national supply. The new technology of production in these industries meant that a half dozen factories dominated the national market. This is why such industries so often became oligopolies where three or four brand names predominated in the market.

Other vertically integrated industries emphasized specialized consumer services for their product. Sewing machines were a notable application. Equipment directed primarily toward businesses included cash registers, mimeograph machines, and typewriters, as well as industrial equipment such as cranes, pumps, conveyors, and electrical equipment.

The Singer Sewing Machine Company was the recognized pioneer in special services in the consumer market. It set up a network of sales offices that included classes in sewing. Singer also maintained repairmen at each sales office. This helped to assure purchasers of sewing machines that they would get their money's worth. There is hardly anything more destructive to sales than a machine shut down by a broken part. Frustrated customers invariably tell potential customers—in great detail—that they should not buy a machine that can't be repaired.

Singer also provided credit through a loan program administered by the branch offices. A sewing machine was a relatively expensive purchase for a nineteenth-century household, so this arrangement was introduced to match payments to the machine's services. Singer discovered that special credit was necessary because the loan market was not yet organized to provide it. For industrial equipment, such as large water pumps and electrical equipment, technicians seldom were available locally so the producer had to guarantee it by lending or training someone.

One or more of these three qualities invariably drove the merger of production and marketing that formed a vertically integrated firm. In some cases firms also found it necessary to ensure their supplies of raw materials by acquiring the suppliers. Diamond Match, for example, integrated back into lumber mills in order to provide a steady supply of particular types of wood. The meat-packing companies maintained their own buyers in the stockyards to provide a steady flow of animals to keep the packing plants running efficiently. Steel firms integrated backward into transportation and iron ore and coal mines in order to have an assured supply of raw materials and foreclose the threat that others might extort their adaptation to particular sources.

Packing companies in the Midwest began integrating toward the customer by developing specialized transportation facilities for their product. Instead of shipping live cattle to eastern markets, paying freight on two and a half times their dressed weight, packers sought means to send only the finished product. The key was mobile refrigeration to keep the meat fresh and palatable. Gustavus Swift and Philip Armour began developing refrigerator cars along with refrigerated warehouses to preserve it until parceled out in the distant markets. Refrigeration technology proved difficult to develop, requiring more than twenty years of engineering. Meanwhile, packing plants were restructured to reap the economies that came with growing volume. They converted the slaughter of animals from what was essentially a batch process, a few animals at a time, to an assembly line—actually, a "disassembly line." This produced significant savings as each worker focused on a particular activity, eliminating the wasted motion of turning from one task to another.

The packers also discovered that their new organization offered a helpful avenue to cope with the vexing dilemma of waste products. A major problem in late-nineteenth-century American cities was disposing of dead animals. Pictures of street scenes from that time not infrequently show a dead horse lying in the gutter. Contemporaries did not prefer this—social styles did not esteem displaying decaying carcasses—but often these bodies were so cumbersome that an owner might be tempted to abandon his six-hundred-pound problem, especially since there was no serial number to trace the owner. (It was the early counterpart of abandoned junk automobiles in large, modern cities.)

The packing plants created so many by-products that disposal costs alone prompted them to spend enormous effort searching for solutions. For instance, it paid to separate out bones to grind into bone-meal fertilizer. They paid more attention to hides, which were valuable when cut and treated suitably. Other uses—such as bristles in hairbrushes and fats converted to glue, soap, and margarine— were found for waste materials. And the packers kept searching for new markets and uses for discarded materials. The cost of disposal doubled the incentive of converting waste products into assets.

By 1890 meat shipped from Chicago or Kansas City to Eastern cities such as New York and Boston was beginning to undersell locally slaughtered meat. As the distribution system was refined, the product also won a reputation for quality. Once the system of distributing fresh meat was standardized, it yielded a better product than many of the various offerings of local butchers. The major packers promoted a perception of quality by advertising their own brands and backing them with guarantees—a tactic frequently adopted by vertically integrated firms.

The cigarette industry also integrated forward toward its customers, but did not build as elaborate a marketing structure as that of fresh meat or other perishable products. James Duke, a producer of smoking tobacco in North Carolina, upended the industry when he introduced the Bonsack cigarette machine in 1884. It cranked out so many cigarettes that it swamped both the nascent market for that product and the existing system of distributing those semiperishables. Duke moved to strengthen demand by extensive advertising, mounting a national campaign as large as any seen to date. In addition, he developed a network of branch offices and manufacturer's agents to bolster the chain of independent wholesalers and retailers who delivered the product. But unlike delivery systems for perishable products such as fresh meat, beer, and bananas, this system supplemented, rather than supplanted, the traditional structure. Duke's agents monitored inventories of wholesalers and retail stores. While they sought orders they also placed strong emphasis on collecting information about factors influencing the demand for individual brands in their locale. This up-to-the-minute information helped the factory coordinate production with sales. Agents also helped educate retailers about displays and inventory procedures, the latter being especially important for product quality given its tendency to deteriorate. The agents worked alongside the product as it moved to the retail level, showing the retailer sales techniques and dealing with customer problems. Thus the system tied production into distribution, not so elaborately and specialized as that developed for meat packing, but still achieving the same overarching coordination.

Given Duke's outstanding success, his single, dramatic failure illustrates a key point about the nature of his operation. He concluded that being in the tobacco business required him to add cigars to complete his product line. But cigars continued to be made by hand and their marketing differed greatly from that of cigarettes. There were few economies of scale in cigar production anything like those that drove the cigarette companies. Thus when Duke tried to impose methods drawn from cigarettes upon cigar production, diseconomies in supervising production developed. This demonstrated that although there were compelling reasons for vertical integration in certain products, countervailing forces were more powerful elsewhere. The forces that had developed in the cigarette industry by 1880 did not appear in the cigar industry until well into the twentieth century and, even then, were much weaker. Firms in other traditional industries, such as rope making and sugar refining, which attempted vertical integration, also soon retreated to their original structure.

The Ultimate Sources of Vertical Integration

The development of large, integrated firms serving the national market in the late nineteenth century was so dramatic and novel that many questioned the reason for its appearance. A ready, popular explanation was the malevolent robber baron thesis to which we shall return in Chapter 8. But scholars have also examined this relation in their own deliberate ways.[4] The most robust explanations now turn on the costs of making transactions between different types of organizations and how tightly resources must be locked into these respective channels. For example, internal coordination seemed to improve the flow of information by allowing participants more freedom to discuss their situations. This was most apparent in those industries in which limited suppliers dealt with a few producers. That monopsony environment compels producers and suppliers to bargain with one another much as in poker, improving their positions by bluffing and withholding information from opponents. But within an integrated structure such information can flow more freely because employees benefit from the gains of others in the company. When such coordination becomes important, firms are encouraged to integrate the units. That appears to be the case with American Tobacco when it synchronized production runs with up-to-the-minute reports of demand in the market. When wholesalers scheduled their own orders of cigarettes, they ordered too much at times, such that some cigarettes became stale, or, at other times, too little, leading to rush orders and inefficiency at the factory.

Firms also were likely to absorb those activities employing workers who specialized in that company's operations. For instance, when Singer began selling sewing machines, there weren't many repairmen prepared to service them. But a person acquiring such skills became dependent on Singer's actions. Similar considerations applied to servicemen of other types of specialized equipment. It was risky to be independent when most of your business came from one source.

A third advantage of integration was internalizing information to aid in developing new products and improving production processes. From 1870 to 1890 the integrated firms underwent rapid growth and assembled huge facilities for the first time. It was important for them to grasp every improvement, and one way to do so was by listening to customers and suppliers whenever possible. Integrating forward toward the market puts representatives closer to customers, providing better insight into what should be produced. Consider the situation of American Tobacco, whose plant in North Carolina was turning out cigarettes by the boxcar. The manager of that operation might have congratulated himself on his production and efficiency. But if the product, no matter how efficiently produced, did not satisfy the customers, he could have quickly gotten into big trouble. Worse than a small operation losing money is a big one whose losses pile up faster. Thus maintaining communication with customers is crucial. This provides perspective, keeping operations aligned with what the consumer values and not enamored of its own technology and production processes.

These three forces explain much of vertical integration. They also proved to be enduring forces because most of the major companies that integrated vertically at that time continue in business—indeed, often dominate their line of business—a century later. We still have Kellogg's cereals, American Tobacco, Procter and Gamble, Campbell Soup, and Heinz Pickles. These big companies persisted because they developed structures that utilized the key strengths of their markets.

7

Entrepreneurs Adjust to the Expansive Economy

By 1865, which marked the end of the Civil War, the economy had come a long, long way from its colonial origins. Understandably, that required drastic changes. Entrepreneurs also had to devise appropriate strategies. One of the best examples was Andrew Carnegie.

Carnegie seems to confirm the stereotype of an entrepreneur, although some of his qualities that have been most publicized were not central to his success.[1] He came from a "Horatio Alger" background. His poverty-stricken family was forced from the Outer Hebrides, the depressed islands off northwestern Scotland, in 1848. When they came to the United States, Andy began working at the age of twelve as a bobbin boy in a textile mill. Without question he worked hard. He was promoted through several jobs because he developed a reputation for dependability. He graduated to telegraph operator, which, in the 1850s, suggested special abilities. It was a new technology, requiring some analytic skills and a certain flair. The telegraph attracted people who, in important ways, were the counterpart of computer programmers today, individuals who liked technical puzzles and might pursue such challenges passionately. It is not unusual to find that successful businessmen in the last part of the nineteenth century went through this apprenticeship.

Carnegie next worked for the Pennsylvania Railroad, which, we now recognize, provided excellent training because it was pioneering management systems for a large, integrated rail system. By 1860 the largest railroads were running scores of trains simultaneously over hundreds of miles of track. This created complicated scheduling and, until solutions were devised, frequent accidents. By the 1860s the Pennsylvania Railroad's track extended from the East Coast well into the Great Lakes area. It combined a sophisticated centralized structure with district superintendents to coordinate traffic. Not only was Carnegie exposed to such techniques, but he also worked as a personal assistant to one of its best managers, Tom Scott. Soon thereafter, Scott became the president of the railroad. Scholars of the development of the industry know that he contributed significantly to the methods of running a large railroad.

Scott also helped Carnegie by working with him personally. As we understand the relationship today, Scott became Carnegie's mentor, a coach who has succeeded in the organization and is willing to share his insights with his juniors. Aspiring young managers are often advised to find a mentor to help them develop. It is better to heed another's experiences than to learn through making the same mistakes. Most individuals like to talk about their experiences and they enjoy helping others, so a symbiotic relationship can develop through which both parties benefit. Carnegie was an apt student who rewarded Scott's efforts with rapid progress. Under Scott, Carnegie advanced to become a division manager of the Pennsylvania Railroad when he was twenty-four. Talk about the "fast track" on the railroad.

Characteristically, Carnegie did not stay with the Pennsylvania or even competing railroads, which would have gladly used his skills. His urge to create his own enterprise was overpowering. He judged that railroads would not provide the advanced challenges he sought, so he had been investing in other businesses on the side, including a sleeping car manufacturer, which proved to be very successful. He also organized bridge construction projects as well as other partnerships connected with the iron industry.

Carnegie left the Pennsylvania Railroad in the late 1860s to become a consultant. He helped businesses requiring expertise about railroads, iron, and related interests. From this broad perspective he drew many of the guidelines shaping his success in the steel industry. Steel was just getting under way in 1870, and was at the point where, for example, computers were in the 1950s. While not the first manufacturer, Carnegie began in the industry's formative period. He sensed that the industry was very promising, and his managerial instincts and experience prepared him for the challenge. He was ready when the industry was.

Carnegie formed a partnership with a few carefully chosen investors. They were willing to tolerate the stringent conditions he imposed on membership because his operations soon proved so profitable. Unlike many companies, which had to turn to outside funding, Carnegie never had to plead his case in a public forum. Steel didn't require as much vertical integration as some other industries, but still his operations became one of the nation's largest. For the remainder of his career, Carnegie's operations were self-financed. Efficiency provided the enormous cash flow that fueled the next move. Recent sentiment has questioned whether we demand too quick a return on publicly owned companies, thereby forcing them to act shortsightedly. Andrew Carnegie had a solution to such a dilemma.

In the early phase of steel, the critical task was prodding the enterprise to reduce costs. An industry beginning to process so many raw materials was a prime candidate for cost-reducing streamlining. Besides, the sensitivity of demand to price made this a logical competitive tactic. Carnegie's challenge in 1870 was to develop an organization that improved efficiency as rapidly as possible. This turned not so much on inventing technology to produce steel, as on building an organization whose instinctive, primary focus was to reduce costs.

Some of Carnegie's innovations are so widely employed today

they have become standard topics in management textbooks. One was the development of *profit centers*. Businesses understand that they must make a competitive return on their resources in order to survive. But in large companies it is easy for departments to follow their own interest to the detriment of the interests of the overall organization. This is a chronic problem in bureaucracies. One antidote is to extend down into the ranks incentives that correspond to the interests of the organization overall. Carnegie turned each of his operating units, steel mill, coal mine, coke oven, and so on, into an independent profit center. Each was given a specific goal for output and rewarded accordingly. This was a precursor of the modern practices of quotas or management by objectives. Based on their performances, Carnegie's middle managers each received bonuses, promotions, or—not infrequently in Carnegie's operations—dismissals. Carnegie followed a sink-or-swim philosophy. If associates succeeded, he rewarded them well. Many of his managers became millionaires.

To make profit centers more effective, Carnegie refined accounting classifications to improve measures of the company's operations. Although businessmen before Carnegie kept accounts, they seldom employed them in ways that we would recognize as cost accounting, where costs are scrutinized in order to be predicted and reduced. Carnegie contributed to analytic accounting. He extended concepts that he had used on the Pennsylvania Railroad to decompose costs into fixed and variable components. In this regard, he anticipated a forthcoming central theorem of economists. The distinction was particularly important for steel because the relatively large costs locked into capital meant that the variable costs, which should be the gauge for daily operations, were easily obscured. Thus Carnegie encouraged marginal cost decision making. The furnaces could not produce anything other than steel, so the most profitable output occurred where the controllable costs equaled—but didn't exceed—the net revenues from additional production. Thus Carnegie was likely to utilize existing equipment more efficiently than his (marginally illiterate) competitors.

Sharper accounting also alerted Carnegie to which of his activities were the most profitable and should be expanded, and to those which should be curtailed. He could measure the performance of a particular mill or piece of machinery better than the competition. One pattern that emerged from his analysis was that he almost always beat other steel companies in adopting new technologies. It was not that he was fascinated by new methods so much as that his cost calculations kept telling him that it was a profitable move. Typically, new techniques speeded the flow of materials through a facility, decreasing the proportionate costs to all the resources employed. Accounting calculations alerted Carnegie to such relations and prompted him to implement appropriate technology first. His organization did not develop much new technology itself. Rather it surveyed its appearance worldwide and adopted those whose numbers were promising.

Carnegie made a third contribution, which the twentieth century can especially appreciate, by applying scientific skills directly to the production line. Until then when iron ore was exposed to coke in a blast furnace, the material frequently turned bad. Ironmasters learned through costly experience that combining iron ore and coal from particular deposits was destructive. They didn't understand the source of the calamities, but trial and error emphatically taught which ores and coal could be used together.

In the middle of the nineteenth century scientists began to understand how the structure of a molecule determined its chemical properties. Adverse reactions, therefore, were simply chemical reactions of elements within the coal and iron ore, which overrode the desired metallic properties. Chemistry also suggested solutions. When samples of coal or iron ore were assayed, destructive combinations could be pulled back before wasting a charge in the blast furnace. This procedure further suggested employing chemistry to turn destructive materials into useful resources. Carnegie hired chemists who ran tests on materials as they came into the mill and prescribed corrective procedures, for example, adding appropriate reagents to counteract harmful phosphorus or sulfur. Thus, rather than being limited to those sources of iron ore and coal that experimentation had proved amenable, Carnegie now could use almost any source by applying the appropriate remedies. This is also a vivid example of how new knowledge expands the supply of economic resources. It is not that more mineral supplies appeared in the world, but that much of that large quantity which had been held hostage was released by new knowledge. Employing that innovation, Carnegie could draw on a wider supply of iron ore and coal than his competitors, at least until they understood his achievement and copied the practice.

These three major innovations were worked out through experimentation rather than arrived at instantly. They were put into use by an organization structured to encourage such innovations by clearly rewarding them. When the managers kept reducing costs, the company stayed ahead of its competitors. Carnegie employed pricing tactics to make the most of this margin. His advantage in productivity meant that revenues generally exceeded his marginal costs. Thus he ran his mills flat out, recognizing that each unit of output up to the limit of capacity added to profit. Marketing was not necessary. Prices could be lowered enough to move all output; competitors with higher costs would have to absorb the adjustments. Thus Carnegie was the price, as well as cost, leader and could always win the sales up to his current capacity.

As he guided his organization, reducing costs, Carnegie constantly plowed back his profits into new facilities. He did not like to pay large dividends (another reason for insisting on maintaining close control of the company). Given his high return on capital, however, this was a wise strategy. Consequently, the Carnegie operations kept expanding, in bad times as well as good. Historians have noted this consistency and sometimes have sought to explain Carnegie's success as that of a smart buyer, buying facilities cheap during recessions. But a growth industry continues to expand irrespective of whether the rest of the economy is expanding or contracting. It was worthwhile for Carnegie to expand during the downturns because consistently from 1870 until about 1895 his facilities produced steel cheaper and earned profits greater than the average. It took that long for the competition to replicate all of his innovations. When Carnegie sold out and his organization merged into the U.S. Steel Company at the turn of the century, his personal wealth was worth in excess of a half billion dollars—in 1900 dollars!

Carnegie not only created enormous wealth for himself but also provided the means whereby many of his associates did relatively well. When U.S. Steel was formed, for example, three of Carnegie's top officers, John Phipps, Henry Frick, and George Lauder, held stock worth, respectively, $50 million, $27.5 million, and $18 million. The managers were valued because, though Carnegie was a dominating personality, his organization was not a one-man show. He developed the organization to be greater than himself and to operate without him. Starting in the 1880s Carnegie usually took a half year away from Pittsburgh each year, traveling extensively. His absence proved it was not necessary to have one person directing everyone else. The structure of the company automatically encouraged employees to do their best and pushed achievers to the top. By virtue of providing challenges and rewarding success, Carnegie attracted some of the best and most ambitious people in the industry.

U.S. Steel, which was the capstone of Carnegie's effort, was not as vertically integrated as some companies that emerged about that time. But it employed the most important elements of such large, complicated organizations. It passed the ultimate test by having numerous employees working diligently within it. In other words, bureaucracy was defeated by finding a way to push incentives down into the ranks so that many employees could, and would, contribute. This depended on blending people with different skills so that they yielded more than the sum of their individual contributions. Thus while Carnegie built a large social organization in which disparate people worked toward a common interest, it was an organization that encouraged a notable degree of uniqueness and initiative. It encouraged people to try different things, to keep innovating. It struck a balance between a structured organization working toward a clear objective and individuals willing to use creative discretion in the ranks.

Becoming Rich as a Rockefeller

John D. Rockefeller also exemplified the critical entrepreneurial qualities necessary to build a large, integrated firm.[2] He clearly understood the urgent centrality of cutting costs. But Rockefeller was able to transcend the particular demands of that environment to lead his organization through the subsequent transition into a mature phase. Thus his life is doubly instructive. Not only does he complement the lessons of Carnegie's experience, but he demonstrated ideal qualities for entrepreneurs generally.

Among America's great entrepreneurs John D. Rockefeller had some of the most modern—and engaging—qualities. He was personable. A good share of his success was attributable to his working with others, motivating them and providing a sense of purpose and direction. Rockefeller worked hard, beginning young, but in his midfifties began a phased retirement, taking frequent sabbaticals. He retired in his sixties, moving to Florida near Daytona Beach and living actively until he died at ninety-eight. Thus his was a precursor of the modern life-style, which values early retirement and/or a second career, anticipating a long, fulfilling life.

Rockefeller was as creative in retirement as he had been in building a business. Some individuals parcel out their largess casually, but he spent his money very thoughtfully. For instance, he was responsible for the renovation of Williamsburg, Virginia, probably the premier attraction of its type in the United States. He funded restoration of Versailles in France, which was then a neglected, dissipated relic, nowhere near the international attraction that it is today. He supported the University of Chicago, which in a very short time became one of America's best universities. This was exceptional because most of America's top universities, such as Harvard and Yale, owe their excellence to a long momentum and continuity built over hundreds of years. Rockefeller's intelligent philanthropy short-circuited much of that gestation. He also acquired major properties that were turned into two splendid national parks: Grand Teton, in Wyoming, just south of Yellowstone, and Acadia, in Maine. So his philanthropy resulted in enduring, international treasures. These achievements contrast with those of other entrepreneurs who spent sizable amounts on "peace" ships, sending them around the world to urge people to get along with one another, and having no lasting effect other than making themselves appear foolish.

Rockefeller was born in Richford, New York, in 1839 and, like most boys of his era, began working in his early teens. Beginning as a stock boy, he worked his way up in the grocery business, becoming a partner in a Cleveland, Ohio, store by the age of twenty. This proved to be the right place at the right time, because in 1859 oil was discovered nearby in northwestern Pennsylvania. It wasn't really a discovery—some had been observed oozing from the ground for centuries; but that year drilling techniques reached a level whereby oil could be extracted from the ground economically. Meanwhile, others had worked out techniques to distill the oil to extract kerosene, the superior lighting fuel of the day.

Rockefeller could have elected to capitalize on this opportunity in several ways. Had he been a flamboyant promoter, he probably would have gone into the oilfields, buying property and drilling wells. Being early in that developmental stage was an obvious way to acquire wealth. But Rockefeller declined. He seems to have conducted a thoughtful appraisal of the industry's development, concluding that the later stages in transportation, refining, and marketing would become relatively more important. He may have recognized that the demand for kerosene would be large and repetitive, requiring an extensive distribution network reaching out to households. He may also have sensed that the long-run payoff further along in the delivery system might be substantially higher. The gain from larger operations with the consequent opportunities for innovation could dwarf the returns on a successful oil well or two.

Rockefeller bought into a partnership in an oil refinery in Cleveland in 1862 (although Cleveland now sounds like an unlikely location, it remained the center of American oil production until the turn of the century when giant fields were discovered in Texas and California). As Rockefeller became acquainted with refinery operations, he began to show the qualities that would undergird his success. He judged that the operations were subject to further increasing returns, so that expanding capacity would reduce unit costs and raise profits. But his partners either were not persuaded of this logic or were timid. Whichever the case, they resisted expansion. Rockefeller forced the issue and said, in effect, "We have fundamentally different visions of this business. You buy me out or I'll buy you out." The latter choice was risky because Rockefeller didn't have nearly enough capital to finance the entire operation. He would have to borrow most of it, in effect using what is now called a *leveraged buyout*. He was betting on his entrepreneurial vision, which is to say he saw the world differently from most others and was willing to assume the risk of acting on that judgment.

Rockefeller bought out his conservative partners and expanded operations. He soon reduced his costs below those of his competitors, an advantage he generally maintained over the next twenty years. His primary winning strategy was working down the learning cost curve ahead of his competitors. Because the market price was set by the cost where most producers operated, Rockefeller made substantial returns on his investment with significantly lower costs. Rockefeller continually devised ways to reduce his costs even while competitors were adopting his techniques and adding others of their own. But the competition usually lagged behind him, yielding a moving competitive advantage that translated into larger profits.

An important ingredient of Rockefeller's success was his being able to visualize where the industry was moving and thus prepare for developing conditions. But he was more than a visionary. He was also a pragmatic businessman who, while not possessing the technical skills of a petroleum engineer, had a good sense of how refining operations worked, including the relative costs of different functions. This honed his instincts so that he was quickly able to assess the likely result of possible changes in operations. Nowadays the Lotus 1-2-3 computer program makes such a capacity to simulate much more widespread, but someone like Rockefeller who has a good sense of proportions and causes still has an advantage over computer programs. Rockefeller leveraged his own inventiveness by constantly broaching possibilities with his employees, encouraging them to find ways to reduce costs. He was a business leader in the sense we understand the concept today, one who builds a team to extend his own capabilities and keeps the team's energies focused toward clear goals. It was, in other words, a strong company culture, which goes a long way toward explaining Rockefeller's team's staying ahead of the competition.

Rockefeller's basic strategy naturally carried him beyond the refinery in the 1870s to tap emerging economies of scale within the distribution of petroleum. As sales grew, the refinery managers noticed how much time and money they were spending on railroad transportation. Rockefeller purchased tank cars as substitutes for barrels to reduce costs. (One of his larger errors in judgment occurred during this phase. When the volume of petroleum transported becomes large enough, pipelines become the cheapest means. But Rockefeller resisted this innovation, only shifting to them when competitors seriously crimped his growth with them.)

The forward integration toward the customers continued into the 1880s as Rockefeller began to take over oil refineries in other cities in the Northeast. Some historical treatments have portrayed Rockefeller as pursuing acquisitions ruthlessly, but the record suggests the opposite. In the majority of cases the firms approached Rockefeller, asking to be acquired. He had more applicants than he could absorb. The explanation is straightforward: Rockefeller's costs were lower and the other firms simply couldn't expect to compete very long, so independence meant inevitable bankruptcy. Critics also have accused Rockefeller of competing unfairly by selling below cost, but he wasn't selling below *his* cost, he was just selling below most competitors' costs. His costs were lower. And so competitors who examined the situation had to conclude: Either we can join the Rockefeller organization and use our assets to the extent that they can be redeployed within that organization or we can remain independent, thereby losing all our assets. A good share of competitors logically decided to sell their facilities to Rockefeller, allowing him to meld them into the broader organization. Thus Rockefeller effected economies of scale not only in production but also in the broader system of distribution that evolved into a regional, and then national, system.

Rockefeller is also recognized for significant advances in the operations of large, functionally specialized businesses. By 1890 Standard Oil was divided into divisions, according to their place in the sequence of product delivery. Engineers supervised refineries; transportation managers dealt with railroads, pipelines, and international steamship lines; marketing kept in touch with customers; financial people ran the accounting department and raised capital; and the scientists toiled in the research labs. It becomes a major task to coordinate these divergent specialties so that they work with, rather than against, one another.

One approach is an executive committee that brings representatives of each major specialty together at the top level of management to ensure that all important considerations of major decisions are represented. Rockefeller began with an informal committee, which we might term a kitchen cabinet. Its members included the major technical and functional specializations within the company. This, for example, avoided decisions that would have completely destroyed the marketing effort by producing a product that consumers would not buy even though the engineers insisted it would be cheaper. And the group avoided adding types of production facilities that the research-and-development staff believed would be made obsolete by developing technology. The comprehensive range of expertise of such a committee should reflect most of the important elements affecting a decision.

Rockefeller's innovations with the executive committee illustrate his success as a "people person" par excellence. He was good at communicating, persuading, and leading. The importance of these qualities becomes particularly evident when students first enter business. The classroom provides a tightly structured agenda for the material to be mastered each day. Exams and deadlines for papers are laid out well in advance. There's no syllabus after college, however, and creating one's own involves much more than taking notes at lectures. You must talk to others, enlisting them to support your ideas. You must elicit information from a wider range of sources than listening in a classroom. Every business organization is ultimately a human organization, a collection of people working together. Therefore, leading it becomes the task of getting people to cooperate toward reaching goals. Rockefeller proved particularly good at such skills.

Moving On to Mature Business

The formation of large, vertically integrated firms is characterized by decreases in average cost as production increases. The onset of this phase varies among industries, depending on the respective technology and demand. Some industries began as early as 1850, as in the case of McCormick's reaper; others came later, such as in the 1870s when Andrew Carnegie helped develop the steel industry. Other companies appeared in the 1880s, such as in cereal, canned goods, soup, and pickles. Each new industry characterized by high-volume processing passed through this phase while the coalescing technology and organizations slashed costs.

The entrepreneurs who succeeded in this environment had an intense—often passionate—focus on reducing costs. This bearing down on costs to the exclusion of other business pursuits appeared as marked tunnel vision. This tactic often became a self-fulfilling prophecy in that cost reduction yielded cost leadership, which in turn "sold" the product, allowing the entrepreneur to neglect marketing and other elements of consumer care. The latter condition also encouraged entrepreneurs to run their own show, exercise considerable power and discretion, and generally behave in flamboyant ways. These leaders usually had technical expertise in making the product or, at least, a clear sense of how the technology worked. In other words, they focused on the mechanics of production even when they lacked technical training in it.

As firms succeeded in reducing costs they inevitably moved into a new phase.[3] In this phase further opportunities for reducing costs remain, but the firm reaches a point where it has captured much of the advantage from such a strategy. When John D. Rockefeller began selling kerosene, for example, it commanded a dollar a gallon. Of course, that made it a luxury purchase on most mid-nineteenth-century budgets. By the late 1880s he had succeeded in reducing kerosene prices to about ten cents a gallon. In other words, a reduction of 90 percent. This completely changed the game, opening up an entirely new market by allowing the majority of Americans to afford kerosene for lighting. The flip side was that further reductions in the price below ten cents would not be nearly as effective in winning customers. Squeezing out further savings had lost much of its competitive oomph. The initial, primary strategy runs into diminishing returns, forcing competition into other avenues.

After firms achieve the greatest possible cost reductions, they must shift their attention to other types of competition. Consumers seek amenities in a product beyond cheapness, such as better styling, more features, financing, and more attractive displays. A wide range of initiatives can be undertaken to make goods more attractive. As a product approaches its minimum production cost, its advantage over competitors shrinks and other features become more important to consumers. Henry Ford illustrates the danger of neglecting this transition.

During the early 1920s other automobile companies, including General Motors and Chrysler, duplicated much of his production technology. But they also added other features to their products. General Motors, for instance, instead of simply matching Ford's low-priced offering, the Model T, filled in more expensive lines to serve wealthier consumers. Even the basic Chevrolet outdistanced the Model T by adding a heater, hydraulic brakes, and an enclosed cab.

Henry Ford wasn't persuaded people required such "luxuries." Buyers of Model Ts who strongly desired such features had to buy and install them separately. Ford's attitude is epitomized by his reply to an executive who is reported to have said to him, "Henry, the competition is offering different colors in their cars while we are only offering black. We could sell more cars if we started painting some different colors." Henry Ford's response was, "You can paint them any color you want as long as they're black."[4] In other words, he wasn't going to budge, and he didn't. But when the competition offered such choices, the consumers started going over to them. Finally in the late 1920s the competitors compelled his organization to offer such options in the new Model A, which incorporated many other common innovations.

A firm moving into the mature phase of the product must offer consumers greater variety and other features to enhance its sales. Not infrequently this collides with habits ingrained in the entrepreneurial phase to reduce costs. Consumers willingly pay more for features unavailable in the cheaper, basic model. So marketing, advertising, better design, and additional features become more important in the mature phase. The entrepreneur who remains stuck in a production mentality, only thinking about reducing costs, encounters trouble. Failing to adjust to this selling mode, he keeps thinking: We're turning out a great value, the consumers should appreciate it.

If only we persist they will come around to see the basic value in it. But increasingly, consumers are not persuaded; they buy others' products. Those manufacturers who cannot break free of preoccupation with low-cost production perish.

The following phase demands different tactics and managerial styles as competition shifts to other dimensions. Invariably the shift pushes firms into major reorganizations. One of the earliest indicators is the structure of management itself. Formative firms are usually entrepreneurial, characterized by loose, informal management. The founder, who usually owns a good share of the stock, is clearly in command. He probably has an informal executive committee— perhaps a half-dozen associates who work regularly with him. Oftentimes they lack formal titles, or the ones they use don't describe the important parts of their activities. Some employees with seemingly insignificant titles may exercise considerable responsibility in such organizations. Such informal structures can be very effective during the formative stage. The grouping is flexible, innovative, and can respond to changing conditions quickly. Some of the best people in the industry are likely to be included because they believe they can learn a lot and have a major impact on society.

As operations grow, the informal organization begins failing to cope with major problems or to miss opportunities. The management group often is held together by the founder's zealous vision. As the business becomes larger and more diverse, he can no longer keep his personal grip on everything, so coordination suffers. An entrepreneur in a smaller company is like a one-man band. He sets the tone, plays a number of instruments, and, by virtue of talent and energy, maintains momentum during the formative growth. But problems develop as the company grows further, expanding beyond the equivalent of three or four instruments. It ceases to be a combo and turns into an orchestra, which requires much more coordination to make the instruments work together.

The founder who has become conditioned to behaving like a one-man band but now has an orchestra, faces two—probably uncomfortable—alternatives: he can become a full-time conductor, which means giving up playing individual instruments, or he can choose to remain a musician. Focusing on coordinating the entire operation doesn't allow one to spend much time on specific details. The best entrepreneurs succeed in making this transition. Andrew Carnegie and John D. Rockefeller made the switch gracefully. Each had a good overall perspective, which told them when it was appropriate to step back into the role of conductor. Occasionally entrepreneurs look at the choice dispassionately and conclude that they want to remain a musician, playing a particular instrument. An example is Edward Land of Polaroid. He decided that even given the importance of directing the company, he still retained important strengths in research. This required spending considerable time in the lab because quality research requires intense concentration and a perspective different from that necessary to run a company. But Land's experience indicates that even with the most careful preparation it still is difficult to fulfill both roles simultaneously.

Entrepreneurs who attempt to continue doing everything find themselves jerking from one instrument to another, playing each badly, and disrupting the music's harmony. Again, a classic example of a failure to adjust to the mature phase occurred with Henry Ford in the 1920s. He was clearly an exceptional formative-phase entrepreneur, but never adjusted to the new environment he did so much to create. He was unable to switch to the more encompassing role, but attempted to manage the Ford Motor Company in the 1920s much as he had begun its operations twenty years earlier. As a result the company slid toward chaos and had to be rescued by others from what was on the verge of becoming one of the biggest business failures in American history.

There are numerous modern variants of this theme. Recently large American businesses have begun promoting the advantages of entrepreneurial attitudes in their employees. In other words, they wish to retain the desirable properties of management in the formative stage: flexibility, innovation, attention to reducing costs, and keeping operations directly focused on primary goals. Thus the task is to promote that form of management and behavior into organizations that have passed into the mature stage. Businessmen have not been so foolish as to attempt converting mature companies to formative organizations, but they have attempted to graft elements of the latter onto the existing structure.

One of the most notable experiments was People Express Airlines, which epitomized the formative phase and attempted to perpetuate that style as it moved into the more mature phase. It became a highly publicized model watched by business scholars to test how far such innovations might be taken. Founded in 1981, it achieved sales of $2 billion within four years. By then it was the seventh-largest airline in the country, and one of the fastest-growing American companies in any sector. Don Burr, the principal founder, attempted to maintain the spirit of a small, entrepreneurial operation while the company became a national, indeed international, airline. Some observers called this approach "Quilting Bee Management" after the manner in which Colonial women used to position themselves around a quilt, stitching it together. No one exercised command, each of them knew what she should do, taking up the obvious task in front of them and, when finished, moving to the next apparent task. People Express attempted to retain a nonhierarchical structure, but encountered severe problems as it grew and acquired other airlines. It is difficult enough to scale up to a large company with this style, let alone meld in others. Its unhappy absorption by others suggests how difficult it can be to maintain successfully that structure of management in a large organization.

Another change typically accompanying the transition to the mature state involves the capital structure of the company. Companies in the formative phase usually are proprietorships or closely-held corporations. In other words, their stock isn't publicly traded. This structure served well earlier when the founder who made most of the decisions also owned a large share of the company. Furthermore, the company was likely to be earning sufficiently high profits to finance expansion internally. The founder did not have to plead to the bank for a loan; he had the cash. He could build a new factory, buy new machinery, set up a sales office or whatever else he believed necessary. In such circumstances the founder has considerable control, so the personalized capital structure is appropriate.

As the firm expands, exhausting the potential of the new market, its cost advantage over competing firms is likely to shrink, reducing its margin of profit and return on its assets. In other words, the firm moves toward the prevailing rate of return on capital. This is not to say that the original founder doesn't have huge wealth from past profits, but rather that profits are no longer coming in as fast. Now when costs don't fall as fast, but the firm must still expand capacity or finance new services to remain competitive, internal funding is not as easy as before. More likely the firm must turn to external sources. And borrowing from a bank or underwriter requires undergoing scrutiny. "What will you use the money for? Let me see your financial projections. Which assets can you offer for collateral?" and so on. Thus the founding entrepreneur must, in effect, surrender some of his control over his company.

Another way to raise capital is to sell shares of stock to the public. Often this is a major symbolic goal entrepreneurs aspire to: making the enterprise sufficiently promising that investors will publicly ratify the company's worth. Entrepreneurs also go public to facilitate their own exit from management. As they grow older they want more time off, probably retirement. Often the founder can't decide who should assume control because younger managers haven't developed sufficiently. Thus the entrepreneur thinks: If we issued stock it would be easier to tap our wealth as well as attract professional managers.

When the stock of the company is publicly traded, however, investors outside management acquire more influence. Their presence, even if they hold the stock passively and do not trouble management, complicates management. Being listed on a stock exchange requires filing regular financial reports and abiding by numerous regulations, including the conditions under which the stock can be traded. This further dilutes the freedom of the founder. It is understandable that few large, older corporations are owned by their presidents or chief executive officers (CEOs). Too many forces erode management's hold on ownership for such concentration to endure.

A fourth characteristic of moving into the mature phase affects the managerial structure of the company. An entrepreneurial company typically operates at one location, often using one factory. Management can look out its office doors to keep tabs on most proceedings. As companies grow larger, however, they usually add other facilities, dispersing them around the economy to take advantage of raw materials or local markets. Some companies develop international operations. Companies must adopt more complex management structures and reporting procedures.

Firms that integrate vertically create additional groups, which must be coordinated and supervised. In addition to production operations, large staffs must be assembled to support sales, manage branch offices, and coordinate the product's flow toward the consumer. Frequently, research divisions are added. Research-and-development groups will often be removed from company headquarters in order to draw on technical expertise near academic centers. Each such influence encourages the company to branch out, making it more difficult for management to supervise operations. Founders who attempt to retain close control find affairs slipping through their fingers. Inevitably firms institute more bureaucratic and hierarchical controls.

A common feature of this increasing complexity in structure is the appearance of a distinct level—middle management—spanning the level between headquarters and the foreman on the shop floor. Middle managers typically supervise a factory, a sales office, a research lab, or other departments of the business that provide a specialized function in the organization. As a company expands into the mature phase, the middle managers begin to take on a distinct identity as a group. They are managers, but also often function as technical experts within their particular professional specialties. Nowadays college graduates with ten to fifteen years of successful experience earn that kind of responsibility for coordinating a large operation—such as a factory—but one that still requires an appropriate technical or professional background properly to direct its performance.

At the same time, top management undergoes a comparable restructuring, developing its own brand of specialization. Formative-phase entrepreneurs must act as generalists; they turn from one task to another while keeping an eye on the overall picture. As the company grows, however, sections thereof are necessarily parceled out to specialists. One division is likely to be production—the factories and foundries. Another is research—those responsible for the next generation of products and the technology to keep the company competitive for the next ten or twenty years. And so the company overall takes on a specialized structure with representatives in the top-management group for each major function: vice presidents of production, marketing, finance, oftentimes international programs, product development, and—these days, increasingly—public relations, stockholder affairs, and government affairs. Thus the top management of the company reflects the developing specialization and the necessary structure for coordinating it.

These major changes suggest that the role of a leader in a mature company is very different from one in the founding phase. The leader of the large company has to direct through example and vision, rather than keep his hands in everything. He must shift from a preoccupation with cutting costs to one in which service and other product features are more important. He has to operate within a capital structure over which he has less control, reporting to numerous outside parties. And finally, he has to deal with a more complex, specialized administrative structure. This drastically alters his style. He must break the conditioned responses that proved so successful in the early years of the company. Now he must lead through symbols and persuasion, convincing associates to leverage his efforts.

It is very difficult for most entrepreneurs to make this transition, as evidenced by how large a proportion of them fail. Indeed, it is one of the largest sources of entrepreneurial failure. But the great entrepreneurs such as Andrew Carnegie and John D. Rockefeller have the personal qualities to surmount the transition. Both Carnegie and Rockefeller had sufficient breadth and perspective so that when the time came for them to step back, they could assume a more detached role. They were able to discipline themselves so that their respective companies successfully formed around a larger group to carry on the operations. It is a tribute to both men that they had numerous successful underlings who not only played an important role within the company but went on to create sizable enterprises of their own, providing that they had an independent entrepreneurial capability. This is the central role the entrepreneur must provide at this point: enabling the larger organization to take over and to develop as he steps back from the forefront of the action.

8

Public Perceptions
of Entrepreneurs

The public could not help but be awed by the appearance and endurance of large vertically integrated firms in the late nineteenth century. The companies were much larger than anything before. They were also closely associated with the entrepreneurs who founded them, and who seemed larger than life. These developments did not fit into the world as Americans had come to know it. As they struggled to comprehend, they concocted one of the most widespread, enduring legends about American history, that commonly called the *robber barons*.

It is clear that these entrepreneurs attracted far more attention than American businessmen normally do. Few Americans can name more than one or two businessmen before the Civil War. And as few can name the top officer of today's largest companies, such as General Motors and Exxon. But the names of John D. Rockefeller, Andrew Carnegie, J. P. Morgan, and Jay Gould are widely recognized, much more than the presidents of the era. How many, for example, can name Rutherford Hayes, James Garfield, and Chester Alan Arthur as the presidents from 1877 to 1885 in the heart of this era? This suggests that the business environment, which could elevate businessmen into such unusual prominence, must have been exceptional.

A closer examination of the era argues that the role associated with the major entrepreneurs was not an accident. An unusual convergence of economic forces prompted an exceptional environment and, therefore, exceptional operations.[1]

Rapid population growth contributed. By the beginning of the Civil War there were already 30 million Americans, a tenfold increase over the Revolution, translating into ten times as many customers. Population growth continued, reaching 110 million by 1914 on the eve of World War I, increasing potential customers and market size by another three and two-thirds times. By itself this was the largest pool of buying power in human history. Even the increase over 1860 was larger than any other economy.

Rising per capita income bolstered domestic spending even further. Personal incomes rose as technology improved, markets became more cohesive, and other refinements worked their way through the economy. Considering the improvement in the quality of consumer goods as well as their quantity, real incomes probably rose two and one-half to three times. Americans were significantly wealthier in 1914 than in 1860, leveraging the effect of population growth, raising spending power in the economy. Improving transportation furthered this gain by reducing the cost of shipping goods, and better information allowed a closer match between resources and opportunities.

The rapid increase in the American market boosted it well into the lead as the largest in the world—where it has remained ever since. Leadership, in turn, gave the economy another advantage. Larger markets raise the prospective return on inventive activity because there are more customers to purchase new or improved products. Thus it was predictable that about the time of the Civil War the United States passed England in creating new technology.

The American market became the most fertile ground for investors and entrepreneurs in which to grow new methods. This gave the economy an added fillip, speeding up the pace at which improved products and methods were put into use.[2]

Entrepreneurial Strategies for a National Market

The burgeoning market drastically altered the operations of those businesses serving large markets. A firm contemplating national distribution in 1914 faced a market at least ten times larger than that of 1865. The new environment allowed—indeed compelled—the firm to tap efficiencies that were obtainable only at those larger levels of output. Such economies of scale reduce the average cost of output as output grows. Learning to implement this opportunity was one of the most important challenges for American entrepreneurs after the Civil War. It opened up sophisticated opportunities to use large-scale production, particularly in vertically integrated firms such as Cyrus McCormick had begun assembling before the Civil War.

The best candidates for such entrepreneurial remodeling were industries handling materials in large volume and, therefore, promising larger gains from economizing on processing operations. This implies manufacturing as distinguished from services. Steel, which expanded rapidly from 1870 to 1895, is a good example. The process burns coal to transform iron ore and smaller amounts of other materials. As the iron ore is pushed through the blast furnace faster, more steel is produced relative to the fuel expended. Cigarettes offered similar opportunities. The handmade cigarettes on the market before 1880 were very expensive. When machinery became available that automatically shaped tobacco into long strings, wrapped it in paper, cut it to the length of individual cigarettes, and packaged them, one factory could turn out millions per week. Other consumer products whose manufacture was reshaped included breakfast cereals, bakery goods, canned goods, meat packing, fresh milk, soap, matches, soft drinks, and beer. Among light consumer machines were typewriters, sewing machines, and bicycles. Industrial equipment included pumps, elevators, conveyors, and electrical equipment.

Opportunities for cost cutting are particularly fertile in the earliest stages of an enterprise. The largest, most obvious gains are attacked first, so that costs usually fall quickly. Frequently, the entrepreneur who first seized the opportunity continued to lead the industry, reducing cost. That gave his firm an important, running advantage over competitors. Of course, no entrepreneur earning large profits was left unchallenged; imitators tried to appropriate some of his gains for themselves. The successful founders were only able to maintain a dynamic gap over competitors by keeping their organizations focused on reducing costs.

The cumulative profits from this progression could be very large. Rapidly growing output, leveraged by the widest net margin in the industry, could yield huge profits. Andrew Carnegie's operations were worth more than a half billion dollars when he sold them to the founders of U.S. Steel in the late 1890s. Adjusting for changes in the value of a dollar, Carnegie was as rich as any American since that era.

The key for large, formative businesses was reducing costs before competitors. The typical entrepreneurs who succeeded in this environment were people preoccupied with—indeed fanatics about—cutting costs. John D. Rockefeller, for example, was a pleasant person, at least compared with some counterparts. Nevertheless, he made his organization understand that costs were the villain. He toured his refineries with a notebook in his hand. While he wasn't a trained engineer, he was very observant, with an instinctive sense of how a good organization should appear and thus where things might be improved. He wrote his questions and suggestions into his notebook and passed them on to his aides. Employees would scramble around for months thereafter answering questions and implementing suggestions.

In this environment entrepreneurs developed a one-track mind, focused on cutting costs. As long as they were able to keep costs below the industry average, profits flowed in and the enterprise had resources to pursue its mission. This environment encouraged entrepreneurs to specialize. When they succeeded in reducing costs, they almost guaranteed that increased sales would absorb the burgeoning production. Andrew Carnegie exemplified this. He didn't pay much attention to the multitude of things that might have affected his business but he watched costs in the company scrupulously. Today it would seem shocking to find a company president who said he did not worry about the market for his product. But Carnegie's practice was to set the price of the product so that everything produced was sold. He forced others to worry about the market. He could compete at whatever price the market determined because he was the lowest cost producer. Thus, lowering the price until everything was sold was his operating rule. He could safely ignore many influences that troubled other enterprises. It was a self-fulfilling strategy while it worked.

The novelty of this entrepreneurial environment is underlined by its contrast with other periods of American history. For a Colonial businessman to plunge unreservedly into a new type of business was dangerous, indeed reckless. The economies of scale that could make the first, dramatic commitment in the post–Civil War period pay off so well did not exist, so that the risks of becoming so specialized were enormous. In such a climate, it is probably wise to wait until the situation becomes clearer. One waits, allowing others to sort out what works, and then builds on their successes. Portions of the modern electronics industry have followed this practice because it takes some experience to determine how new technology performs in consumer products. IBM, for instance, often lags in introducing the newest technologies into their computers. Rather, they monitor competitors' introductions, incorporating successful elements in the next model. IBM's organization is designed to deliver a complete package of services along with their hardware, so caution in introducing technologies that might upset some of the other service elements is warranted, even if the machines sometimes lag behind the latest techniques.

Most opportunities for Colonial entrepreneurs to innovate promised only marginal gains for the immediate future, which meant the risk in hesitating was not large. The greatest opportunity to make profits was in moving goods among locales as prices fluctuated. This rewarded short-run assessments of market conditions, skills that differed sharply from the long-term process of building organizational efficiency. However, in the late-nineteenth-century American environment there was a much larger payoff to being first. The entrepreneur initiating the technology of mass production in a particular industry gained a decided advantage over competitors.

The wealth that this advantage promoted released entrepreneurs from many of the financial constraints normally confronting businesspersons. They didn't have to ask bankers for a loan. Their profits allowed them to operate however they desired—and many accepted the opportunity. Carnegie, for example, laid down the rule that anybody investing in his firm must obtain his approval and abide by his rules. Despite being the head of one of the nation's largest firms, he operated his enterprise as a limited partnership rather than a public corporation. He accepted only investors whose business judgment he respected and who agreed their holdings could be sold back only to the company at book value. There would be no disagreeable stockholders. King Gillette, who popularized the safety razor, spent much of his energy promoting a utopian, socialist model of society. Kellogg's cereal company grew out of an interest in health foods that W. K. Kellogg continued to promote throughout his career. With fewer forces trimming their sails, these entrepreneurs were more inclined to yield to their flamboyant instincts, and that has colored depictions of this era.

Such situations still occur, as was evident at Apple Computer a few years ago. Their first personal computers, which contained a couple of hundred dollars' worth of parts, could be sold for $2,500. Steve Jobs, the president and major shareholder, was frequently publicized for his ascetic life-style. Major business magazines pictured him sitting in the middle of his huge, virtually vacant, California house meditating—the complete opposite of how the president of a major company might be expected to behave. His aberrations were tolerated because his company was making enormous profits and serious competitors had yet to emerge. Success freed him from many of the obligations that those who are just keeping pace with the competition feel. A similar pattern emerged in the behavior of Kemmons Wilson, the founder of Holiday Inns, who opposed acquiring casinos and had Billy Graham address the stockholders' meeting.

Of course, Steve Jobs is no longer with Apple. As the company exhausted cost reductions, the competition caught up. Apple lost its big margin of profit. While it has not done badly, it certainly is not nearly as profitable. And the managerial style appropriate in the present phase departs sharply from the dedicated cost cutters necessary earlier. As a firm enters the latter phase, flamboyant managers become less tolerable. Mr. Jobs was eased out of his "own company" when his life-style and management philosophy became more of a distraction than a contribution.

Consequently, the period between 1870 and 1910 is distinguished by the exceptional expansion of the national market producing an equally large surge of entrepreneurs of large firms. The growth of the market encouraged—indeed dictated—their visibility. Their behavior was not unique to this period, but the conditions that encouraged so much of it were. Some historians have called this period the era of the robber barons. The term was coined in the 1930s, but the concepts it expresses have been common ever since the late nineteenth century. The description *baron* conveys the impression that such individuals had considerable power. They are believed to have had, in effect, their own fiefdoms. The above discussion shows there is some basis in fact for that label, at least as a transitory phenomenon. Historians also have commonly assumed that the power was ill-gotten and used in socially degrading means. They interpreted the entrepreneurs' wealth, often observed in lavish, pretentious displays, as further evidence that something was wrong. Hence, the other half of the term, *robber.*

Those who choose to explain entrepreneurs through the robber baron model actually are basing their interpretation on a more general thesis, which is best described as the "zero-sum game" view of human affairs.[3] It assumes that the total amount of resources or opportunities available at one time is fixed, so that the gain by one party can only be obtained by taking it from another. This view also typically assumes that it doesn't make much difference how the fixed supply of resources is employed. In other words, particular managers or structures of incentives don't make much difference.

This view of the world contrasts with the positive-sum approach, which entrepreneurs exemplify when they create new possibilities. Entrepreneurs assume that they can improve things, and when they succeed they do so by making resources produce more or by utilizing resources that previously were useless. John D. Rockefeller's contribution in converting the sticky, black goo in northwestern

Pennsylvania into a common household product is a good example. We also recognize that managerial and entrepreneurial resources are scarce and valuable because the ability to make judgments in complex, uncertain situations is uncommon and benefits from sustained preparation.

John D. Rockefeller illustrates how one can apply these alternate views of human activity. On the one hand, it has been alleged that Rockefeller exploited consumers by controlling petroleum products and depressed workers' wages by manipulating the labor market. Rockefeller's enormous profits are seen as prima facie evidence that consumers and workers were receiving that much less. The entrepreneurial view, on the other hand, would emphasize that during Rockefeller's tenure the price of kerosene, the main petroleum product of the period, fell from one dollar to ten cents a gallon and that real wages of workers doubled. By this measure, Rockefeller passed most of the new opportunities he created on to others.

No doubt the most common application of the robber baron thesis is the treatment of mergers and trusts during the era. There appeared to be an unusually large number of such combinations at the time, and many commentators have interpreted them primarily as a device to gain control over industries and markets. Firms at the time felt compelled to expand the scope of their operations, including integrating forward and backward. They assembled large distribution systems that reached down to the consumer and, in some cases, also back toward raw materials supplies.

There are two basic paths to implement such integration. Build your own network, as American Tobacco did by developing its own sales people, setting up local branches, and establishing an information reporting system. Alternatively, a firm could purchase established organizations that had already developed such services. While this requires meshing different business structures and cultures, it can provide a head start over building such structures from scratch. This is why so many vertically integrated firms were created through mergers. Both parties to the merger discovered that the combination would enhance what each had been attempting to accomplish by itself. Often these mergers included horizontal combinations to capture economies of scale in production as well. An overall account of mergers is complicated by some firms using the procedure to attempt to monopolize the market and increase profits by reducing competition. The problem is to distinguish between the two cases. Motives are elusive, but the correlation between the type of merger and its success is much clearer. When mergers actually improved efficiency, the new organization was much more likely to survive because it acquired advantages that the individual firms did not possess previous to the merger. Indeed, competitive forces would compel smaller firms subject to such efficiencies to merge. Competition would soon eliminate smaller firms that continued to deliver products at the higher cost.

In contrast consider the result when there are no such economies—that is, no reductions in cost when two firms are combined. At best, costs would not increase. It is much more likely that the additional overhead required to coordinate the production units would increase average cost. The lack of synergistic production gains means higher costs, putting the firm at a competitive disadvantage. Thus there is a market test of mergers. Those that promote efficiency are much more likely to survive. Those firms that are formed primarily to raise profits by increasing their clout in the market soon fade. Efficiency, rather than size, determines whether an enterprise will be able to compete.

Late-nineteenth-century trusts provide ample examples of firms merging with little prospect of improving efficiency. They attempted to control such basic industries as sugar, textiles, rope, and hardware. But the technology and market structures of these sectors had not undergone the powerful changes that prompted vertically integrated firms. There were no further economies in production or advantages of incorporating marketing. Thus these new organizations sacrificed efficiency, and losses forced most to disentangle to their premerger forms.

Firms organized as trusts attempted to operate as monopoly producers, surveying the total demand for the product and attempting to set the output and price that made the most overall profit. The tactic quickly lost its effect, however, because competitors soon appeared. They are attracted by the excess of the administered price over the cost of producing additional output. In every case these tactics were tried, new firms moved in. Sugar refining became a comedy of errors. The sugar trust agreed to raise prices through coordination. Competitors appeared in the West, making sugar from beets. Others opened in Louisiana, making cane sugar. Other brokers simply purchased supplies from abroad. As new suppliers appeared, the price fell until further entrants were discouraged. Then the sugar trust would incorporate the new firms and the cycle would begin again. After twenty years of such behavior sugar capacity in the United States was several times the necessary level because so much expansion had been encouraged under the price umbrella.

This pattern is essentially what has occurred recently in the international oil market with the Organization of Petroleum Exporting Countries. OPEC never was a true cartel, in that it could not dictate to individual members prices and output, but the prices set informally held up for a decade. It maximized near-term profits for the industry but the dilemma was that while thirty dollars was being charged per barrel, many new sources of oil could be developed for from ten to fifteen dollars a barrel. Moreover, the stimulus to conservation from high prices reduced demand, so a large surplus developed. For a while the OPEC countries adjusted by cutting back their own production, but after a decade that could no longer support the price. Prices collapsed toward a long-term competitive level.

Almost all successful mergers around the turn of the century occurred in three types of industries. The first used large amounts of raw materials, volume production, and energy-intensive processes, such as in petroleum, where huge volumes of oil are processed and transported. The second category employed standardized machine tools or machines made from interchangeable parts and sold in volume. This included sewing machines, typewriters, cash registers, and electrical equipment. A third characteristic was providing extensive specialized services along with the product, as did Singer Sewing Machine. Each of these characteristics could be implemented by variations of vertical integration in which mergers tied different levels together synergistically. In other words, they were more than a group of firms coordinated by a trust. They developed significant economies of scale in their structure, which reinforced their operations.[4] Waves of mergers have reappeared periodically in American history with similar forces determining their success. In the 1960s, for instance, mergers creating conglomerates became common. They were characterized by combining firms from dissimilar industries and structures. They clearly violated the entrepreneurial rule of thumb of "sticking to your knitting," not going into another business unless it brings enough expertise or value to offset the costs of absorption and added supervision. Conglomerates depended on production facilities remaining separate while gains were made integrating top management, particularly financial planning. By reallocating capital from lower returns to better uses the company would become more profitable. But many such firms were later returned to their original structure in disappointment. Those that continued have usually undergone further sizable reforms in order to mesh other aspects of their operations.

In contrast, consider some recent patterns of mergers in the 1980s, which appear to be grappling with the fundamentals. It remains to be seen whether they call upon forces sufficiently strong to prevail, but the logic motivating restructuring appears sound. Petroleum has become a declining industry; its market is shrinking and the value of assets tied to it has declined. But some oil firms were slow adapting to the new environment, keeping assets in production, refining and distributing oil after their returns had dropped. They should have been actively searching for better opportunities to employ them. An entrepreneur would instinctively ask, Other than oil, what is that land good for? or, How could those distribution facilities be redeployed? We don't know yet whether such a strategy can be successful, but that's what drove entrepreneurs like T. Boone Pickens.

Mergers also can be productive in a contrasting case, the growth sector of airlines. Interstate deregulation in 1978 opened up huge, new opportunities. As airlines experimented in the new environment, they discovered that consumers valued ready access to the national market. In other words, there are economies of scope in providing one service over a large area. The important forces appear to be gains in scheduling and connecting flights from larger operations. It seems particularly important to include major markets of the country so that passengers stay with the airline. As a result there have been numerous mergers, such as Eastern's being acquired by Texas Air, Ozark by TWA, Piedmont by U.S. Air, and Republic by Northwest. Industry executives believe there are efficiencies that can be mobilized by these combinations.

The experience of late-nineteenth-century mergers suggests that when there are compelling efficiencies the merged airlines will be more competitive and, therefore, more likely to survive. If the economies are not important, the mergers are likely to unravel. Future entrepreneurs would then find it advantageous to split off parts of companies, returning to the smaller structures preceding the mergers. Thus the forces that prompted mergers in the late nineteenth century appear to continue developing, and no doubt will do so into the future.

Many accounts have assumed that the mergers at the turn of the century necessarily reduced competition. This premise could not be properly tested until recently, when an operational concept of competition developed. The formerly held, now obsolete, view equated the amount of competition directly with the number of suppliers within the industry. Chapters in introductory economics texts once postulated that competition was fostered by a large number of sellers providing a homogeneous product, which would provide sufficient competition to keep the price down at the average minimum cost, the most efficient level of output. We now understand that it is not essential to have many sellers to assure competition. Smaller numbers often work quite well. One or two aggressive competitors can keep all others on their toes. Besides, powerful competition often comes from related, substitute products. Competitors need not be identical to be effective; indeed, differences sometimes make them even more attractive.

Moreover, the number of firms selling in an industry understates possible competition. A better indicator is the ease with which additional competitors could enter the industry. Economists have recently introduced the concept of *contestability*: the number of firms that would supply the industry if returns made it worthwhile. This is a better criterion for competition, which should be seen as a dynamic process of potential rivalry between firms. By this standard there was much more competition at the turn of the century than the number of firms within industries and the merger activity suggest. According to the old interpretation, two firms merging into one must mean less competition because one competitor disappeared. But the new firm is an opportunity to employ resources better, thereby intensifying the competition for that product, as well as resources generally. In this context, markets were quite competitive at the turn of the century.

Actually competition is much more likely to be dampened where legal prohibitions prevent competitive activities. This is ironic given widespread perceptions at the turn of the century. In 1890 the Sherman Antitrust Act was passed with the intention of blocking anticompetitive behavior and environments believed to prompt such. The federal antitrust division was established to monitor industries to ensure they remained competitive. We now realize, however, that much of what the antitrust division attempted to promote was counterproductive because, growing out of a misconstruction of competition, it promoted a structure of the economy that was actually less competitive.

This was illustrated about 1970 when the antitrust division decided that IBM was not sufficiently competitive. It was a dubious premise because most authorities have considered IBM one of America's most aggressive and competitive large firms. The argument was that by controlling a large portion of the market, IBM preempted competition. Anyone who has seriously examined the computer market in recent years would be astonished because competing firms keep nipping at IBM's heels and carving out their own niches in the expanding market. Recently the government finally had the good sense, after ten years, thousands of court hours, and millions of dollars in lawyers fees, to realize that they didn't have a case.

One of the reasons the Justice Department dropped the IBM case is that they learned more about competition. You don't promote competition by curtailing competitors; rather, you attack the barriers to competition. For example, the biggest monopoly in the United States today is the United States Postal Service, employing 760,000 people. It is protected by a law that prohibits anyone else from delivering first-class mail. No one would claim that the United States Postal Service is competitive or efficient! Over the last thirty years they have raised prices much above the average. Other suppliers could have begun operating, providing these services much more cheaply. Some would begin quickly now if allowed. More than the paucity of firms within an industry, the prohibition on new entrants curtails competition.

Another telling example is that airline deregulation reduced fares on average by a half and even more dramatically in certain cases. The number of airlines increased from thirty-five to more than one hundred. The regulation approach had assumed that existing firms in an industry must be protected to prevent those thirty-five airlines from being squeezed down to five regional monopolies. But when the barriers to competition were removed, the number of competitors expanded threefold. Thus the greatest barrier to competition is usually preventing new firms from entering a market. A good share of antitrust activity discouraged firms entering new industries. For a long time the antitrust division held the view that certain firms were too big and shouldn't expand anymore. So when they acted competitively the antitrust division went after them, creating a major barrier to competitive behavior.

9

Creating Opportunities and Controlling Choices

Conceptions about economic power lie at the heart of discussions about the robber barons. Most accounts assume that major entrepreneurs were able to use their large enterprises to gain significant control over their respective markets. The claim is often supported by citing industries dominated by a few firms. Steel, oil, copper, railroads, and corporate underwriting are examples commonly offered. But several large assumptions lie between observing a limited number of firms and concluding that they necessarily wield considerable power.

A common misstep is to assume that two or three competitors in a late-nineteenth-century market represented a significant break with past conditions. Earlier American markets also typically could support only two or three suppliers. It was exceptional to have so many competitors serving a market that one of them could withdraw without being noticed. When markets expanded, it allowed the firms in them to grow correspondingly larger. Thus two or three firms dominating a national market were merely counterparts of the situation that existed previously in local markets. For example, consider meat packing. By 1900 four nationally integrated meat-packing companies had replaced many of the local butcher shops. But of the latter, probably no more than three or four had ever been within reach of a typical consumer. In other words, market concentration, measured by the size of demand relative to the number of competitors, did not change significantly.

Moreover, the number of firms serving a market is not the best indicator of competitive conditions. As we noted above, a more comprehensive and appropriate measure is potential rivalry—the range of competitors who could offer suitable services if returns warranted it. The function of economic systems is to cope with scarcity, which is to say that as long as people can't have all the goods and services they want, every use of a resource competes with those unfulfilled desires. An individual wanting an automobile discovers that each dollar spent on food, clothing, housing, entertainment, and saving for retirement postpones that goal. In an economic system every good is ultimately a substitute for every other one.

In the late 1800s steel became relatively cheap and, therefore, entrepreneurs developed widespread applications including railroad tracks, bridges, high-rise buildings, office equipment, locomotives, and tin cans. Used in construction, the steel in skeletons of buildings intensified the competition against the traditional materials of stone and wood. Employed in tin cans, it competed against barrels, wooden boxes, baskets, and pottery. In other words, the new material was superimposed across established zones of competition, cutting through old market boundaries. Thus competitiveness in an industry can only be assessed dynamically. The introduction of new products both carves out new markets and restructures existing ones.

The lack of a clear conception of power has allowed inflated assertions about the amount held by the robber barons. The newly-weds who discussed how they should manage their family affairs suggests a useful perspective. Electing to follow a traditional division of responsibility, they agreed that the wife would control domestic responsibilities, which, by their reckoning, included where they would live, the jobs they would take, how to spend their income, and how to raise the kids. The husband was to have responsibilities for larger issues. He would decide if the United States should participate in a nuclear freeze, whether taxes should be raised in order to eliminate the federal deficit, whether there should be a state income tax, and all other equally significant issues. As one readily infers, the husband's choices are meaningless because he cannot influence them. He can have opinions, but no control over such questions. Likewise for economic power: one must distinguish between cases of large size and those where significant choices exist.

The Treasurer of the United States probably supervises more money than any other person in the world, more than $2 trillion annually. But the individual holding that position is seldom recognized, except as the answer to a trivia question that asks us to identify his or her signature on a dollar bill. We don't believe that position possesses much authority, because he or she mostly carries out the directives of others. In contrast we pay attention to the president and Congress. The salary of congressmen is less than $100,000 a year, or about as much as that of a typical middle manager in a major corporation. So why do we follow the words of congressmen while the national media seldom publicize opinions of the manager of a factory or sales office? We obviously believe that the power Congress wields is much more significant. Thus the first step in understanding power is to separate absolute size from meaningful choices.

Economics employs simple concepts that can directly explain economic power. It is well understood that markets tend to move toward equilibrium, where prices cease rising or falling because forces become balanced. In that situation each resource is also paid a return competitive with its next best use. Of course an equilibrium seldom endures long because changes inevitably intervene, but markets adjust, including altering the compensation of the resources they employ as is necessary to retain each. Labor, natural resources, and the stockholders, therefore, tend to receive their competitive return. In equilibrium a manager or owner does not have much discretionary power. If he pays a resource less than its competitive return, it is likely to leave for greener pastures elsewhere. And there is strong reason *not* to pay more, because that would not leave enough to pay other necessary resources. A manager in such circumstances cannot change things much no matter how much he wishes. Even the largest firm in the world is frozen into its structure and policies in that state. The individuals who built the company can be wealthy by virtue of their equity, but the firm doesn't have power to do much other than what it is currently doing. Owners can sell the company and workers can move to other jobs, but they can't alter operations without jeopardizing its existence.

An individual can wield significant power, however, when the product or service he provides yields more than the opportunity costs of the necessary resources. Profits above the average rate of return in the economy cover costs and allow some spare resources. After paying labor and other costs, including the opportunity costs of capital, the remaining margin provides the leverage. It may be reinvested in the firm to build up operations or it may be spent on additional research and development to develop new products, outdistancing future competitors. Profits above the normal level, produced where competition has yet to force conditions to equilibrium, provide discretion. This is power in an operational sense; owners can choose a different course if they desire. Returns on resources below normal are just the opposite of having power. When capital is being dissipated by not earning the going rate, it is not long until the bankers arrive to lock up the remaining assets for security. Bankruptcy is not power or a meaningful opportunity. Advantageous situations whose by-product is power are precisely what entrepreneurs are seeking to create. By devising novel products or cheaper means to provide a service, they raise consumer satisfaction, thereby earning a higher return than others employing such resources. Thus entrepreneurs gain power during the lag between their implementation of the improved methods and others' adoption of them. Historians' judgment that the late nineteenth century exhibited concentrated power is correct in this sense. Power existed as long as profits were above normal, which was until the innovations had been generally assimilated. Once competition asserted itself, however, and pushed profits down to the equilibrium level, that margin of power disappeared. Power in business is much like running a canoe through the rapids. As long as the boat is pushed along faster than the current, it can be maneuvered. But riding with the current puts one at the mercy of every rock or cascade in the way.

While an industry is in the early stage of development—in other words the firms are rapidly reducing costs—the leading firm processes power. Its choices are wider than its counterparts in industries that have reached a competitive equilibrium. However, once competitors replicate its advances, it loses its margin of discretion and special leverage. Even though the owners may be enormously wealthy, their ability to use the company has lost its previous edge. Power remains effective only as long as you remain ahead of the competition—and only to that degree.

Late-Nineteenth-Century Railroads: Power in Transitions

After the Civil War the rapid growth of railroads resumed, expanding almost sixfold in the number of miles of track—from 35,000 in 1865 to 207,000 in 1900. But the sector's prosperity masked the beginning of a maturation process and the restructuring that necessarily followed it. When such adjustments began, they surprised many who, lacking any apparent explanation, concluded that they must have been foisted upon the industry by outside manipulators. But an industry that grows by 80 percent in a decade, as the railroads did from 1870 to 1880, is bound to require some remodeling.

Two major forces were at the heart of the adjustments. First, railroad technology continued to improve. Many of the gains originated outside the industry. Cheaper steel allowed longer-lasting rails and thus saved on maintenance. Steel also replaced wooden trestles and much of the materials going into railroad cars. Stronger materials and improved engineering produced more powerful locomotives and, therefore, larger and longer trains. Block signals allowed more trains to use a segment of track without running into one another.

The overall effect was a steady increase in productivity, lowering costs, which kept traffic expanding.

Utilizing the gains in productivity was an important stimulus to the second, central change: restructuring the railroads' management. Like other large firms in emerging industries, the railroads had to adapt their structures to larger operations. They had to coordinate denser traffic over longer distances and give more attention to polishing operations rather than planning new facilities. And they had to be attuned to the new technology being developed elsewhere and how best to appropriate it. This was a complicated environment, but it also offered major opportunities for entrepreneurs, and thus the chance to create sizable amounts of power. Two who made the most of this transition illustrate how it could be done.

JAY GOULD: STOCK MANIPULATOR OR SYSTEM BUILDER?

Before 1870 the standard wisdom among railroaders held that coordinating operations on systems larger than 500 miles of main track became prohibitively costly. In other words, railroad managers expected diseconomies of scale, with the cost per mile exceeding that of shorter lines. This judgment was shaped by previous experience as well as people's instinctive expectations that bureaucratic inefficiencies must stifle operations beyond some size.

The mid-nineteenth-century consensus about optimal railroad size recognized that coordinating traffic over longer distances became hazardous because complexity meant more opportunities for mistakes—meaning collisions. Supervision of traffic had to be decentralized for safety's sake. This, in turn, meant that more distance had to be allowed between trains, reducing the capacity of the system. Thus as a railroad approached about 500 miles, it was assumed that it should cease expanding and hand further traffic over to connecting, independent lines.

In the 1860s railroads adhered to this rule of thumb by passing traffic from one line to another through cooperative arrangements. But this environment was upended by a very dramatic railroad entrepreneur.[1] Jay Gould is considered to be one of the best—or worst, depending on one's interpretation—examples of a robber baron. After working as a surveyor and managing a tannery, he became a broker on Wall Street. Gould quickly learned the mechanics of railroad finance because the stocks and bonds of that sector were the most common securities. As he was to prove repeatedly, Gould had one of the sharpest analytic minds in business. Thus his familiarity with railroad finances soon blossomed into a probing, perceptive understanding of its structure and operations. This provided him with a critical edge when many managers in the industry assumed that their traditional approach remained correct.

In the 1860s and 1870s the major east-west railroads, particularly between New York and Chicago, sought to raise their profits by cooperating in setting freight rates. These informal monopolies had no legal force behind them, and thus individual railroads frequently found it worthwhile to subvert the arrangements to siphon off more traffic. But the railroads kept patching up the arrangements because they expected that cooperation was more profitable than aggressive competition.

Jay Gould's first foray into management was with the Erie Railroad during its famous struggles with Cornelius Vanderbilt. The latter had shifted from coastal steamboats to the brighter prospects in railroads, assembling a continuous line from New York City, through Albany, to Buffalo. He was one of the first to see advantages in combining shorter lines. But Gould also appreciated how the basic forces in the industry were changing and he was never one to draw back from the logical response. He bid against Vanderbilt for strategic parts of the east-west line and did exceptionally well for an underfunded novice, although he didn't win permanent control of a major line.

In attempting to assemble a main east-west line Gould discovered the potential in such an arrangement for exploiting other railroads when they attempted to act together as a cartel. Gould continued assembling alternative throughlines, purchasing control of smaller lines and connecting them to bypass sections of established main lines. The process was often sophisticated; some lines were leased, and sections were even sold back to the competition. In other words, when Gould created competitors, the existing cartel had the dismal choice of either buying him out or ceding him some of their profits. He took advantage of the vulnerability of a monopoly when it boosts its prices above the cost of production.

Gould worked west probing for pockets of opportunity. Starting from the lines in Pennsylvania and New York, he moved into their connections in Ohio and Michigan, which ran parallel to the main Cleveland-to-Chicago line. Then in 1873 he purchased a large stake in the Union Pacific, whose stock was cheap in the aftermath of financing its recent transcontinental connections. Gould's behavior at the Union Pacific belied one of his most pervasive images, namely that he was only a manipulator and trader of railroad securities, allowing operations to depreciate during his tenure. Gould remained president and a major stockholder for six years. During that time he spent a good portion of his time developing branches and local industries to build traffic along the empty spaces the main line passed through. He also made major progress in reducing costs and improving facilities. He made several extensive inspections of the system. (Such contributions are easily overlooked because, during the same time, Gould's exceptional energy allowed him to continue what would appear to be a full-time program in other acquisitions.) Gould also used the Union Pacific as the base for building an integrated continental system stretching all the way from Boston to Denver. One measure of how he increased its value is that the stock sold for about five times its purchase price when he sold it in 1879.

When Gould was blocked from taking control of a railroad, it was often because the target found another, seemingly less threatening, merger partner. This is now known as the *white-knight strategy,* because it repulses the dreaded "dragon." Whether or not they succumbed to Gould, their response acknowledged that he introduced an improved means of organization, which had to be accommodated. If the acquirer was threatening to impose an unprofitable structure, the move would lack credibility and targets could ignore it. But Gould's threat was substantive, forcing his targets to adopt his improvements.

White knight or not, a basic change in the opportunities facing railroads is necessary to prompt such widespread reorganizations, something as fundamental as the structure of costs. This had to increase the mileage at which diminishing returns set in, encouraging rail lines to embrace larger systems. Thus the appropriate tactic is to merge smaller lines into larger ones. Gould proved to be the catalyst forcing many railroads to make the move.

It is not clear what produced the larger economies of scale. If it came through better coordination, for example, why would railroads not have achieved this in 1860 as well as in 1875? The telegraph appeared in the 1840s, so presumably its consequences could have been incorporated earlier. There didn't seem to be any major improvements in the railroads' technology. Continuing refinements allowed larger locomotives, stronger steel trucks, heavier cars, and longer trains to take advantage of efficiencies, but it is not clear how this translated into serving wider markets.

When railroad managers discussed the reasons for merging at that time they raised many of the same points that airline managers have recently raised. They stressed the advantage of providing larger systems so that the traffic from local routes continued on main lines. In one sense they were attempting to enclose the market. In transportation, horizontal combination can play much the same role that vertical integration did in industries such as petroleum, in effect integrating marketing and production. What appears to have developed in railroads—as it has more recently in the airlines—is a number of advantages in connecting major markets. Not only did railroads merge into larger regional and national lines, but they also acquired related businesses such as steamships. It appears there were economies of scale in handling traffic in volume over a distance, and the threshold was reached about 1870. Jay Gould obviously was a catalyst in bringing this about, although some combination of entrepreneurs would have accomplished the same restructuring later if Gould hadn't. So while he was not indispensable, he certainly was the leader in galvanizing these changes into new environments.

Jay Gould died in 1892 at the relatively young age of fifty-six. The immediate cause of his demise was tuberculosis, but those who knew him understood that he worked himself to death; his small, frail body could not accommodate his intense intellect and ambition. Even at that age his estate of $80 million put him among America's half-dozen richest men, this during an era that was producing rich men copiously. Andrew Carnegie and John D. Rockefeller became much richer, but then they lived to eighty-four and ninety-eight, respectively, and much of their wealth compounded after they were fifty-six.

No doubt Gould would have been much richer in another decade. Up to his death his personal wealth had to be greatly leveraged in order to control large railroads. This consumed considerable ingenuity and energy that he could have turned to running his enterprises had he possessed unquestioned control over them, as Carnegie or Rockefeller had of their ventures. Gould had to borrow much of his capital and, therefore, often had to make concessions that didn't allow him to stay with a business as long as, or to apply his authority to the full extent, he desired. He operated from such a small capital base that several of his business ventures didn't last long enough to reap the harvest. To a critical, or even untutored observer, this verified the common claim that he was only a stock trader.

Historians have often characterized Gould as a scoundrel. He wasn't. The ethics of some of his stock trading were questionable by modern standards, but were normal for the time. He performed the classic entrepreneurial function of seeing things differently and taking appropriate action. But most contemporaries were not inclined to view him in that manner. To some he personified the dangerous interloper. Railroad managers viewed him in much the way that modern oilmen hate someone like T. Boone Pickens. They saw him destroying the world they had spent much of their life patiently assembling. The outsider not only challenges their position but their whole view of life. That is difficult to cope with dispassionately.

But even more, Gould became a symbol of what was believed to be wrong with the uninhibited expansion of the economy. The New York City newspapers, in particular, singled out Gould as a shorthand expression of pernicious trends. They were so convinced that his operations led to evil that they soon ceased verifying the details of their accounts of his activities. As Maury Klein, author of *The Life and Legend of Jay Gould,* has abundantly documented, not only were many of their reports incorrect, but most subsequent histories of the man have largely repeated the accounts uncritically. Gould was the perfect choice of a target. He seldom spoke out in public. As befitted a man with his quiet, analytic skills, his passions were reading and raising orchids.

The elevation of Jay Gould into a symbol of all that was evil in the robber baron era was not an accident. It helped many cope with their deep-seated concern that society was getting out of control by providing a personification of a new environment in which ordinary individuals were losing control of their lives. A strong indication of the attraction of this approach was that it was applied to almost every famous entrepreneur of the era, including the one who took up the role of Jay Gould in railroads, Edward Harriman.

STREAMLINING THE RAILROADS

Edward H. Harriman came to the railroads through a route similar to Jay Gould's.[2] He was the son of a minister in New Jersey and received a traditional education in a private school in New York City. But about the age of fourteen he decided the classical curriculum wasn't taking him where he wanted to go so he left school, becoming an office boy for a Wall Street firm. He worked his way up, so that by the age of twenty-one in 1869 he had purchased his own seat on the New York Stock Exchange. He spent the next ten years as a successful broker, building assets and acquiring skills and contacts in the market.

The route that Harriman was following was similar to that of Jay Gould for good reason. During this era the most common security on Wall Street was that of the railroads and the key problem in creating railroads was financial. They were still in their growth phase, when constructing and managing the systems could take a back seat to raising capital. An entrepreneur putting together a railroad could expect to make profits off the leverage of borrowed money and worry about tidying up the operations later.

In 1880 Harriman, at the age of thirty-two, made his first entry into railroad management. He became a director and partial owner of a small, upstate New York line. At that time the line was neglected and unprofitable. But Harriman showed two approaches that he was to pursue for the rest of his career: namely, he improved the operation of the railroad as well as analyzed its strategic importance to see how it could be used in a larger system. When the other directors and investors of the line rejected his recommendations, he purchased the entire operation and within a couple of years was able to resell it at a profit to the Pennsylvania Railroad.

Armed with his experience and capital gains, Harriman moved

up to a position on the board of the Illinois Central Railway. The Central was a slumbering operation that had been conceived before the Civil War to collect farm products through downstate Illinois. But by the 1880s the competition of the new east-west lines and improvements in railroad technology dictated that management should change tactics. Harriman advocated improving the system with new equipment and expansion in order to provide better services. He also understood that railroads were moving into the mature phase, where ups and downs in the economy would now be reflected in the demand for railroad services. Therefore, he also warned about the timing of such expenditures, anticipating opportune movements in the economy for the line's investments.

As Lloyd Mercer has shown in his book, *E. H. Harriman, Master Railroader,* Harriman was a very perceptive steward of the Illinois Central. The return on the line rose well above the national average. Harriman took advantage of the economies that were implicit in the use of improved locomotives and track, and larger trains. In 1896 when Harriman assumed a position on the board of the Union Pacific, he again undertook the reconstruction of facilities. On an inspection tour of its western lines in 1896—which he made famous by placing his car in front of the locomotive to improve the view—he noted all the deficiencies and set about rebuilding the line. Again, the profits on the line improved dramatically in response to his new management.

Soon thereafter he began acquiring positions in neighboring lines such as the Southern Pacific, which controlled the Union Pacific's main outlet into California. He also attempted to acquire the Northern Pacific, which ended in the famous Northern Securities arrangement of joint ownership with rival James J. Hill in 1901. Because of these larger acquisitions, he was labeled a monopolist who attempted to control railroad markets generally. But Harriman saw it simply as an extension of his efforts to complete railroad systems, as was the trend nationally, to take advantage of the efficiencies therein.

His record clearly indicates that he improved the operating efficiency of his railroads and in doing so not only improved his own position but also that of the stockholders and bondholders in the respective lines. Thus he performed the fundamental entrepreneurial function of creating value. This also created new opportunities that hadn't been available to those enterprises and their owners previously. While some outsiders interpreted those opportunities as allowing him to become a monopolist and exploit consumers, the opportunities would not have existed had he not created them in the first place.

Like Gould, Harriman became a symbol of developments that worried much of the population. They believed that he had too much power. But like Gould's, his power could only come from the creative contributions that he was able to bring to the enterprises he managed. Moreover, his power was transitory and soon eroded by imitators. Gould and Harriman represented a new environment with which Americans had not come to grips. Through all previous history they had been able to relate to almost everyone, the merchants, the farmers, and even the teamsters, who touched their economic life. But as the market grew large and impersonal, they felt that much of what was occurring was moving beyond their personal control. They also suspected that markets could be manipulated to their personal disadvantage. Therefore, entrepreneurs such as Gould and Harriman were seized upon as shorthand stereotypes for the dangers of a large integrated economy.

Viewed overall the ability of such people as Carnegie, Rockefeller, Harriman, and Gould to control markets was much less than the creative contribution that they made to their respective industries. They only gained "power" to the extent that they pioneered creative contributions. Much of that eroded quickly as competition assimilated their inventions. Thus consumers benefited directly through lower prices and better services, and the ability of entrepreneurs to charge customers excessive prices was severely restricted. John D. Rockefeller might have been able to raise kerosene prices above their competitive level of ten cents a gallon in the 1890s, but it would have required an unimaginable effort to put them back up to the level of one dollar a gallon, where they were when he began operations in the 1860s.

10

Developing Twentieth-Century Financial Mechanisms

Jay Gould could not have moved to reorganize railroads nearly so adroitly without being able to tap the markets for railroad securities. The latter were just forming before the Civil War; in fact, they were coalescing even as Gould demonstrated new ways of employing them. Nowadays it is difficult to conceive of organizing large enterprises without financial markets to raise large quantities of capital.

The supply of capital increased rapidly in the United States in the late nineteenth century, per person, as well as total. As economic growth gave Americans more to spend, they elected to put some of it into assets to increase future well-being. This corresponds to the worldwide pattern in which improving material well-being accompanies capital deepening. Capital markets were a logical application of this growth, as well as a reflection of the general trend toward interdependence in the economy. The development of the markets improved the allocation of capital within the economy, raising its return. This, in turn, made saving even more attractive. It doubled as a percentage of gross national product (GNP) by 1900.

The growth of capital markets prompted individuals to cut back on placing their own investments and hand them over to specialized agents. Earlier, in the absence of such markets, borrowing and lending money were difficult. A party wishing to earn interest on his savings had to arrange the loan and keep tabs on the debtor—typically a costly, awkward process for an individual. Much American borrowing took advantage of the commercial mechanism by which goods were imported from Europe, where credit was piggybacked onto foreign trade because it didn't pay to develop a separate channel to mobilize capital. This was less productive until larger volumes allowed a specialized system to become feasible.

Specialization in nineteenth-century capital markets developed in three major areas: insurance, banks, and stocks and bonds. Each grew faster than the economy overall and each contributed to better utilization of capital. People have always sought to cushion themselves against life's major risks. Insurance companies appeared in the United States right after the Revolution, but well before that time, Americans created cooperative self-insurance schemes. Neighbors banded together to spread over the group such major risks as a house burning down. Shipowners typically bought fractional shares of several ships. They understood that particular voyages were risky with some likelihood that a ship crossing the Atlantic would founder. Purchasing a one-sixteenth ownership in each of several ships would buffer the loss of one. Such devices for self-insurance were common well before individuals found it worthwhile to turn to companies specializing in insurance.

The Insurance Company of North America (which operated almost 200 years before recently merging with Connecticut General to form CIGNA) was founded in Philadelphia in 1792. It was the first organization to have sufficient capital reserves to undertake underwriting beyond its neighborhood. After a few years it moved beyond its initial base of ocean shipping to the other large segment of the market for insurance then—fire insurance.

The company developing some of the most valuable innovations in fire insurance was The Hartford. Its first twenty-five years after its founding in 1810 were mostly spent offering policies in southern New England. Operations were often lackadaisical. The part-time secretary did not promote sales, but rather expected policy buyers to seek him out. One important innovation did evolve, however, which was an agency system such that representatives in other towns sold policies for a commission. This is still the structure for much insurance sold today. That network of self-interested agents and the dispersion of risks across the region kept The Hartford going for its first quarter century.

In 1835, in response to several severe losses, Eliphalet Terry took over as president. Very quickly he faced a make-or-break crisis. In December, a fire destroyed much of lower Manhattan, making the company liable for losses well in excess of its net worth. Several other companies in similar circumstances declared bankruptcy, paying their policyholders only a fraction of their claims. Terry, however, set up a special office adjoining the razed area of New York City and advertised that all verified claims would be paid. The company paid out the unprecedented amount of $85,000 but quickly discovered that a surge of new policyholders more than covered the cost. Terry's bold move of personally going to New York to personify The Hartford's dependability convinced many people who up to that time had (rightly) distrusted the dependability of insurance in a severe crisis. By his personal integrity—he pledged his own assets to pay off claims—Terry demonstrated the importance of both trust and marketing in selling policies. Thereafter, fire insurance became a common service in America as other major companies adopted these insights.

Continuing development of the national economy created other major risks. The Travelers Company of Hartford—as its name suggested—initiated coverage for domestic travelers, particularly those using railroads. Thus insurance evolved along with the economy and the consequential major risks that people wished to control. At the beginning of the nineteenth century the largest demand was for fire protection, but then life insurance became progressively more important. Individuals grew more concerned about assuring continued support for their family. In the twentieth century automobiles stimulated major amounts of insurance because, in addition to their becoming a large component in the economy, their mobility allowed them to run into one another or be stolen.

The demand for insurance typically rises along with individuals' incomes. The value of life insurance in force, for example, rose from $5 million in 1840 to more than $2 billion in 1870 to $20 billion on the eve of World War I. Though some risks are sought—gambling, skydiving, purchasing stocks—people tend to insure against risks that are not sought—such as death, fire, floods, accidents, and disability. One of the largest forms of modern insurance covers medical costs. Consumers seek protection against catastrophic illness and the huge charges that can result from a serious illness.

Insurance companies receive premiums for policies, which they expect to repay later in claims. In the interim, the reserves provide a pool of investment capital. Reserves were increased further when large amounts of life insurance that contained a savings component began to be sold. Consequently, during the nineteenth century insurance companies became major custodians of capital. Thus it is not surprising that they were major buyers of securities such as bonds issued by railroads and state and municipal governments.

Like many industries gearing up to serve the national market in the nineteenth century, insurance companies tended to agglomerate in one locality, which in their case was Hartford, Connecticut. This was especially true of stockholder-owned companies, as distinguished from mutual companies owned by their policyholders. The Hartford companies provided the basic insurance function of spreading risks by selling across the economy, using the equity of their stockholders as a buffer against particularly bad years. Diversification was particularly important in the nineteenth century because the damage from a fire could become catastrophic. Large wooden buildings were side by side and the fire apparatus was little more than hand pumps. Once an inferno began, the only recourse was to create firebreaks and wait for the flames to burn themselves out. Every major American city, including Chicago, San Francisco, Boston, Philadelphia, and New York, had a huge fire prior to 1910. Such a catastrophe could ruin a company that had written substantial coverage in that city. Many insurance companies were bankrupted by the great Chicago fire in 1871, for instance, because they had written so many vulnerable policies that they did not have sufficient reserves to cover claims when put to the test. The Hartford companies issued policies across the country—property in the city of Hartford itself being insignificant relative to the nation. They also subcontracted many of their policies, reselling them to other companies in order to reduce concentrations of particular risk.

Making Money—Better

Banking also was a growth industry throughout the nineteenth century. Its basic function was providing the medium of exchange, allowing commerce to expand. And the growing specialization of the economy kept increasing the amount of money each person required to accomplish his transactions.

Almost all of the paper money used before the Civil War had been issued by private banks, much as personal checks are drawn on specific banks today. The banks put their currency into circulation when they initiated loans. As long as consumers accepted the currency it continued to circulate from hand to hand. To the extent that the banks were able to maintain this floating supply, it provided services similar to having another stock of capital. This served Americans by facilitating the exchange of land, goods, or services. Paper money saved, dollar for dollar, resources that would otherwise have had to be diverted to maintain an equal stock of gold and silver coin.

In addition, by accepting deposits banks could mobilize capital. Average balances became, in effect, permanent assets of the banks. While individuals deposited or withdrew money, the balances that banks retained on net could be lent. They consolidated small deposits into larger loans, lowering the costs of transactions through volume. Banks assumed an activity many individuals were eager to turn over to them, namely arranging the investment of their money. Millions of small accounts whose owners would not otherwise have found it worthwhile to search for a high rate of return were placed in the best use by intermediaries.

Banks also increase the liquidity of assets in an economy. When one individual lends money to another, that asset is locked in until repaid. Even to borrow, using the loan as collateral, is often difficult. It is much easier to recall money from a bank deposit. An individual depositor is not tied to a particular loan, because as a bank continually turns over such assets it can repay an individual depositor from any recent deposit. In effect, the bank creates liquidity by converting a personal asset into a fungible one.

Taking Stock in America

Markets for stocks and bonds also grew very rapidly in the nineteenth century. A regular forum in which to exchange securities provides owners with liquidity not available to owners of a private company. Suppose a founder wishes to use some of the wealth he has developed in his company to endow a foundation. In a proprietorship, one must take out a loan on the business or find a partner willing to purchase part of the business. Partners can be awkward— they often start to think that operations might be run differently. Incorporation eases such eventualities, particularly in turning operations and/or ownership over to the next generation. Incorporation allows each share, representing a portion of ownership and its corresponding claim on income, to be traded separately. This makes the ownership of a company more liquid, just as using a bank account for investments makes it easier to reclaim assets.

Liquidity also broadens potential ownership. It is risky to hold a major stake in a partnership without keeping close tabs on it. Stockholders, in contrast, can own small portions of the company without having to follow the day-to-day management of the company. This greatly expands the number of potential owners by including those who have small amounts to invest but lack the experience or interest in running a business. Selling shares in a public forum significantly broadens the market, thereby earning a premium (relative to each dollar of earnings) compared to a privately-held company. A rule of thumb in the late nineteenth century was that taking a company public would raise its value three times relative to selling it as a proprietorship to investors. This encouraged entrepreneurs like Carnegie and Rockefeller, who operated closely-held companies, to convert them into publicly traded corporations.

Such incentives are still strong. Most entrepreneurs developing a business look toward the milestone when they can sell shares publicly because that substantially increases the value of their company. Even while retaining a sizable stake, they release shares into the public market. This provides a public valuation on the company as well as a convenient channel to sell additional shares later.

The development of capital markets broadened Americans' opportunities to invest. It also improved the means available to businesses and individuals to borrow, improving the allocation of capital in the economy. Americans understandably began saving more. Prior to the Civil War Americans saved about 5 percent of their income. Improving capital markets doubled the rate to 10 percent of income. The capital markets made Americans more thrifty by offering them more on the use of resources.

J. P. Morgan: Creating the Capital Goods of Capital

J. P. Morgan is undoubtedly America's most famous financial entrepreneur.[1] In contrast to the other celebrated entrepreneurs of the period, such as Rockefeller and Carnegie, he began in favored circumstances. His father, a manager and partner in a major international financial house that dealt in foreign exchange and securities, spent a good share of his time in London. Thus J. P. Morgan grew up in the environment that he later chose as a career. In addition, he received a first-class education. His most important schooling was received at the University of Göttingen in Germany, where he majored in mathematics. There he came as close as was then possible to today's M.B.A. program, absorbing heavy doses of quantitative analysis that bolstered his critical skill of making financial calculations and assessing their interpretation. One of his prime strengths proved being able to detect the important forces working in a given organization and judging the changes appropriate by quickly scanning the financial figures.

Morgan began his career as an intern at a brokerage and foreign exchange banking house (not his father's) in New York. He became a partner and then the major partner as he built up his own capital and developed a reputation for rock-solid dependability. His banking house dealt mostly in foreign exchange; that is, it swapped currencies back and forth across the Atlantic and acted as the financial agent for foreign traders by settling balances of currencies and arranging loans. Firms with interests such as Morgan's naturally became involved dispersing stocks and bonds, because, at the time, America was a large, net borrower. The higher return on capital in the United States prompted Americans to borrow continuously from Europe.[2] (Some perspective on the recent foreign trade deficit may be provided by noting that the United States ran a deficit for 310 years, from 1607 to 1917, during which time the economy outgrew the rest of the world.) Financial houses served this market by selling American securities in Europe. Morgan honed skills in this trade that were to serve him very well later.

Morgan's career can be divided into three phases corresponding to three major developments in the capital markets. The first, from the middle of the Civil War to about 1880, was shaped by substantial trading in federal securities. The Civil War required unprecedented federal borrowing, two and three-quarter billion dollars in order to finance the military operations. The value of these securities was huge relative to peacetime issues and required two decades to be paid down to an orderly level. The outstanding debt had to be frequently refinanced by new securities as existing issues matured. Thus the market for government debt was large in proportion to the economy, presaging post–World War II conditions.

Trading in federal securities was complicated because the financial strains of the Civil War were so large that the United States was driven off the gold standard. Until its suspension in 1863 the American dollar was linked to gold, adhering to the prevailing international gold standard whereby the domestic currency contracted or expanded in response to changes in the domestic holdings of gold. Gold settled net differences in the balance of payments among countries via its link to each currency. The northern government issued huge amounts of greenbacks—paper money not backed by gold—to finance the war. This complicated finance by creating dual circulating currencies, with the greenbacks passing at a discount from gold dollars until the United States paid down the federal debt sufficiently to redeem enough greenbacks to return to the gold standard in 1879. Meanwhile, a large market was created to handle trade in federal debt, so it is little wonder that Morgan spent much of his early years concerned with these securities.

Beginning in 1870, railroad securities assumed increasing importance, prompting the second phase of Morgan's interests. Railroads continued to expand and, being capital-intensive industries, required a large amount of investable funds. The large blocks of stocks and bonds they issued required underwriting—that is, to be prepared and marketed. There was also an enormous amount of reorganization of the financial structure of existing railroads as the market for railroad services matured. Railroad mergers and the streamlining of existing lines were typically associated with refinancing and restructuring. Morgan developed much of his professional reputation in these endeavors; in fact, people began to use the term *Morganization,* which meant the reorganization of the management and structure of a business in a particular way.

Morgan's third phase was the large market for industrial securities that developed with the mergers of large companies toward the end of the century. He and his organization led in developing these securities and the procedures necessary to implement them.

Morgan's basic function was that of a broker. Though he sometimes acquired equity in the companies he served, he became wealthy primarily by bringing other buyers and sellers together. He located investors, matching them with companies seeking to borrow. Essentially his task was building a bridge between the parties by creating the appropriate arrangements. A broker-underwriter requires several interconnected skills, many more than the routine act of compiling a list of potential buyers and sellers, and then matching names. Underwriters develop considerable expertise about particular industries, as well as keep current on market conditions. Morgan's primary service was developing financing, but to reach that end he had to supply numerous complementary services.

Morgan's role could also be characterized as the counterpart to vertically integrated firms, which appeared about this time, when the firms discovered that they also had to provide complementary services in order to sell their primary product. Morgan provided the full services that investment houses have since routinized in their role as creative intermediaries. Suppose, for example, that a railroad believed it required a major infusion of capital. It would probably sound out an investment house about the feasibility before placing an issue in the market. Most likely an officer of the railroad would go to a firm such as Morgan's, explaining to the senior partners: "We see the need for this much new capital in the next three years because while this revenue should be coming in, these securities are coming due. We expect these investments will be warranted, so this is the net amount of cash we need to raise." Morgan's typical procedure was to probe deeper. He asked the company to justify its plans so that he could judge the feasibility of the proposed securities. Underwriters must ascertain the prospects of the money being repaid in order to be able to assure lenders that the securities are good investments. This requires developing a good understanding of the operations and prospects of the company. So underwriters, assuming the role of consultants, evaluate the prospects of a company in much the same way as its own management should.

Oftentimes underwriters imposed conditions on a company, such as reorganizing its management, before sponsoring an issue of its securities. Morgan examined potential offerings, reshaping them to deploy their assets most effectively, therefore assuring investors the soundest possible investment. The terms of securities were typically polished before releasing them to the market. Of course this was done in the context of a competitive market, which consisted of other brokers also seeking such business. Thus, unless Morgan contributed good value by the requirements he imposed to produce a compensating increase in the value of the enterprise, a company would turn to other brokers.

It is useless to prepare securities unless they can be sold. As an underwriter Morgan constantly cultivated potential buyers. He understood, for example, the interests of portfolio managers in the insurance companies. And he knew what qualities were important to other investors, particularly those in Europe, where a good share of the demand came from. He constantly updated his inventory of demands and watched the emerging supply of securities, noting where good matches might be made. When he brought a stock or bond to market, he usually had major buyers already committed. Failing to obtain such assurances made him doubtful that the security was proper yet.

Morgan's participation didn't end with the sale, however. He worked to guarantee the value of his securities by maintaining a watch over client companies. One practice—often a condition for issuing the securities—was to place an associate of Morgan's firm on the board of directors. This allowed Morgan to monitor developments and press for realignments, assuring buyers of securities that their interests would be safeguarded. By a strict interpretation of liability such safeguards were unnecessary but were undertaken recognizing that securities buyers would be more inclined to purchase securities he sponsored.

THE ECONOMICS OF HONESTY

Morgan, like most professionals, strove to build a commendable reputation, which becomes a form of capital, an earning asset. There are numerous situations in life where one can't specify the response to all conceivable events, and often we must depend upon the judgment of an appropriate professional. People recognize they must defer to doctors to prescribe medical remedies. A similar ignorance governs the choice of an underwriter because most investors lack the expertise to assess such a collection of influences. Thus one turns to a professional like Morgan to assess events.

Certain types of business situations tempt participants to default because it is not costly to their own business to take advantage of another participant. But in a profession where the demand for services depends heavily on a demonstrated record, such tactics have greater long-term costs than short-term yields. That's why top managers so often say that one must play it straight. When much of the perceived value of services depends on people's confidence in one's judgment, delivering consistently is essential.

Some situations are tailor-made for shirking commitments. A market supplying products to infrequent buyers invites deceit. For example, it's unlikely that you'll ever deal with the party who buys your house again, so misleading them won't damage your future transactions. Home buyers find many defects after the sale because sellers have a strong incentive to hide them. If you inspect the house in the summer they will not admit that there is six feet of water in the basement each spring. When the furniture comes floating up the stairs the following year, however, the neighbors verify that this has happened every year.

In such a market sellers gain from concealing harmful information because the buyers can discover it only after the sale. But buyers who purchase frequently from the same seller will quickly grow suspicious of dubious claims and more circumspect in dealing with him. When buyers purchase an item repetitively, so that each purchase informs the next, the seller's reputation for completing service becomes very important. And that is what Morgan accomplished. When he said, "I will safeguard it," buyers of securities bet their wealth that he would follow through. In some cases he salvaged securities to which his obligation had almost certainly expired, more than fulfilling the spirit of his implicit guarantee. Morgan might have elected to promote bonds with higher returns, pushing their yield as an attraction. But he understood that such securities usually carried a correspondingly higher chance of default, so the buyers would be much less likely to return.

J. P. Morgan's name is often associated with those who are wealthy and the special financial services they might require. But ironically his contributions tended to broaden financial services, making them accessible to those below the elite. Morgan, in effect, standardized securities, reducing the special requirements of information and monitoring that previously were necessary. He provided an early form of the Good Housekeeping Guarantee label, which indicates that products have been tested before their sale and that their performance will be backed up afterward.

Morgan is probably most widely known for the large mergers he arranged late in his career. In addition to reformulating railroads he assembled AT&T, General Electric, U.S. Steel, and International Harvester. But his contribution went well beyond merely swapping securities. For instance, a typical railroad had laid down considerable track earlier, when railroads were very profitable and most new ventures appeared promising. Railroads also were highly leveraged;

that is, they had borrowed much of their capital relative to that contributed by shareholders. As in other maturing industries, however, the competition intensified and the returns on each line, and the parts thereof, fell. The large fixed charges on debt became a threat to solvency each time the economy—and therefore the revenues of each line—slowed down. Under such conditions, leverage would have hurt rather than helped the company. Morgan typically shifted from a financial structure heavy on debt toward one relying more on equity. In other words, he cashed in many of the bonds, exchanging them for new issues of stock.

Morgan also modernized management structures. Some railroads had not absorbed all of the lessons that progressive lines like the Pennsylvania Railroad had discovered. It was often possible to reduce costs, speed up travel, and attract more traffic. He also rationalized the route structure. He might say: "This branch line is not paying its way. It should be dropped. But your main line should be improved by putting in new steel rails and double tracking this particular section." Thus he prodded the reorganized company to operate better, which was an important component of the package of services that came to be called Morganization.

Morgan, of course, tried to raise profits by controlling competition as much as possible. He used the term *orderly competition,* but essentially he sought cartels. Though these often didn't endure competition very long, their profits could justify the efforts. The process of reorganizing railroads typically merged individual lines to increase profits by both greater efficiency and control.

Morgan followed the same strategy in forming industrial companies, fashioning viable companies out of outdated structures. Thomas Edison's industrial ventures were merged into General Electric, becoming the world's largest electric power and equipment company. Edison, weak on administration, had not aligned his operations to market demands. Competitors were outdistancing him. George Westinghouse would have captured the bulk of the market within a few years if Edison's management had not been rectified. Morgan examined the situation, concluding that to supply electrical equipment properly a firm must provide the full array of services required by customers. This included not only electric power generating equipment but also the services necessary to support it. The firm should provide repairs, financing, and related services that developed in other vertically integrated firms. Morgan's success in reorganizing General Electric has been proved by time: it is still one of the most successful large companies in the United States today.

11

Merchandising to a Large, Affluent Society

When foreign visitors are given a tour of an American steel mill they might politely say, "That's interesting." But oftentimes this is out of deference to their hosts, since they can see similar operations at home. But the place where foreigners truly marvel at American civilization is upon entering a supermarket for the first time. Americans are so accustomed to such variety and convenience that they are surprised when others find it marvelous. Besides, historical accounts have focused so much on industrial revolutions or, more recently, information and service revolutions, that commercial activities are treated, by implication, as relatively unimportant. But the American flair for commerce is fundamental, extending well back into the nineteenth century. As the premier market economy, the United States became the world model of responsiveness to consumer demands.

While the American economy was expanding robustly in the nineteenth century, commerce was growing even faster. The growth of specialization increased the proportion of goods and services exchanged outside households. Rather than individuals consuming much of what they produced in their household, they bought and sold more. Thus the economy moved out of local self-sufficiency toward greater specialization and interdependence. And the exchange of goods and services between neighborhoods, particularly between regions, became an obvious growth sector.

This prompted a major reorganization in business. The port merchant, holding the central position in the Colonial trade network, had stocked a wide array of products. He also was forced to assume the functions of commodity dealer, banker, postmaster, landlord, and industrialist for the small markets. But as markets grew, specific functions were hived off to specialists.[1]

One of the first divisions to emerge was that between the merchant's functions as a retailer and as a commodity dealer. The latter collects the farm produce—an early example being the cotton factor. This type of broker appeared early in the 1800s; he purchased cotton, arranging to have it shipped or stored, insured, and, frequently, pledged as collateral for a loan to the farmer. He became an expert in organizing the delivery of cotton to the factories. A comparable specialization developed later in the north-central states, where brokers specialized in grain, particularly wheat. As exports increased, it became worthwhile for individuals to work full-time expediting the supply of wheat from the farms to distant markets. Brokers called *commission merchants,* working at the textile mills, began arranging the delivery and sale of their products. Commodity dealers appeared spontaneously in a locality as it developed a marked specialty in a product.

Brokerage operations are still the predominant means of selling securities or real estate, for instance. It is impractical for a merchant to purchase an inventory of homes to offer for sale. Each is unique because of its location and features. Most people seeking real estate employ a broker. A good agent keeps current on selling opportunities and understands the pricing of particular kinds of property as well as the best financing available. The broker's information makes buying more convenient and efficient. Sometimes buyers resent paying brokers' commissions but, of course, they have the option of providing those services themselves if they do not think the costs worthwhile.

Brokers typically appear in markets where current, specialized information is important in making a decision and there are economies in its repeated application. A cotton factor, for example, followed developments in cotton markets full-time. He had to know where cotton supplies were available, which types were in demand, their respective prices, and the best current means of shipping and storing them. Any cotton farmer could arrange each of these services independently if he wished, replicating the factor's services, but he usually found that employing the latter was more efficient. Many types of brokers appeared in the first part of the nineteenth century in the major markets for industrial products, consumer goods, and agricultural produce. While providing information and bringing buyers and sellers together they also demonstrated that the domestic market had grown large enough to employ markedly new institutions.

Innovation in Retail Specialization

The growth of the market in the nineteenth century almost completely eliminated general stores from larger cities. They divided into shops that took over particular components of the former range of offerings. Some outlets provided groceries while others handled what were called dry goods: cloth, accessories, and clothing. There were also hardware stores, pharmacies, and other specialists filling out the range of retail purchases. Such an array had developed in every large downtown area by the middle of the nineteenth century.

Before 1850 the distinction between retail and wholesale operations often was blurred. Then certain merchants began to make the break, selling only to retailers. But at the same time another major innovation in retailing appeared, running counter to the trend toward specialization. The department store began consolidating the specialties of retail stores or departments—as they were called—into one operation. Consumer convenience was the driving force. Retailers have always understood that good locations attract customers. Therefore they clustered their shops in downtown areas or at crossroads. The department store built upon that principle, becoming a forerunner of the modern shopping mall, which provides extensive choice under one roof. This convenience was so appealing that within a decade after the Civil War department stores appeared in all large- and medium-size American cities and, indeed, as scaled-down versions in smaller cities.

Department stores developed using either of two basic strategies. The first strategy was having the entire store, with all its departments, owned by one company. Such an enterprise expanded by adding further products. Stewart's Department Store in New York City, the largest in the nineteenth century and one of the most innovative, employed this approach. Using the second approach, many department stores collected individual businesses that leased space and managed their own product lines in a common building. Typically, entrepreneurs erected a large, multi-floor store, renting out space to merchants who offered the requisite variety of products much as in modern shopping malls. The fact that both approaches succeeded suggests that it was the convenience of a wide collection of products together in one location that was the prime attraction. Such imperatives continue to characterize American retailing. Sellers must provide consumers with services that enhance the intrinsic value of the merchandise. Merchants attract customers by displaying goods appealingly and making it convenient to purchase and use them. Department stores suggest that, at least up to a point, the value of such amenities offsets the benefits of specialization. Consumers are willing to trade in some of the reduced prices, which specialization provides, for other amenities.

Implementing a true department store involved more than clustering small retailers together, however, as the accomplishments of the two major entrepreneurs of the formative period indicate. Alexander T. Stewart came to New York City from Ireland in 1825.[2] He established a dry goods store and soon acquired a reputation as one of the most perceptive merchants in New York City. Stewart's first major contribution smacks more of a modern discount operation than a department store, however. He recognized that the growing city meant that more goods would be sold, so the store that expanded could reduce its inventory costs through a more rapid turnover of goods. Stewart aggressively pursued this tactic, lowering prices to sell more cloth, which in turn lowered costs and reinforced the tactics. By the 1870s the store was the largest by far in New York City, with annual sales in excess of $60 million.

Stewart integrated back to the suppliers, establishing buying offices in Europe as well as purchasing textile and accessory factories in the Northeast. An astounding measure of the depth of his involvement was that his single store accounted for 10 percent of all imports into New York City, which meant at least 5 percent of the value of all imports into the economy. (By way of comparison, McDonald's, which has more than ten thousand outlets, uses less than 5 percent of America's output of potatoes.)

While Stewart was developing the high-volume, low-price approach he was also developing special services aimed at the upper-income bracket, or "carriage trade." Stewart was among the first to offer money-back guarantees. Until the 1840s and 1850s goods were sold "as is" with no further implied promises. The watchword was "Let the buyer beware," because once out of the store the good was his, no matter what. Of course, such practices would not have survived without being based on important considerations. Before 1860 it was difficult for stores to ensure the quality of many of their goods. Such commodities as flour, coffee, and cheese came in bulk from different sources and vintages. Each purchase had to be inspected to ascertain its quality. It was necessary for the buyer to judge a good's value and thus negotiate an appropriate price.

Department stores began the shift toward fixed prices. In effect they claimed, "Here's what we believe is a fair price and if it turns out that the good is defective, we promise to refund your money." The change particularly appealed to wealthier buyers, who most resented time spent haggling over prices or worrying that their purchases would be satisfactory. They preferred an organization that guaranteed its goods, even at the cost of higher prices.

Department stores sold enough to become a major player in the markets for their goods. Stewart, for example, actively elicited his customers' preferences and instituted the desired features into his offerings. In effect, he introduced store or "private" brands of goods. This intensified competition in retailing, providing a fuller portrayal of consumer preferences. Thus department stores took on functions of vertically integrated firms by reaching back to suppliers. In so doing, they pioneered a practice that has since become commonplace in which American retailers shape products rather than passively pass on the creations of manufacturers.

While A. T. Stewart developed the most publicized model of the department store, he didn't provide all its features. Credit for that goes to John Wanamaker in Philadelphia.[3] He had been a partner in a men's clothing store in the 1860s, helping develop it into the largest of its type in the nation. But his ambition outran that store, so he added a high-fashion branch in 1869. The experience he gained with different types of goods helped him envision an outlet carrying the comprehensive array of products that we now associate with a department store. In 1876 he opened the Grand Depot, named after the old freight depot of the Pennsylvania Railroad, which he rehabilitated for that purpose. (This demonstrates that the modern concern for historical recycling has had long-standing antecedents.)

Wanamaker expected that merchants would want to establish specialty shops in his building, but when they demurred he proceeded on his own, filling out product lines. It was a huge risk because had the operation not succeeded he certainly would have been bankrupt. (His gutsy, make-or-break move evokes young John D. Rockefeller, who recognized that competitiveness dictates size, which, in turn, dictates a large, specialized undertaking.) But the abundance of goods he offered attracted so many customers that within a few years the store became a model for stores throughout the country. Wanamaker also pioneered in the fixed-price policy across much of his product lines and was also one of the first to use extensive advertising in newspapers.

CHOICES TO THE REMOTE

About the same time another major form of retailing, tailored for just the opposite circumstances of the department store, was

—— 169 ——

developing in the Midwest. Mail-order stores also followed several embryonic paths before coalescing into their successful pattern. The most important entrepreneur in the formative stage was Aaron Montgomery Ward.[4] He managed a general store in Michigan before moving to Chicago to work for Marshall Field, the most advanced department store in the Midwest. Not yet satisfied, he became a traveling salesman of dry goods operating out of St. Louis. There his experience in merchandising helped him envision bypassing the limitations he encountered in the existing structure of rural distribution.

In 1872 Ward opened his mail-order operation, selling goods from the loft of a livery stable in Chicago. His medium was a single-page flyer. Right from the beginning he emphasized his promise to refund any unsatisfactory purchases. This was crucial, because it assured customers who were ordering the goods unseen at a time when accepting unproved goods invited disappointments. Moreover, some items were difficult to portray completely in the catalogue. Clothes and shoes came in standard sizes but, not infrequently, either the product or the person proved not quite standard. Successful mail-order stores had to promise to resolve such complications quickly. When Sears Roebuck began in 1886, it adopted the slogan "satisfaction guaranteed or your money back" to assure customers that it would make adjustments until the buyer was satisfied.

In his second year Ward received a big boost when the Grange, the farmers' association, began using his services in their cooperative-purchasing program. They were convinced that the country stores were exploiting them, so they attempted to create an alternative supply. The idea proved unfeasible—the rural shopkeepers didn't have much monopoly after all—but the outlet added important, marginal sales for Ward. The increase in the turnover in Ward's warehouse reduced inventories relative to sales and reduced costs by earning discounts on quantity purchases. Customers also benefited because the centralized inventory provided more selection than country stores. The typical rural shopkeeper could not afford to finance anything like the choices provided in the catalogue. By 1876 Ward had added so many lines of merchandise that his catalogue reached 150 pages.

Like the department stores, mail-order firms used the clout of their quantity purchasing to shape products. They began developing their own lines, such as in appliances, tools, and—later—automobile parts. Their purchasing agents actively refined product offerings by specializing in particular products, devoting full time to developing them. The companies even developed their own testing facilities and research labs.

Mail-order houses added installment credit so households could acquire expensive items. Sears pioneered providing foreign-language translators. The company's growth coincided with the largest immigration to the United States, so there were many potential customers with limited English. Sears told its customers, "Send your order in any language, we'll fill it." They employed clerks fluent in at least twenty-five different languages.

JOINING SERVICE AND LARGE-SCALE EFFICIENCY

The general store was a long-standing, American institution carrying a wide sampling of goods intended to meet the basic requirements and occasional luxuries of an isolated community. But this necessitated severe drawbacks in customer choice, cost, and quality. Its low turnover made the markup of prices over cost high. As long as distance sheltered the general store from competitors, local necessity perpetuated it. Mail-order companies eroded that shelter by introducing delivery from a distance.

The third major development in late-nineteenth-century retailing was the chain store. It also sought many of the customers that the general store had served. While some outlets were in large cities, the prime targets were smaller towns. Chain stores added to the attack on the general store by standardizing retail services such that they could be provided farther from the supportive environment of larger downtown markets. Each chain organized its outlets around a centralized supply, providing a standardized array of products. Each also developed uniform store designs and trained managers according to a standardized curriculum. Thus they attempted to routinize many of the one-per-store activities that otherwise would have had to be undertaken from scratch each time, such as arranging for the site and building, store furniture, suppliers, and creating and learning store procedures. Because of its experience, an organization that does this repetitively can economize by this learning among stores—an advantage denied to just one store—and thus reduce cost and improve quality.

Chain stores developed in all major product lines. A & P expanded from its initial base in tea retailing by adding related lines, much as department stores found it worthwhile to provide consumers with wider choices. There were also variety stores, often called five & dime stores, carrying numerous small items, as well as drug and hardware chains. Many major product lines were represented by several chain stores. The degree of its product specialization determined how small a market each chain could enter. In groceries, for example, A & P could move into relatively small communities and neighborhoods, not quite as small as country crossroads, but much smaller than the central districts of larger cities. Variety stores such as Woolworth's typically stayed in larger markets.

Each of the three major retail types—the department store, the mail-order house, and the chain store—are variations on a fundamental theme. They take advantage of the gains from size while remaining responsive to consumer demands. This strategy reflected such fundamental forces that it continued into the twentieth century, reappearing in franchise operations. Much like the chain stores, they bring uniform services to each outlet. McDonald's, the best-known franchise, provides help in site selection, design, fixtures, training, supplies, trouble shooting, and advertising the product locally, regionally, and nationally.[5] An entrepreneur starting a franchise is really starting an independent business in the sense that he must raise the capital and operate it successfully. The difference is that he operates it in conjunction with a large, experienced "partner" who has developed a comprehensive package of supporting services. McDonald's owns some outlets, but the majority are the property of individual investors. McDonald's insists the latter remain active in their franchises to inject energy and care into the operation.

McDonald's exemplifies the franchise's strength in product development. They can spend millions of dollars developing and testing a new product before committing it nationally. Chicken McNuggets and Egg McMuffins were studied extensively for production feasibility at the Chicago headquarters and then tested extensively in selected local markets for consumer response. A single outlet could not afford anywhere near that large an investment to groom a new product. Not every franchise succeeds—all uncertainties cannot be engineered out—but it will probably encounter far fewer surprises than a firm starting out by itself. What franchises do for product development, they reinforce through advertising. It's hard to forget a "Big Mac Attack" or Wendy's "Where's the Beef?"

Franchises, of course, charge a fee for their services, typically a percentage of sales, say 5 percent. Their rapid growth since World War II suggests that the payment is generally seen to be worthwhile. While McDonald's is the largest and best known, franchises are now ubiquitous, having appeared in automobile repair, lawn care, cleaning services, as well as most types of food. Basic business forums such as *The Wall Street Journal* regularly advertise a large cross section of franchise opportunities. This reduces the risk for someone desiring to own his own business who can raise some capital and is willing to work hard. It is, in effect, organized entrepreneurship. It provides critical assistance to those who couldn't construct such businesses by themselves. It expands the pool of potential entrepreneurs. There are numerous individuals who would like to own a business, are willing to work hard, and have the capital but could not afford to develop the required skills on their own. Franchises ease them into the market.

Franchises imply that business structures can be created enabling individuals to accomplish more than they could do on their own. Thus it is a counterpart to the effect of the corporate structure. When a business moves beyond the formative phase to the mature phase it typically becomes a public company, thereby greatly widening the range of potential investors. Before their stock is issued publicly, owners have to remain closely involved in management. Shifting to the corporate form taps wider sources of capital. A franchise works analogously but on another aspect of business. Corporations allow individuals to participate in ownership without managing, as well as vice versa. Franchises allow individuals to manage and own an operation without working for a large company or developing all its necessary supporting structure for themselves.

New structures provide people with new opportunities, new ways of getting things done. The American commercial sector has been outstanding because sellers are put to the test every day. Any day the customers don't come in means serious trouble. Each commercial institution has to be very responsive to customers' desires. The basic strategy must be to devise new arrangements that provide better, cheaper services. Each time something better—such as a department store, mail-order operation, chain store, or franchise—provides consumers with a better opportunity, they return to buy again. And they'll keep coming as long as the service is best.

Ponder the fate of the proprietor of the general store. In 1840 the local market was shielded from direct competition, so when someone asked for a pound of coffee he could say, "The coffee is a dollar fifty a pound. I've had the stuff for some time, ought to be well seasoned by now." And the consumer did not have much choice. But when alternatives developed, such as chain stores and mail-order stores, the consumer gained substantive choices, ensuring he would receive much more value.

12

Constructing Institutions
for Modern Science

Thomas Edison is a household name in the United States, right along with George Washington and Abraham Lincoln.[1] It does not take much reading about his creative life to understand why he earned the epithet "The most useful American." It is obvious that Edison passionately enjoyed invention from the time he was quite young. His zest for his work propelled him, shouldering aside all obstacles that daunt most people. He became immersed in any mechanical device, seeking to know how it worked and might be improved. Edison also had enormous energy. The confluence of the two qualities was exceptionally productive, driving his curiosity through one discovery and on to the next.

Early on Edison knew that he wanted to devote his life to invention. In one sense the choice was inevitable because he would have been invariably neglecting any other responsibilities in his pre-occupation with research. But in the mid-nineteenth century it still was a drastic move. Conditions contrasted sharply with the present, where sizable numbers of scientists and engineers are employed full-time at such pursuits. There were very few positions, or the institutions to support such interests, in the mid-nineteenth century. There were scarcely any research institutions or research facilities in businesses. College teachers, for example, spent more time in classes with correspondingly less energy for research. Thus it is likely that someone determined to make his living by inventing would have been thrown back on the problematic rewards of his own discoveries.

While most were intimidated into pursuing more conventional careers, Edison steadfastly plowed ahead. He worked at a series of jobs, just enough to support his interest. Like Carnegie, he became a very good telegraph operator, although he was fired several times for neglecting his responsibilities while he was conducting experiments. By the time he was twenty he was producing enough useful innovations to support himself. (He did not require all that much. Edison was content with a cot in a corner of a lab and basic food.) Among other innovations, he improved the telegraph system. His familiarity with the equipment's use helped him visualize means to send messages faster over existing lines.

By the time Edison became self-supporting, his reputation for being able to solve problems had become widespread. His emphasis on results had been instilled by one traumatic disappointment. Edison had become intrigued with building a machine that would record votes in legislatures by means of a crude punch card system. When it was completed he assumed legislators would quickly adopt it to speed up their proceedings and provide an official record of decisions. The machine functioned well mechanically, but the politicians would have no part of it. Edison overlooked the fact that politicians frequently didn't want their votes recorded because politics involves convincing as many people as possible that you're helping them while hiding the costs.

The obvious implication was that inventions must meet a genuine demand in order to be worthwhile. A professional inventor, dependent on earnings, must contribute toward ends that users value enough to purchase. Inventions created primarily to satisfy the inventor's curiosity are properly understood as recreation. Edison never forgot that lesson. Thereafter, he never undertook a major project without satisfying himself that a commensurate payoff existed. And he went on to prove that he could keep his innovative curiosity fully engaged while pursuing applications with commercial returns.

Edison's revelation illustrates a crucial lesson: entrepreneurs cannot be controlled by visionary worlds. They must create innovations that are so desired as to be remunerative. Even when candidates pass that test, most attempts to innovate do not yield market successes, so entrepreneurs must constantly refocus their efforts toward what they discover consumers want.

By the time Edison reached his midtwenties his skill as an inventor was widely recognized. The next twenty years were his most productive period. He pioneered motion pictures, a duplicating machine, transcribing equipment, the phonograph, and, of course, the light bulb. He was so well regarded in the 1870s that the day it was announced that he had begun sustained work on electric lighting, stocks of gas lighting companies lost one-quarter of their value.

Clearly Edison was bright and creative, but he also worked very hard. An old saw says that successful entrepreneurs work half time: twelve hours a day. By that standard Edison worked at least two-thirds time, and oftentimes three-quarters time, sixteen or eighteen hours a day, and seven days a week as well. This persistence multiplied his talent into prodigious dimensions. For instance, Edison's most famous success, the electric light, did not require exceptional technical skill in that the requirements necessary to make it work were commonly understood. Experiments with prototypes had established that sending electricity through a wire or filament produced good light. The major drawback was that the wire would quickly burn in the oxygen in the air. A solution, then, was to evacuate the air from a glass bulb enclosing the filament. The invention of an improved vacuum pump in the early 1870s was widely recognized as the enabling step. Edison, among others, immediately set to work, focusing on finding a suitable material for the filament. Edison and his assistants in his lab in New Jersey worked through more than ten thousand different materials, one right after another, until they found one with the requisite qualities. They simply out-tested everyone else. Such persistence characterized Edison's work. He claimed that the formula for success was 1 percent inspiration and 99 percent perspiration. Of course, successful people must have sufficient talent to create new approaches but, almost invariably, they enjoy their work sufficiently to put in the long hours crucial to success. The driving passion that Edison exemplified succeeds in almost any profession.

Failure and the Single Inventor

The invention of the light bulb marked the end of Edison's most productive period. Another force increasingly diminished his achievements, as it would have hampered any independent inventor or small research lab using his strategy.[2] Edison was able to continue supporting his operations, but his laboratory reaped only a tiny fraction of the ultimate value of its inventions. Most benefits went to others who pushed the discoveries along toward useful products. Edison's greatest effort, the electric light, illustrates this lopsided division of rewards.

Electric lights were not practical without the development of electric power systems. Edison understood that requirement; even while his lab was feverishly pursuing a working light bulb, he was designing a basic system to generate power and carry the current to dispersed users. First at his lab in New Jersey, and then in downtown New York City, he built power stations with a grid of electric wires, switches, and rudimentary transformers. But he soon encountered roadblocks as he moved beyond invention into the challenges of management—which was clearly not his forte. He was excellent at fashioning products in the formative stage, but failed in the implementation of large, complicated delivery systems. A powerful example occurred in the choice of a mode of transmitting electric power, which pitted Edison against George Westinghouse. Edison designed his systems to use direct current, whose power quickly dissipated with distance in transmission. It was impractical to send electricity much beyond a mile. Thus Edison's technique restricted power systems to areas where users were concentrated, which—in practice—meant business areas of large cities. Even then, however, distribution costs were high.

At this time the electric transformer, which could raise or lower voltage, was invented. At higher voltages much less power is lost in transmission—which has been the standard practice ever since. But transformers require alternating current to function. George Westinghouse, who was also developing electrical systems, quickly grasped this opportunity, shifting to alternating current to adopt transformers. Edison simply could not believe the arrangement could work. How can current go back and forth, he asked, and yet go anywhere or accomplish anything? He became so fixated on direct current as to ridicule Westinghouse and spread malicious stories about insidious effects of alternating current. He could not bring himself to accept the contributions of a competitor, and was thus an early victim of the "not-invented-here syndrome." But no single inventor, no matter how brilliant, can provide all the varied contributions necessary to complete a system as large and complex as electric power distribution. This necessitates a range and depth of expertise that only the sustained efforts of numerous professionals can supply.

Edison also backed into other managerial cul-de-sacs until his efforts to develop power distribution systems and manufacture electrical equipment had to be salvaged by others. Edison, the formative-type entrepreneur, had to give way to managers with broader perspectives who could cope with commercial and organizational forces. He had become so enamored of particular aspects of the technology that he failed to develop the comprehensive perspective necessary to service large markets. J. P. Morgan was called in to save Edison's handiwork by drastically reorganizing it into the broader organization, General Electric.

Edison's experience illustrates the problems that an independent, for-profit research lab is likely to encounter pursuing basic technologies. By its nature, research is very unpredictable. Solutions intended to solve the initial problem more often than not prove applicable to entirely different activities and often should be employed by other types of organizations. Research labs can market some of their discoveries but typically only reap a small part of their potential because other types of organizations must assume considerably more work and risk before useful products result. Thus, to make his inventions pay off commercially Edison would have to have drawn together expertise from much of the span of commercial knowledge. This is an important reason why much research is now organized through nonprofit organizations and independent research labs, which tend to focus on particular specialties and work on contracts from others. This environment intensified after 1870, making it progressively more difficult for Edison to produce basic, yet profitable, research. He succeeded for much of his lifetime because his exceptional productivity meant that only a tiny fraction of his results was sufficient to support his efforts.

A second force working against Edison was that he operated as a generalist while science was becoming more specialized. In some cases he read extensively in current scientific literature and—remarkably—kept pace with the professionals in the field. But even for Edison, it was impossible to keep current with a broad array of technological advances in the late 1800s as they fragmented into distinct, professional specialties. Utility fielders, such as Edison, are excluded by the long training period required to join particular disciplines. Indeed, even coordinating the work of diverse specialists has become a major challenge in managing research. Edison's strategy of finding applications was a serious handicap for managing research professionals. Production line workers can be ordered to do specific tasks, but scientists—as well as doctors, lawyers, and professors—determine the product by their work and thus must be allowed latitude to depart from preconceived goals.

The basic problem bedeviling Edison was that science was converting innovation into a two-stage process. Commercial payoffs became unforeseeable until research was well under way. While discoveries might be very important, they are also nearly impossible to convert to specific applications in the early stages. Similar considerations operated in reverse if one started from the specific problem and attempted to develop the relevant scientific principles. The linkages had become so diffuse and unpredictable that Edison's "invention factory" could no longer manage much of it. Others, however, were working to develop a mechanism for the new environment.

Du Pont: Systematizing Innovation

Large companies whose product technology was being reshaped by emerging sciences also had to grapple with Edison's dilemma. General Electric and Union Carbide were in the vanguard, but possibly the most illustrative example was the Du Pont company.[3] Each discovered that there were particular bodies of science that could contribute—indeed were essential—to their commercial products. General Electric, which defined its mission to be all applications of electricity, developed a complete line of components ranging all the way from light bulbs and electric appliances through electrical switches and motors to transformers, turbines, and power plants. Such a concept of a market drew upon a broad range of technologies and specialists. An analogous situation developed in chemical companies that converted basic materials, such as petroleum, sulfur, and chlorine, into a wide array of products. Such companies learned that science and its practitioners were indispensable to their operations; indeed, they learned it was necessary to shape their basic market strategy around them.

The du Ponts fled the French Revolution, arriving in America just after independence.[4] Their traditional craft of making black powder, the basic material of gunpowder and blasting powder, proved quite welcome. At the same time, the technology of their craft imposed a social isolation that characterized the company and family throughout the nineteenth century. Even with the most exacting care, production was dangerous, marked by recurrent explosions and casualties. The du Ponts located their powder mill on the Brandywine Creek, *safely* outside of Wilmington, Delaware. To assuage workers, du Pont promised family security, providing a pension to dependents. In other words, nineteenth-century Du Pont offered privately many of the services that are common benefits provided in the twentieth century.

The technology of powder manufacture also shaped the organi-

—— 181 ——

zation of the company. Production skills were acquired through practice. No school offered courses in black powder manufacture; an apprentice learned the trade working beside experienced journeymen. Du Pont perpetually had to restore their supply of technicians, giving them sufficient time and opportunities to develop their skills. This reinforced the company's inclination toward paternalism in the nineteenth century. This insular environment also shaped Du Pont management. The family kept expanding during the nineteenth century, producing an ample supply of prospective officers. A candidate had to bide his time in a not-too-demanding position in the company waiting for openings in top management.

As the nineteenth century drew to a close, several changes destroyed the basis for this self-contained world. Dynamite, an improved explosive that was much less susceptible to accidental discharge, was developed. The introduction of smokeless powder also cut into the market for black powder. Du Pont had lost its secure market to competitors with novel, seemingly unmatchable techniques. At this time, Pierre du Pont joined the company.[5] Unlike most of the family, he was appropriately prepared for the emerging environment. He earned an engineering degree from MIT in 1890, even then one of the premier colleges for engineering and science in the United States. MIT was also among the first to realize that engineers often use their technical skills only a decade or so before moving into administration. The college provided business studies so that its technical graduates had more skills organizing and managing a business. In addition, Pierre's father was killed when he was fourteen—another explosives mishap—so at a very young age he assumed the stewardship of substantial family assets. Some of the holdings proved to demand considerable restructuring. Thus by the time he joined Du Pont, Pierre had considerable financial and managerial experience as well as technical skills.

On joining the company, Pierre was horrified to find a complete lack of modern business methods. Production techniques were craft operations, little updated in a hundred years. After coming from MIT, where modern management and science were second nature, walking into a Du Pont plant was almost like stepping back in time a hundred years. Pierre's accounts leave no doubt that he had enormous reservations about the manner in which the company was being operated. Only by turning out a specialized product, which had been cushioned from close competition, had the company survived. But that margin was quickly eroding as better substitutes appeared. It was clear that the Du Pont company would have to improve drastically in order to continue.

Pierre du Pont soon found that two of his cousins with college training had assessed the situation similarly. The three confronted the management committee, arguing that quick remedial action was necessary to save the company from bankruptcy. At first the older governing du Ponts suggested that the company be sold to a rival dynamite company, with the proceeds divided among the family owners. But the young turks wanted the family tradition of operation perpetuated. They insisted that they, as family members, be given the first opportunity to turn things around. They fashioned what is now called a *leveraged buyout,* where a group of managers assumes ownership, financing their purchase mostly by borrowing.

Of the three who took over the company, Pierre du Pont quickly assumed leadership. He pushed the company toward a modern managerial structure, inspired by the practices developing in similar industries. The company was grouped into three divisions around major product lines, each with separate managerial hierarchies organized according to functional specialties. This meant plant managers and engineers supervising production, financial specialists setting up cost accounting, and—in a very novel gesture for the company—marketing people working with customers. In another move that was significantly symbolic, scientists were hired for long-term, systematic research.

Embedding a financial structure in the restructured organization was a drastic step for Du Pont, which until then had treated accounting as little more than double-entry bookkeeping. Receipts and expenditures had been recorded, and the difference at the end of the year was the profit, if positive. Du Pont began instituting closer controls on costs and analyzing them carefully in order to increase margins. Practitioners began discovering how much it would cost to produce particular products and, therefore, which were actually profitable. This often produced surprises, because while some operations proved lucrative, others had apparently been losing for decades without anyone recognizing the burden they imposed on operations.

Du Pont also began creating a scientific infrastructure. Quality control of production had been almost entirely informal. Black powder workers developed their judgment through work, using little scientific equipment. Pierre du Pont had seen the value of modern facilities at Carnegie Steel and General Electric. He also recognized that, fundamentally, Du Pont's business was in chemicals—transforming materials into new, more useful forms. Du Pont erected research labs for each major product area and began to coordinate each project with the respective production and marketing staff. Thus when the latter returned with reports that the customers wanted a particular quality in the product, the technical staff could develop such features in the materials. Or the research people might ask the production people which production bottlenecks they would most like to eliminate. Such interaction began to speed the flow of products to market.

Pierre du Pont also recognized that one of the key problems in the new company was allocating its scarce capital. Until the 1890s Du Pont was a very small company whose yearly sales did not equal the *profits* of the largest companies. But the drastic restructuring of the company—adding new products and updating existing ones—created enormous demands for capital. There was no way that the company could satisfy everyone, so the problem became to choose the best uses from among conflicting requests. College economics and finance courses now regularly teach the answer. Capital should be allocated to those uses that have the highest rate of return of anticipated future revenues less costs, all discounted back to the present. But the formal techniques had not yet been developed in Pierre's time. Entrepreneurs such as Carnegie, who used the best available cost accounting, employed the concept of a payback period to calculate the number of years it would take to recoup the initial investment. The shorter the payback, the more attractive the investment. But this result is not as accurate as calculating the rate of return. The fastest payback may not be the best investment because it ignores returns after the initial investment is recouped.

Pierre du Pont was the first manager in a major American

business to make rate of return calculations an integral part of the central decisions of his firm. A division requesting capital funds was required to submit estimates of the distribution of sales and costs in the future and calculate the return on the project. This emphasis led to further discoveries, particularly that many early forecasts of demand and production costs proved well off the mark. Though predictions never reached perfection, they improved substantially with practice. By approaching the process systematically, Du Pont began to alert its managers to factors that were likely to affect projections. This focused planning on important, controllable factors. It also had unanticipated benefits. Soon most Du Pont managers began focusing on increasing their return on capital. In recent years company cultures have been highlighted because of transmission of qualities that are believed crucial to a firm's success. In Du Pont that culture emphasized facility in calculating the rate of return and developing proposals that maximized it.

Profits at Du Pont climbed rapidly. Better utilization of capital was important, but Du Pont also discovered lucrative new markets as chemicals became a growth sector. The success built on the new scientific technology, combined with a company structure that made the most of it by pinpointing the best opportunities, yielded impressive returns.

Du Pont was in the forefront of large firms implementing scientific and financial techniques between 1900 and 1914. This proved to be ideal timing because the organization was soon put to an extraordinary test during World War I, which dramatically increased the demand for powder and explosives. The European conflict began in 1914, so that even though the United States did not become a belligerent until 1917, Du Pont sold enormous quantities of powder to England and France. The years from 1914 through 1918 were, not surprisingly, very profitable. Hard-pressed countries agreed to pay top prices for Du Pont's output. But the flip side was that World War I put the Du Pont organization to a severe test. It became obvious that had the company not completed its drastic reorganization, breaking from its nineteenth-century style, it would not have been able to respond anywhere nearly as well. Lacking flexibility, it would have produced much less. The American government might have felt compelled to take over its operations, as they did with the railroads. World War I proved that Pierre and his group, in the comparative isolation of Delaware, had worked out a very robust model of management. It quickly expanded output, responding deftly to major changes as well as performing very efficiently.

The du Pont family emerged from World War I several hundred million dollars richer, enough to buy a commanding share of General Motors. That company was still quite small, disorganized, and—in retrospect—a risky investment at that time. The du Ponts discovered that, in the process of buying into the company, they were entangled in managerial problems no less complicated than the original problem they had faced earlier in their own company. Pierre du Pont was compelled to take an active hand in the management of General Motors for several years, reorganizing and turning it over to competent management. And so he converted two major companies into historical models, a record few other American entrepreneurs can match.

13

Creating
Twentieth-Century Mobility

The transportation technology of the late nineteenth century made some forms of travel much more desirable than others. For longer trips trains were an attractive, even obvious choice. They ran frequently and were generally pleasant, dependable, and comfortable. Some were quite posh. But railroads were often awkward for local trips. The economics of their operation dictated large numbers of passengers in order to sustain a given route. Meanwhile Americans were becoming less tolerant of the personal inconveniences necessary for gathering such concentrations: walking to the local station, waiting for the train, making connections, and living in the congested corridors astride commuter routes. Commuters on steam railroads were looking for something better.

Between 1880 and 1900 numerous experimenters sought such a convenient means of transporting people. Electric trains, streetcars, subways, and elevated systems, among others, were tried. Another major effort, which suggested much that consumers sought, was the safety bicycle. It was actually the design we now assume is standard, with two wheels of equal size. The name distinguished it from the preceding model, which had a large front wheel; though picturesque, it had been dangerous because it flipped unwary riders over the handlebars. This caused "headers," named after the part of the human anatomy that was bashed. It is not surprising, then, that when safety bicycles were introduced in the 1890s a large, newly enfranchised portion of the population bought one. Bicycles gave individuals versatility and freedom. Released from the train's timetable they could leave when it suited them, cycling directly to many of their common destinations. Bicycles became omnipresent in large cities during the work week and a common sight in the countryside on pleasant weekends. And it sure beat the next best alternative—walking.

While rising incomes were providing many Americans with the resources to purchase more convenient transportation, technology proved to be slow delivering the opportunities. It was widely recognized that consumers would gladly purchase services such as those that the automobile eventually provided. Inventors, both in the United States and Europe, were experimenting with numerous prototypes in the 1890s. Different sources of motive power were tried, including the steam engine—which had the advantage of a century and a half of experience. The ultimate winner began as a long shot. Gasoline was not the cheapest fuel, but its output of power relative to its weight was the critical advantage. (There is actually more explosive power in one gallon of gasoline than in a half-dozen sticks of dynamite.)

The gasoline engine opened the way for inventors to develop other amenities in the vehicles. The demands of buyers strongly influenced manufacturers from early on. Early body configurations, for example, frequently borrowed bicycle parts, as the famous picture of Henry Ford sitting in his first model illustrates. Such components work for bicycles, and even light automobiles at slow speeds, but stronger, specially made parts were necessary to satisfy consumers' preferences for heavier and faster cars.

During the early stage of an industry, the technology is still developing and the system for delivering the product incomplete. This makes the product expensive and, therefore, restricts its use to wealthy consumers. During the 1950s, for example, the only firms that found computers worthwhile were making inordinately complex calculations. Likewise in the early twentieth century, automobile manufacturers sought luxury niches, building small batches of distinctive cars. Racing proved to be one of the most attractive markets because cars promised to go much faster than anything previously. Horseracing was a major attraction in the nineteenth century, but horses cannot exceed 45 miles per hour and tire within a mile. Race cars, however, soon exceeded 80 miles per hour for hours at a stretch. Automobile producers discovered that such competition could win enormous publicity. Victories were a powerful recommendation, in the same manner that trophies on the European Grand Prix circuit recommend a Ferrari or Porsche today.

While most producers focused on expensive, limited-production autos, some visualized a low-cost-through-volume strategy. Henry Ford was not the only manufacturer to depart from the conventional wisdom. Ransom Olds and the Dodge brothers also sought to spark a mass market. But Ford proved to have the most creative persistence, forcing the abstract concept into working reality.[1] He expected that reorganizing production methods could substantially reduce the cost of producing automobiles, thereby pulling in entirely new levels of buyers. While others sought the carriage trade, Ford saw the middle class, and even poorer folks, affording automobiles. Of course that meant dropping some luxury features that the existing market took for granted; but a car that was reliable, easy to drive and service, as well as less costly, should create its own market. That was Ford's vision and—the crucial step—what he hammered into reality. It was undoubtedly one of the most influential visions of the twentieth century. After pervasive effects on the United States, it is proceeding to restructure much of the rest of the world.

Henry Ford was the central entrepreneur during the early years of the auto industry. But more than that he is probably the best known of all entrepreneurs in American history—for good reason.

The product that he created is one of the most valuable, with a corresponding impact on the economy. The products developed by entrepreneurs like McCormick, Rockefeller, and Carnegie, notwithstanding their fame, were much less valuable per capita. Modern consumers spend almost as much on automobiles as they do on housing or food. Understandably, Ford was among the wealthiest of American entrepreneurs. It's hard to appraise his wealth because most was held in a private company, beyond the appraisal of the market. But by the early 1920s he was conservatively worth a billion dollars, which means at least five billion dollars in today's prices, ranking with the largest contemporary fortunes.

By themselves, wealth and influence would have drawn enormous interest to Ford, but an additional element helps to explain, for example, why literally shelves full of books have been written about him. Ford worked hard to maintain the image of an ordinary American. He sought to be regarded as the unspoiled, common man and a principled holdout against the enticements of the establishment. Most individuals mellow as they accumulate assets and social standing and develop associations with others in similar circumstances, but not Ford. As a result several generations of Americans, particularly the blue collar and poor, honored him for remaining true to his roots. They believed that Ford worked for their interests, steadfastly resisting being co-opted by the establishment. The truth behind the image is less certain, but the perception has endured, reinforcing Ford's legend. Thus it is not surprising that he is probably the most publicized, albeit not uncontroversial, of American entrepreneurs.

Like Eli Whitney and Robert Fulton, Ford was a natural mechanic, likely to shine in environments rewarding mechanical innovation. He never overcame his temptation to tinker with machinery, even after he headed a huge company. In the early 1900s Ford was widely considered a crackpot. He went bankrupt twice, taking down partners who had supplied much of the enterprises' capital. But he persisted in believing that a cheap automobile was feasible. Any prudent banker would have told him, "Henry, you tried it twice. We can't risk our depositors' money." But Ford persevered long enough to turn his dream into the tangible form of a profitable, complicated production organization. In particular, he developed an assembly line that produced automobiles in a repetitive, cheap fashion. This required extended experimentation and frustration. There were probably ten failures for each success. Thus Ford had to tolerate frustrations, not the least of which was people recalling his early failures.

Ford faced a challenge similar to that of Eli Whitney. Whitney understood the concept of interchangeable parts but never achieved the technology necessary to implement it. Ultimately such technology was completed after his death in several decades of further work. Ford began with an appropriate concept, but then succeeded in working out much of the required technology in fifteen years. Ford is widely credited with developing the assembly line, but that element of his system had already been employed, most notably in meat packing. His specific contribution was constructing a system that applied interchangeable parts far beyond the complexity undertaken by any organization before. The automobile was—and still is—the most complicated, mass-produced consumer product. Ford's organization worked out a technology employing standardized parts to create cars that were not only easy to assemble but also to operate and maintain thereafter as well.

The system required fifteen years to implement because an automobile uses several thousand parts. Modifying only one in the search for improvements typically required adjusting several others. Ford went through an extended learning process from 1908 to the early 1920s, implementing hundreds of refinements each year without stopping the production line. The annual model changes, which General Motors began in the 1920s, drew the public's attention, but Ford, in effect, practiced daily changes while continuing regular operations. The paradox was that he continually changed the production organization even while doggedly sticking to a standardized product.

Ford's complicated assembly process achieved a steady, synchronized flow of standardized parts, drastically reducing the labor necessary for assembly. Most of the cost of automobiles before 1910 was in the labor of assembling them and manufacturing their parts. Ford accomplished in the automobile industry what mechanization had achieved in the textile industry a century earlier. In the mid-1700s labor composed 90 percent of the final cost of cotton cloth.

Each thread was spun by hand and then woven, again by hand, into cloth. Much of the dramatic cheapening of cotton cloth between the late 1700s and the mid-1800s derived from perfecting machines that mechanized those steps. Machine spinning, for example, could spin sixty threads simultaneously, multiplying the output of an operator correspondingly. When the transformation was completed labor costs had been reduced from about 90 percent of the finished cost to less than 10 percent. The market price was reduced accordingly, making the product far more accessible to consumers.

Ford performed the same transformation for the automobile, except that the technology implemented was much more complicated. In textiles, spinning, weaving, and auxiliary processes were mechanized. For automobiles about 5,000 parts had to be designed, coordinated, and assembled in complicated sequences. This was achieved before computers or much in the way of industrial engineering techniques were available to rationalize such an enormous undertaking.

Ford did not pull it off all by himself. Like other successful leaders, he supplied a commanding vision. Quite possibly his major contribution was articulating his idea to his associates as they toiled to implement it. Not only was Ford a master mechanic, but he also played the role of an evangelist, urging his employees to pursue the goal of reducing costs and building a utilitarian automobile. His efforts attracted some of the more inventive talents in the United States, such as Charles Sorensen, Edward Martin, and William Knudsen, who went on to demonstrate their skills independent of Ford. Sorensen was one of the few who put up with Henry's quirks all the way to World War II, becoming the de facto CEO. Knudsen moved to General Motors, where he continued playing an important role in developing the industry.

Aspiring professionals naturally gravitated toward the Ford Motor Company. They wanted to become a part of that very challenging organization and have an opportunity to make a major impact on society. Working at Ford between 1905 and 1920 was much like working at Apple Computer during its formative years between 1978 and 1981. An individual could undertake an important project and soon see widespread, tangible changes. Very talented people joined up because they believed they would be challenged and re-warded. They contributed significantly to Ford's success. The prom-ise of participation overrode Henry's disruptive mistrust of organiza-tions.

Ford developed a group of close associates into a kitchen cabi-net, working with them almost every day. They became acknowl-edged experts at making assembly operations productive. Each as-sumed a particular specialty such as coordinating incoming parts, designing assembly lines, or working with parts suppliers. But all were close to Ford, operating within the vision he personified. In effect, they constituted an informal management committee similar to that which Rockefeller formalized in Standard Oil. The Ford organization was able to pool into a synergistic whole the contribu-tions of people working from different angles.

The style of Ford's organization is characteristic of entre-preneurial firms—that is, organizations whose primary focus is creating technology to satisfy an evolving market. Such an organiza-tion usually coalesces without an explicit organizational chart. No one finds it necessary to sketch out the hierarchy of the company on paper because employees instinctively move into self-evident niches, coordinating operations informally. The early Ford organization was not a one-man show. One man imparted the vision, but an organiza-tion of people working together contributed much of the tangible advance.

Ford's organization directed virtually all its energy toward re-ducing cost, largely ignoring other objectives. The goal was to reduce the cost of manufacturing a standardized car. In 1907 Ford froze the design of the Model T, blocking major changes until the introduction of the Model A in the mid-1920s. Thus he produced a standard product for almost twenty years. For the first decade at least the strategy was optimal. Ford's greatest advantage was reducing costs by learning how to squeeze the most out of his production facilities. He reduced the cost of producing a Model T from about $1,000 in 1908 to $250 per car in 1925, a reduction of 75 percent. That was in addition to the Model T already being positioned at the bottom of the market in 1908. This is particularly noteworthy because costs are usually reduced by introducing new products based on new technologies. Ford extracted his standardized output from fewer and fewer inputs. Since his achievement, this phenomenon has been shown to be powerful and widespread and has been given its own name, *learning by doing*. This is now routinely expected to develop in the production of commodities such as computer chips. Production can be streamlined after experience detects wasteful steps. In the case of computer chips, for example, more chips are squeezed from a given sheet of silicon or the processing machinery is speeded up. A good portion of such techniques for reducing costs can be developed only by experience. While some of this learning results naturally in the course of production, Ford's organization was set up to maximize its likelihood. Freezing the design of the Model T forced the staff to focus their full creative energies on improving its production. By doggedly sticking to that strategy, Ford kept moving down the cost curve ahead of his competitors for a decade and a half.

Had Ford frequently redesigned the Model T—à la General Motors—he also would have shifted from the learning curve specific to one model to that of another. Each model would have required changes in organizations, so that considerable organizational learning and cost reduction would have been repeated. Had Ford, for example, shifted from the Model T to the Model A at an earlier date, he would have lost the momentum of reducing the former's costs, and faced selling a much more expensive untried model.

Other automobile companies sought to sidestep Ford's judgment by carving out distinctive niches in the market. General Motors went to the opposite extreme, introducing new models rapidly—too rapidly as it turned out. By imposing new models and purchasing more parts suppliers, Will Durant, the president until 1920, disrupted his divisions' efforts to reduce costs. He also acquired nonautomobile lines, such as refrigerators and diesel engines, which took GM away from its core business. Between 1915 and 1920 such loose ends kept up costs at GM, forcing it into bankruptcy when the economy turned down in 1920. Thus between 1905 and 1920 Ford had the winning strategy. Predictably, he dominated the market for low-priced cars, selling more than 80 percent of them. In fact, Ford was producing more than half of all automobiles in the United States. He controlled the lower range of the market so completely that, in the early 1920s, General Motors wrote off that market, judging that its Chevrolet could never compete with Ford.

Events proved GM's prediction wrong because Henry Ford stuck with his strategy long after it lost its potency. Ford was a determined, even obstinate, individual whose instincts had been reinforced by experience. At several pivotal times in his life when others urged him to pull back, he heeded his instincts and succeeded dramatically. Moving into his sixties in 1923 made him less amenable to change. But in the 1920s the forces driving the industry were changing. Much like squeezing an orange, cost reductions from learning were tapering off. Henry's competitors were pushing their own learning curves, and—critically—intensifying competition by improving their models.

The Model T performed its basic functions admirably. It was inexpensive and easily repaired; anybody with a little sense about its mechanical makeup could usually coax a few more miles from it. It bounced over the poor roads of the countryside. But its very success changed the landscape of America. The growth in the number of cars caused a corresponding increase in road improvements. During the 1920s major highways were reconstructed all across the United States. Roads were paved and straightened, and bridges erected until a comprehensive highway system emerged. Conditions contrasted sharply with pre–World War I, when most roads were unpaved, rutted, dusty in the summer and muddy in the spring. Ford designed the Model T to function as an off-the-road vehicle. Its high clearance rode over obstacles and uneven terrain. Better roads, however, eliminated the necessity of swaying around well above the road. Vehicles could have the lower clearances, making travel faster and smoother.

Other car manufacturers made numerous improvements including heaters, self-starters, improved brakes and tires, and enclosed cabs as well as choices in colors and styles, but Ford allowed few options on the Model T. For a while, Ford's adamant adherence to the basics worked. Lower costs allowed him to undersell other manufacturers, and customers could add their own accessories out of the savings. But other manufacturers closed in on his cost reductions, eliminating that advantage. In fact, competitors' techniques became more efficient in that some features were best built into completely redesigned models. The Model T was neither large nor strong enough to support many of the new accessories, most obviously the enclosed cab. By the mid-1920s, Ford's rigidity was becoming costly. Sales of the Model T fell until it became clear, even to Henry, that drastic changes were necessary. Ford had worked himself out of a job, at least as he originally defined his objective. Initially his product was so attractive that he didn't have to worry about competition. Everything he produced was readily sold at a price that provided a cushion to reach even more customers if necessary. Ford's only problem then was producing *enough* cars. But inevitably the competition caught up. And past production created another form of competition. An active trade developed in used automobiles, which proved a substitute for new ones. Ford, concentrating at the lower end of the market, was particularly vulnerable.

Henry Ford created a new world but didn't recognize the drastic implications of his achievement. While he was justifiably proud of creating a boon to the common man, as he correctly touted it, he failed to understand the wide implications of its effects. Slumping sales finally forced drastic remedies. He stopped assembly for a full year (which raised havoc with his dealers, who were left with nothing to sell). In a remarkable crash program he produced the Model A, which caught up to current industry practices, providing a competitive model. But its luster soon dimmed as the other automobile companies continued refining their models and features. Ford reverted to his old tactic of sticking with a model, pushing the company toward bankruptcy by the late 1930s. Finally during World War II federal officials became so concerned that Henry's practices would hamper war production that they helped nudge him into retirement.

Henry Ford created one of the most famous and successful American companies, but then came very close to destroying it. A few more years of the tactics of the 1920s and 1930s would have dissipated the remaining assets. Thus the Ford company's rebound in a major transformation from 1945 to 1955 was astounding in itself. Ford adopted much of General Motors' structure while retaining some of its historical innovative flair. General Motors also had learned to squeeze the most from the learning curve and economies of scale in production, but it also had developed a managerial system that renewed itself over the long run. It didn't depend on a single entrepreneur such as Henry Ford. It could hunker down during bad times as well as serve an expanding market.

Henry Ford's approach was similar to Andrew Carnegie's. As long as the cost of his product remained below the competition, most other marketing considerations could be ignored. The tactic was better suited for steel, which, being a commodity, could be sold by cutting its price. But when an industry approaches maturity and begins to be affected by downturns in the economy, as autos were in the 1930s, different tactics become necessary. Before 1940 Ford was very vulnerable. But General Motors was structured to ride out the bad years. It encouraged continual refinements in its products and demonstrated its diversity by producing industrial products other than automobiles. The acid test of General Motors' design is that more than sixty years after 1925—when Henry Ford ran out of steam—it is still one of the world's largest companies, even though its individual products have been transformed repeatedly. Ford, in the strongest compliment it could pay to its prime competitor, adopted much of GM's structure.

The Entrepreneurial Organization

Henry Ford is arguably the best-known American entrepreneur. Therefore it seems fitting that the organization which surpassed his creation has assumed a special place in the history of American business. General Motors, as assembled by Alfred Sloan,[2] has probably been the most important model for large American—indeed worldwide—businesses. Most studies of managing a complex organization begin here. While we certainly have progressed beyond the model, both in theory and practice, it is clearly the basic benchmark. Its operation profoundly affected thinking as to how a large organization should be structured and nurtured.

As the Ford organization grew increasingly obsolete during the

1920s, General Motors was developing a better model. Alfred Sloan was instrumental in making General Motors a prototype. It is ironic that Sloan is not well known beyond those familiar with the logic of business structures. (The humorist Will Rogers used to say that Henry Ford had an automobile named after him, as did Walter Chrysler, but poor Alfred Sloan only had a car named after an Indian chief—by which he meant Pontiac.) Ford's name is immortal, and yet Sloan probably has had a greater impact on American business history than Ford by creating a business structure applicable to many more operations. Ironically Sloan probably would have preferred the obscurity history has rendered him, which is consistent with the role he expected of individuals he promoted at General Motors.

Sloan joined General Motors through the back door. His preparation was similar to Pierre du Pont's, in that he earned an engineering degree from MIT. He began work with the Hyatt Rolling Bearing Company when it was struggling to become profitable. The industry was just getting under way and Sloan had to take the initiative to pull his firm through its growing pains. Within a few years he remodeled Hyatt—risking his reputation and wealth as he turned operations around. He learned much about management through this on-the-job training, as his success was to demonstrate.

Having put the company on a sound footing, Sloan could see that it still faced a strategic, external danger. The largest customer for bearings, particularly Hyatt's lines, was the automobile industry. Thus the fate of his small company was strongly influenced, if not controlled, by a few large customers. Such a monopolistic buyer can apply great pressure to a supplier whose facilities have been shaped to produce a specialized product geared to a specific user. Hyatt, structured to produce bearings for Ford's and General Motors' automobiles, was very vulnerable to shifts in their direction. Companies in such a situation typically merge with their customers because long-term efficiency is fostered when management can confidently make the best long-term commitments. Thus between 1915 and 1925 many captive suppliers of automotive parts sold out to automobile manufacturers. General Motors took the lead, acquiring Fisher Body, Delco Electric, and New Departure Bearing in addition to Hyatt. As was typical of General Motors at the time, the last three were combined within a new subsidiary, United Motors.

Sloan examined this environment and concluded that the logical thing was to sell out to GM. He accepted GM stock worth $13.5 million for Hyatt, much of which was owned by his father and himself. At that point he could have sold the stock and retired to Daytona Beach along with John D. Rockefeller. But what probably motivated him—as with most good managers—was that he enjoyed his work. Beyond the paycheck, the joy of solving and creating keeps such an individual working. Thus Sloan elected to stay on within the General Motors organization, even though its future—and his stock therein—was far from assured.

General Motors was poorly coordinated. Will Durant, the president, had not done much to integrate the companies he kept acquiring. He expected that somehow the independent units would merge into a synergistic unit by themselves. Pierre du Pont, whose company had purchased a large portion of General Motors, stepped in to impose order in 1920, turning extensive operating authority over to Sloan. He operated under du Pont's oversight for a couple of years and then assumed full authority.

GM's problem at the beginning of the 1920s was that they had absorbed Ford's central lesson of decreasing costs in automobile production too easily. Durant expected the effect to work even more widely than at Ford, so he assembled seven automotive divisions, of which only two, Buick and Cadillac, were yet viable. Then he added in other divisions, including appliances and railroad locomotives. He believed that as all of these divisions began simultaneous production costs would fall and profits rise. But implementing such complex, evolutionary forces required much more coordination than Durant was able to provide. Henry Ford had pushed the process to its extreme in driving down the cost of the Model T. But he had required the entire energy of his organization to reach that goal. And the scale of Durant's transformation was much more ambitious.

Sloan began to remodel the organization to combine Ford-style economies of scale with techniques of decentralization to build adaptability into the organization. The goal was to reach well down into the organization, encouraging employees to eschew bureaucratic temptations in favor of working toward the company's interests. Those activities exhibiting economies of scale, such as assembling cars, were centralized, but all others were kept as small as possible in order to promote innovation. This remodeling attempted to strike a judicious trade-off between centralization and decentralization. Sloan insisted that decisions in the company be reached at the lowest possible level where all relevant factors were incorporated. They should be made by those closest to such issues, who would be most affected by the consequences.

This balance appears reasonable in hindsight, but Henry Ford studiously avoided it. Beneath his informal top management group he erected one of the most rigid industrial bureaucracies devised. Ford's tactic was to prevent failures by structuring manufacturing to deny an individual worker's discretion. The assembly line was organized such that every step was precisely specified and, therefore, regulated. Ford's philosophy was summed up in his comment that "in the perfect assembly line there are no fitters," by which he meant that workers had no judgments to make when putting parts together because every part fit precisely. Thus, paradoxically, in contrast to Ford's informal and loosely structured top management, the hierarchy below was structured, mechanical, and bureaucratic. This marked division of responsibilities succeeded as long as top management made perceptive changes for the assembly line to implement. But when the top group ceased to respond appropriately, those below were locked into frustrating decline.

One of Sloan's most notable innovations at General Motors was accentuating annual model changes. Unlike Ford, whose Model T remained static from 1908 to 1925, GM offered a 1923 model Chevrolet, and then a 1924 model, a 1925 introduction, and so on. In recent years this practice has been criticized as inefficient. But during the 1920s yearly changes implemented a vigorous stream of improvements including better wheels, brakes, tires, transmissions, engines, heaters, enclosed cabs, and self-starters. Almost every part of each car was redesigned and improved. Had manufacturers held back innovations, such as Ford did for nearly two decades until the Model A superseded the Model T, consumers would have been denied the benefits for a long time. Besides, it is difficult to implement such a large backlog of improvements simultaneously. Designing a substantially new car and committing it to production quickly can invite defects. Thus General Motors chose regular incremental changes in automobiles in order to manage improvements. Each year General Motors' cars were improved, giving buyers more for each dollar. Ford, sticking with the same design, attempted to attract buyers by progressively reducing the price of the same model. Consumers bought General Motors' cars while deserting Ford's product in droves. The buyers were not convinced that lower prices compensated for the innovations that GM was putting into its cars.

The logic of this relation reasserted itself in the 1970s when automobile companies retreated from annual changes. In effect, they reverted toward the old Ford pattern. Many of the changes were imposed by the necessity to respond to new government regulations rather than made as a competitive tactic to attract buyers. With less to promote, automobile companies used continuity of production to reduce costs. Thus the excitement that once accompanied the introduction of new cars each fall faded as external forces commanded greater attention.

Sloan leveraged annual model changes with a comprehensive range of models and options. Ford's strategy of providing only basic transportation had prompted a cottage industry supplying accessories independently for Model T's. When Ford refused to add a heater, others offered units that could be retro-fitted. And when Ford rejected decorative trim, suppliers created a wide array of accessories, including "Phord" name plates. General Motors met such demands directly via new models, features, and options. At the heart of this strategy were five lines, from Chevrolet to Cadillac—which have proved the company's wisdom by their sixty years of service— bracketing the bulk of car markets. GM expected to gain from commonalities of production and distribution, as well as to pass buyers up to more expensive nameplates as their incomes rose.

Sloan also departed from Ford's scheme in structuring his organization to adapt a long-run view. By the middle of the 1920s the industry had exhausted most of the gains possible from volume production. But sixty years later the basic General Motors strategy of competitive innovation is still producing good returns. Sloan understood that in the long run the company could not grow faster than the overall economy, so it had to ride out the busts as well its booms. General Motors adapted some of du Pont's techniques of long-term planning, including projecting the demand for the products. This set the stage for their practice of "uniform" or "standard pricing." They projected their expected volume; that is, the number of cars they expected to sell per year over a typical five-year span. Then they calculated the price necessary to make a sustainable profit. (Economists would term this a *normal* or *competitive profit.*) In slack years they shaded the price, expecting to recoup during prosperous periods. Average prices were set such that the company survived over the long run. In retrospect this seems sensible enough, but at the time Ford was defaulting on it, depleting its assets.

General Motors also sought to promote continuous vitality by avoiding heavy dependence on specific managers. They decentralized responsibility in order to subject programs to continual review. This allowed the brilliant initiatives of more centralized organizations to surpass them occasionally, but consistent internal review kept the company's overall average high. Security proved to be found not so much in avoiding risks as in having more people working on problems and, therefore, increasing potential advances. The General Motors system admittedly tends to produce a bland company style, which some would characterize as compromise. By the time proposals have been exposed to the views of the relevant parties in the organization, much originality has been chipped away. The officers of General Motors were not as distinctive as Henry Ford. But, collectively, they developed a more comprehensive view, which headed off mistakes as well as warned them sooner about developing fiascoes.

In the 1980s General Motors has undertaken a major reorganization. They examined forces working on the automobile industry, deciding to shrink the company from the five traditional divisions down to two. They expect to economize on the overhead costs of engineering and product development. Given the automobile industry's evolution toward an integrated international market, this seems logical. It is noteworthy that this was carried out by a self-appraisal; independent consultants or a dictatorial president would have had great difficulty obtaining the widespread consent necessary within such an organization. The initial results are none too promising, but then the strength of the organization is its ability to learn from experience. This quality has allowed GM to renew itself repeatedly. The present automobile industry is very different from that of sixty years ago and yet the organization is doing reasonably well in the face of vigorous competition because its structure has encouraged continued adaptation.

General Motors is sometimes depicted as a bureaucracy, perhaps not as cumbersome as a large government, but a bureaucracy nevertheless, which connotes sluggishness and insensitivity. Though GM or other organizations may dampen individual instincts or styles, they seek to screen out excesses that are less productive. The positive side is giving individuals more leverage by rallying the organization behind a promising idea. The company provides a forum for many to consider and try out ideas. A productive organization will draw out the special talents and contributions of its members, magnifying their influence beyond what they could accomplish alone. An organization can be more than the sum of its individual parts if individuals reinforce one another's contributions. Thus it is not surprising that the model has been widely copied, not only in the United States but throughout other developed economies as well.

14

The Entrepreneurs
of Growing Government

Historians often have observed that nineteenth-century American governments built public works, erected tariffs, set the rules of incorporation, and generally considered themselves stewards of the economy. They often then infer that the persuasive government role in the contemporary economy is not a drastic change and, therefore, does not warrant much explanation. But the respective magnitudes of government in the two periods say just the opposite. Government has expanded dramatically at every level: local, state, and federal. Nor is the American experience unique, because comparable expansions occurred in all major growing economies.

In 1871 the American federal government employed only 50,000 civilians, less than 0.01 percent of the total labor force. By 1970 it was almost 4 percent, representing a relative four hundredfold gain. In

1870 federal spending averaged 4 percent of the GNP—with a good share of that going toward paying off the Civil War debt—and in 1970 the figure was passing 20 percent. In other words, government has been a major growth sector in the late nineteeth and the twentieth centuries. And as a growing sector it was invariably totally reconstructed as entrepreneurs devised new technologies and delivery systems to satisfy emerging demands.

At first government was blocked from growing to its modern role until the intellectual climate changed.[1] Most nineteenth-century Americans believed that having set the ground rules for social conduct, government should allow individuals complete freedom to reach accommodations within those guidelines. Contracts, institutions, and other mutually agreeable arrangements among people must be upheld by public institutions. This tenet was a logical part of the prevailing philosophy that it was best to allow individuals to pursue their own interests except when imposing unwarranted costs upon others. Personal accountability, it was believed, not only encouraged each individual to promote his own interests but, also, the best interests of society as well. Thus it was believed necessary to restrain government in order to promote substantial economic and political freedom.

This view was not completely unshakable, however. Most adherents could not concretely articulate why it was superior. This contrasts with today, when such tools as supply-and-demand curves in economics, for example, can demonstrate how free exchange maximizes economic welfare. A typical current calculation shows that the cost of restricting automobile imports costs consumers ten times as much as the protection afforded domestic auto manufacturers. Such results, employing modern techniques, help explain why almost all modern economists favor unfettered trade.

Many nineteenth-century scholars also favored free trade, but they could not justify their views so precisely and persuasively. They developed supply-and-demand curves as an analytical tool around the turn of the century in the process of explaining how markets functioned. The generality of the justification, at least up till then, allowed an intellectual counterrevolution to develop in the last quarter of the nineteenth century. More began to say that though freedom was a good thing, there were problems. A blanket view extolling the benefits of freedom became viewed as overlooking some important defects.

Skepticism about the effects of markets and unfettered freedom, however, was not sufficient by itself. There had to be an alternative for individuals to justify more government action. Charles Francis Adams, who gave this outlook a big, early push, seemed an unlikely entrepreneur.[2] He had an aristocratic lineage: his grandfather and great-grandfather were presidents. He attended traditional schools befitting an established family before serving as an officer in the cavalry during the Civil War. An instinctive entrepreneur, he appears to have used the lulls between action to sort out the implications of his schooling and plan his mission. Like most Americans he could not help but notice the rapid growth of railroads and the central role they were assuming in the commerce of the economy. He concluded that the typical market structure in the industry was a great threat to national well-being. He committed his substantial talents to publicizing and reforming it.

Adams turned to writing to spread his ideas and promote his remedies. His greatest success was an article published in 1869 titled "Chapters of Erie," which lambasted the behavior of Vanderbilt on the one hand and Drew, Fisk, and Gould on the other in their struggle for control of the Erie Railroad. It provided considerable impetus to the robber baron conception that chicanery and a disregard for the public interest drove the founders of the large companies.

Adams also developed a prototype for state regulation of the public utilities. He was a founding member of the three-man Massachusetts Railroad Commission in 1869 and soon became its dominant spokesman. He used this forum to publicize his view that railroads tended to become natural monopolies because technology dictated that only one firm of efficient size could serve a market. His implication was that government would have to regulate in the absence of effective competition. Adams rejected government ownership of railroads and detailed regulation of railroads by state legislatures, however, because he understood the perverse incentives that political interests would bring. Therefore, he concluded that railroads would have to be regulated by a board, expert in railroad operations but independent of direct government control. The Massachusetts commission became the model for adoptions in many other states.

The commission lacked power to compel railroads to follow its directives, such as setting rates and prescribing safety regulations. Adams's premise was that investigation, publicity, and reason would push railroads toward the best social policies. But experience generally suggested that "sunshine commissions" failed to compel businesses to behave according to what the regulators believed to be the public interest. Thus, state commissions were generally granted greater powers for enforcing regulations.

Adams left the commission in 1879 to be a railroad manager himself, soon becoming president of the Union Pacific Railroad. (This foreshadowed a twentieth-century concern about regulators being shaped or "captured" by the information and personnel provided by the regulated industry.) In his later years Adams grew cynical about the ability of public regulation to craft the genteel type of cooperative world he sought. But his innovation in Massachusetts proved to be an important way station to greater regulation. The regulatory board embodied the common view that some public intervention had become necessary, although most people had not yet been persuaded that regulation as stringent as was adopted later was necessary at this time.

States turned from using Massachusetts's model of "weak" railroad regulations because, in addition to weakness in controlling railroads, it was also vulnerable to competitive moves in neighboring states. Even when "Granger" railroad regulations, which included the power to set rates, were imposed in the Midwest, individual states still found it difficult to control interstate railroads. Because states were prohibited from regulating anything crossing state lines, much traffic evaded controls, undercutting the power of regulatory regimes. This experience sparked the general conclusion that regulation would have to be imposed nationwide. Thus, in 1887 the Interstate Commerce Commission (ICC) was created. For a while court decisions removed much of the bite out of the ICC's regulatory clout, but congressional legislation strengthened its power in the early twentieth century. Comprehensive railroad regulation became the norm, at least until the 1980s. It also served as a model to be extended to other industries, including trucking, waterways, pipelines, telephones, and airlines. By the middle of the twentieth century, it was generally accepted as a necessity to mitigate the serious defects believed inherent in those markets.

Louis Brandeis: Entrepreneuring at the Federal Level

Louis Brandeis is still considered one of the brightest students to have attended the Harvard Law School.[3] Not yet twenty-one when he graduated in 1887, he had to obtain special permission to practice law before legally becoming an adult. He became known as "the people's lawyer," earning a reputation much like that of Henry Ford, who, as we have seen, was viewed as someone who sought the interests of the common populace rather than those wielding concentrated power in the economy. Brandeis proved to be a powerful agent for change in the economy as well as a superb lawyer. In addition to having considerable energy and curiosity, he was also intelligent and able to work with others.

Brandeis's major contributions to increasing federal regulation began in the early twentieth century. The first milestone was a 1908 Supreme Court review of an Oregon law that stipulated maximum working hours for women. By established principles the law was clearly unconstitutional, interfering with the right of individuals to make contracts among themselves as they saw fit. Brandeis took a completely different tack. Ignoring legal precedents, he argued for the merits of the case, that prohibiting women from working long hours safeguarded their well-being. His case was the first example of what became known as *sociological jurisprudence,* shifting traditional court arguments from the legality of actions to their advisability. Brandeis's victory greatly expanded the range for government action by allowing the government to legislate well beyond its traditional domain of deciding whether the rules of the game were being followed. Now one of its agencies could become an active player whenever it saw fit.

In 1910 Brandeis argued against the railroads' request to the Interstate Commerce Commission for a rate increase. Again, the case clearly was a loser on the basis of legal precedence. The railroads were entitled to an increase in rates, having shown that their costs had increased sufficiently to justify the raise under regulatory procedures. But Brandeis argued that the rate hike was not necessary because pursuing untapped efficiencies in railroads could reduce costs. He organized copious expert testimony from consultants in "scientific management" who were then introducing the use of time-and-motion studies. A particularly effective tactic by Brandeis was coining the expression "saving a million dollars a day," a slogan the press discovered made good copy. In retrospect the cost savings upon which he based his argument proved to be largely illusionary, never appearing. But by shifting the grounds of the debate Brandeis won his case.

Brandeis was also a prime instigator behind the formation of the Federal Reserve Banking System in 1913. He wrote a book titled *Other People's Money,* which became a classic by criticizing the "excessive" fees of underwriters to issue and to trade stock. Such publicity also contributed to the creation of the Clayton Antitrust Act and the Federal Trade Commission (FTC) in 1914. The FTC was significant for instituting the practice of administrative law in the United States. The commissioners could prescribe behavior in their jurisdiction rather than, as in traditional judicial procedures, wait for others to initiate suits before issuing rulings. The FTC was hobbled initially by court and congressional restrictions, but like other regulatory mechanisms tended to gather authority with practice.

Brandeis was appointed to the Supreme Court by President Wilson in 1916, and he went on compiling a distinguished record until his death in 1941. But his earlier role in devising federal mechanisms to address public concerns about society and business was his major entrepreneurial contribution. The basic techniques of sociological jurisprudence and administrative regulation that he created are still the basis for much of (the greatly expanded) current American regulation.

World War I: Experimenting with Economic Planning

The first clear indication that a sizable portion of the public had come to believe that economic coordination beyond that provided through markets was necessary occurred with the onset of World War I.[4] Most Americans continued to maintain that they believed private enterprise should organize the economy—as the majority still do today, having since approved many more compromises. But a better test is how far people are willing to rely upon that organization as apparent threats grow larger. When the United States joined the fighting in 1917, it was commonly assumed that the wartime economy would require national coordination beyond that provided by prices and markets. Many believed that relying on private incentives to mobilize the war effort would also create major inequities within the society.

The focus of the planning effort was the War Industries Board (WIB), which had power to allocate resources believed critical to mobilization, particularly raw materials. Prices were set by a parallel board, so that, in effect, the government assumed the management of much of the economy. The War Industries Board instituted priorities to ensure that "critical uses" would receive sufficient raw materials. Such a system fails to recognize diminishing returns within its categories of priorities, however; thus, it fulfills all of the highest category—no matter how little the last use yields—before any uses in the second category. This creates misallocation among sectors, in that some resources could be moved from high-priority sectors to produce better yields in lower-priority sectors. In World War I the priority system channeled large amounts of natural resources and war supplies into sectors that, while clearly important in the abstract, were not yet prepared to use them. In particular, the railroads became clogged because large quantities of supplies were shipped to shipyards that simply weren't ready to use them to build ships. The planners knew that somehow the shipyards should have priority, but didn't have a means to tell what amount was appropriate, as they did in markets governed by prices.

The War Industries Board attempted to promote other wartime efficiencies, including that perennial favorite of planners—standardization. It assumed that if the number of models or variations of products can be reduced, production costs will fall. This is true to a point, but often such policies simplify the task of the planners at the cost of others. Buyers do not seek special features on goods merely to pay higher prices. They buy those providing worthwhile additions in their applications. For example, the War Planning Board (WPB) thought they could save on spool material by having thread wound onto larger spools. This certainly reduced the number of spools required for thread production. But it also meant that consumers had to buy thread in larger quantities such that on average they held larger inventories. It is not clear there were net savings.

Other federal boards allied with the War Industries Board attempted to control food supplies and untangle the railroads. (Much of the latter mess had been caused by previous attempts at planning.) In each case there was a strong concern that no group should bear a disproportionate cost of the war and, therefore, that price increases should be balanced. But the war brought changes into the economy so large that they could only be accommodated by major shifts among prices. The government's attempt to keep a "level playing field" encouraged consumers and producers to overuse resources that the war had made more valuable.

The attempt to preserve equity in the system via controls introduced further complications. It is easy to assume that government can spot and correct defects in the operation of a market economy. There are such defects, but there are also strong forces that cause government initiatives to go astray. Groups lacking economic clout usually lack political clout as well. The groups who benefited the most during World War I were those able to press for special treatment from the War Industries Board. But these interests often would have done very well for themselves in any case.

The overall record suggests that the attempts to coordinate the economy during World War I were, on net, damaging. Real GNP in 1918, even including military production, fell in comparison with 1917. Given the war's stimulus to the economy, the reverse was more likely. During World War II, for example, the economy was less constrained, so it was able to both increase war production and civilian goods at the same time. The performance in 1918 suggests that planning worked perversely. Some scholars pointed optimistically to this attempt at national coordination as showing that, given further corrections, things might be done right. But the proper lesson is that the very nature of the activity invites intractable problems. Government officials, remembering this experience, established weaker controls in World War II. It is also significant that Americans have since shied away from the thought of overall economic controls.

The Federal Reserve and the Coming of the Great Depression

Just prior to World War I America began another experiment in governmental direction that proved to have an enormous impact on the economy. The 1913 legislation that created the Federal Reserve System was seen merely to back up the banking system in emergencies. It was intended to provide liquidity to keep transactions going during panics. But like so much legislation, the details weren't filled in, in large part because such institutions had never been employed. Unlike a private entrepreneurial venture that goes through a trial-and-discovery process as it adapts to its market, the Federal Reserve was created full-blown without testing. Thus the functioning of the system was subject to considerable discretion. Either a change of Federal Reserve officials or a shift in public opinion could prompt the system to take on a much larger role in the economy.

The late 1920s offered such an opportunity.[5] The financial markets underwent an enormous expansion during the decade and, in particular, the stock market caught the attention of many Americans. The value of stocks rose as more companies were being financed and publicly owned. The improving economy also made existing shares more valuable. But many Americans concluded that shares were becoming too high, making a correction inevitable. It was not understood that such results were normal for a growth sector. There was considerable sentiment for reining in the stock market, which evoked a sympathetic response among generally conservative managers at the Federal Reserve System.

In 1927 the Fed began to unlimber its powers to slow the growth in the money supply and raise interest rates in order to curtail this "speculation." But this approach was using a shotgun where a rifle was indicated. From 1927 through 1929 this policy was unable to slow the stock market because it was one of the strongest and most resilient components of the economy. Rather, tight money began to retard the remainder of the economy. By late 1929 it had become obvious that the economy was sliding into a major downturn. The famous "Black Friday" crash of the stock market in October 1929 expressed that realization. The crash is often seen to be a major instigator of the Great Depression, but most likely the causation is reversed. The stock market's crash reflected the reappraisal of the economy's prospects in that the earnings expected of most stocks had to be sharply marked down for the foreseeable future. Though the crash certainly didn't help the economy, its impact was small relative to the economy and thus more likely to reflect rather than lead it.

Even after the obvious deflation of the economy and the stock market, the Federal Reserve persisted in keeping money tight. Even though its concern about speculative excesses had been erased, it still worried about inflation reviving. In retrospect, this is hard to believe. There had not been any inflation since 1920, and in 1931 and 1932 prices fell by more than 10 percent per annum! The Fed also misinterpreted the current low interest rates as indicating that there was plenty of money to serve the needs of the economy. The governors of the Federal Reserve overlooked that as prices fell; the cost of paying back loans in enhanced dollars increased to equal real interest rates of 15 percent to 20 percent. Lost in myopia, the Fed kept the money supply declining all the way till 1933. This clearly is the outstanding suspect for the cause of the Great Depression.

Money plays the central role in a modern, sophisticated economy as the medium through which exchanges of goods and services take place. It pays for the employment of resources and, in turn, buys back the goods that make such employment possible. When the supply of money is drastically reduced, as it was from 1929 to 1933, total spending is reduced, setting off retrenchments in the demand for resources such as labor and capital. But even worse than allowing a large reduction in the money supply, the Federal Reserve allowed much of the banking system to be destroyed by failing to oppose depositors' panics. Many banks were forced to close while the remainder hunkered down, conserving their reserves in self-defense. Much of the populace retreated to a cash-and-barter society, substantially reducing the amount of checking-account balances, the largest component of money in the economy.

The Fed proved to be an iatrogenic institution, its treatments causing more damage than good. It was created to help the economy during distress. From 1929 to 1933, it made a bad situation into a catastrophe. The Great Depression was doubly bad for business. It shifted public sentiment, giving business another problem on top of depressed demand. Business became a scapegoat for the problems of the Depression, which encouraged government to take further steps to constrain it. Especially affected were financial markets that were subject to much heavier regulation, including the Glass-Steagall Act, which blocked banks from participating in other financial markets.

The Unlikely Entrepreneur: FDR and the New Fiscal Economics

The growth in regulation was paralleled by that of government spending. And the political entrepreneur who vividly showed how to expand that activity was Franklin Delano Roosevelt.[6] In his early years FDR did not show much promise of entrepreneurial breakthroughs. He was never a good student. He graduated from Harvard in 1904 and, although he failed to complete his work at Columbia Law School, passed the New York Bar in 1907. Later, however, he proved to have a remarkable political sense, which included the ability to communicate with others, develop their ideas, and spot new opportunities emerging in the political system. He was first elected to the New York State Senate in 1910, where he quickly became a leader of the "good government" faction in the legislature. His reputation soon carried well beyond the state. He became an early supporter of Woodrow Wilson, so that upon Wilson's election as president in 1912 he was rewarded with the post of Assistant Secretary of the Navy. In addition to the exposure to a wider political environment, this was also one of the largest managerial positions in the federal government. Roosevelt proved to be an active leader who developed considerable rapport among the constituencies of the department.

After being trounced in the primary for senator from New York State in 1914, he patched up his differences with the "Tammany Machine" and never again made the mistake of alienating a large group of potential supporters. He was nominated for Democratic vice president in 1920 and ran an outstanding campaign, even though the ticket was defeated. From 1920 to 1928 Roosevelt, in effect, took refuge in business, waiting for conservative Republican strength in the country to subside. But he remained an active political force, working to keep opportunities open until conditions became favorable. In 1928 he was elected governor of New York and then, of course, in 1932 he defeated the Depression-racked Herbert Hoover for president.

FDR's superb political instincts directed him to a key feature of modern federal government. Scholars have subsequently delineated the mechanism, but Roosevelt employed it effectively to his own ends without coaching. (Perhaps this is the advantage of a man who learned to maneuver through life without the aid of sustained academic effort.) His success can be understood by recognizing how small an effect a voter in an election can have on the government compared with the influence of someone actually working in the government.

Public polls show that Americans are consistently poorly informed about the operations of their government. Fewer than half can name their senators or congressman, their most direct contact with the federal government. Familiarity with individual issues is even worse. Yet the federal government allocates about a quarter of a household's income. It collects in taxes and pays out for programs about what a typical household pays for housing. It is inconceivable that a homeowner would not know his or her address. Those who consistently fail to find their way home have to be committed into the care of others.

No one seriously considers committing more than half of the

populace for ignoring their government—indeed, large, powerful interests benefit from that ignorance. But ignorance is not stupidity or laziness. Many voters correctly judge that the effect of their vote is much less than the effort required to become adequately informed about public decisions. Scholars of "public choice," the study of government behavior when participants are presumed to pursue their own interests, call this *rational ignorance.*

The vacuum of ignorance pulls in more focused, purposeful groups. The special interests—as they have become widely known— learned that influence on governmental decisions was much more effectively applied through groups that have a large vested interest in a narrow issue. Landowners benefiting from reclamation projects, for example, had good reason to become "rationally informed" about possible government aid, expending their time and money to promote it. Direct approaches to the government bureaus and congressmen who stand to gain from the legislation are much more effective than voting and being swallowed up in the crowd.

Today these tactics are so well honed and understood that the three co-participants—the special interests, government bureaucrats, and respective congressional committees—are termed the *iron triangle* for their power to elicit government allocations. The problem now is to stop them from exercising their narrow, concentrated power to the detriment of the public interest. But in FDR's first years as president, the conditions that permitted iron triangles were just forming, so he actually encouraged such connections, dangling the prospects of funding in order to entice special interests to coalesce into operations. Programs such as the Civilian Conservation Corps (CCC) and relief for endangered mortgages created new, supportive constituencies.

Agricultural interests required no prompting, however, because they had been systematically seeking to foster such opportunities for at least six decades. They were the prototype of modern special interest organizations, having already demonstrated the value in winning favors from the federal government. Not surprisingly, the Agricultural Adjustment Act, which subsidized major crops, was one of the first pieces of New Deal legislation.

Although it was declared unconstitutional two years later, the

National Industrial Recovery Act (NIRA) exemplified the special interest activity that Roosevelt promoted. It overrode long-standing antitrust laws by allowing producers and workers in each industry to set prices and wages jointly. The result was predictable—both were raised substantially. Also, predictably for special interest legislation, the costs were borne by the consumers of the goods whose relatively small purchases per capita made organizing counterpressures much less attractive. The ostensible purpose of the NIRA was to promote industry "stabilization" and, therefore, revive confidence in the economy. But the net effect was choking off sales by pricing consumers out of the market.

Since World War II the federal government has continued to grow until today it directly spends one-fourth of the peacetime GNP while significantly regulating the remainder. This generally accords with Americans' view about the appropriate role for the federal government to play; despite its shortcomings, many think that a large government is essential in a complex, modern economy. This holds for both liberals who tend to favor further intervention in the economy and conservatives who tend to want a little less. It also represents a turn of 180 degrees from that of a hundred years ago, when it was believed that government should intervene only in extraordinary cases. Adams, Brandeis, and FDR did their work well, acting as powerful catalysts to create a new social order.

World War II and Perceived Limits

When mobilization got under way for World War II, most Americans were surprised that so much latent vigor remained in the economy. That potential had seemed increasingly remote as the dreary years of the 1930s had dragged on. The economy seemed to have lost its traditional enterprise and resilience. But the economy's vitality during mobilization and continued momentum in the conversion to civilian production erased that presumption. The outpouring of Liberty Ships, B-24s, LSTs, machine guns, 100-octane gas, sonar equipment, and khaki cloth undercut the skeptics. After 1945 the demand for automobiles, refrigerators, single-family homes, freezers, classrooms, and four-lane roads caused all but the most incorrigible stagnationists to raise their forecasts. From 1940 to 1945 the GNP (in constant 1940 prices) rose from $100 billion to $159 billion. This increase occurred despite the diversion of large amounts of manpower to the military. It allowed the production of a generous number of civilian goods, especially when compared with recent standards of living.

The vitality of the economy was evident in several ways. At the height of the war, 40 percent of the economy was devoted to supplying the military. This meant that more than two-thirds of the economy's resources had to be converted to uses that required different means of production, machinery, and even locations. The automobile companies, for example, found themselves producing not only trucks and jeeps but also tanks, aircraft parts, and antiaircraft guns.

Right after Pearl Harbor, when the Americans calculated what they needed to contribute for the Allies to win the war in two theaters, the manufacturers and economists gasped. The projections implied military output far exceeding the estimated capacity of the American economy. If the United States was to become the "arsenal of democracy" it would require a lot more effort and ingenuity than seemed possible in early 1942.

Retrospect allows us to conclude that these ambitious objectives were essentially met. Certain types of production fell behind schedule and necessitated juggling war plans. For example, the effectiveness of German submarines in the Atlantic forced a slowdown in the construction of landing craft in order to build destroyer escorts and sub-chasers. This delayed operations in the Mediterranean and postponed the cross-channel attack on Normandy for a full year. On the other hand, the campaign against Japan ran well ahead of schedule. The coordination of fast aircraft carriers and amphibious operations allowed strikes directly at the centers of enemy power, bypassing the peripheral islands that the Japanese had expected would embroil the Americans.

The output that allowed the margin of success resulted from two serendipitous developments in the economy. First, more resources were forthcoming than the experiences of the Depression had conditioned Americans to expect. Higher wages caused large numbers of individuals such as housewives, students, retired workers, and the handicapped to choose to work. By 1944 an "extra" five million workers were in the labor force beyond what prewar labor participation rates would have predicted.

Output per worker also exceeded expectations. At the beginning of the war the United States Department of Labor made a survey, commonly called the "Five-Million-Six," which estimated the necessary number of workers of each skill. Its dismal conclusion was that only a tiny fraction was available and that the war effort was going to be seriously hampered until many workers were trained. However, employers were able to bypass, and even, in some cases, capitalize on this deficiency of skills. Many followed the traditional tactic of subdividing the production process into sequences of simple steps that could then either be mechanized or turned over to unskilled labor.

The second pleasant surprise of mobilization was that quantity production turned out many war goods much more efficiently than expected. The 210 days required to complete a Liberty Ship in 1942 had been reduced to 41 by late 1943. The number of man hours necessary to produce a pound of aircraft—a strange index necessitated by the great diversity among the products—fell by more than 80 percent between early 1941 and late 1943. Similar trends appeared throughout defense production. Such advances resulted from shortcuts evident only in large-scale production. Today we recognize that the process is both common and important and have labeled it the *learning curve.* World War II was a milestone in that it involved such an enormous increase in production of essentially new products that the process became widely discernible for the first time.

The vitality of the economy also produced considerable innovation and new technology. Many of the developments were military adaptations of longer-term trends in the economy. For example, the proximity fuse (which increased the damage a shell caused by exploding near an aircraft rather than having to score a direct hit) was considered one of the most important advances of the war. It employed printed circuits and miniaturized electronics, forerunners of postwar developments in computers, radios, and television. There were similar military-civilian crossovers in the advances in atomic energy and radar. The military, operating in varied and often unhealthy climates, took a special interest in antibiotics. The most important example was penicillin, which was pushed from a laboratory discovery to everyday availability during the war.

In recent years, "supply-side economics" has been widely discussed as a means to expand total output by improving incentives in the economy. It is, for example, credited with inspiring large cuts in federal marginal tax rates. But by far the largest test of supply-side economics was World War II. An economy that had operated at less than 75 percent of capacity for a full decade was subjected to exceptionally high demand. This prompted work and ingenuity that minds dulled by the dismal 1930s found inconceivable. It showed that entrepreneurial instincts are so deeply embedded that even the worst experiences cannot extinguish them and that providing better incentives can prompt an enormous increase in economic activity.

15

Working with
Mature Governments

Inevitably, the growth of government in the economy has increasingly shaped business decisions. There are now rooms literally filled with laws regulating business behavior. A favorite gimmick of politicians is to stand beside huge stacks of documents all representing federal regulations while making the campaign pitch, "How could business operate amidst all this red tape?" with the promise that they will work to reduce it. But after the election they seldom fulfill such commitments because strong vested interests continue pushing for regulation. (A cynic noted that when government sets out to cut red tape, somehow circumstances always guide the scissors lengthwise.)

Current regulations span the full range of business concerns, including regulating holidays, overtime, sick leave, terminations, hiring, and promotion of employees. Products are restricted as to their safety, warranties, and advertising. To begin an enterprise or expand an existing one, licenses, zoning, and other authorizations must be obtained. Raising capital is likewise subject to legal requirements. Production techniques must be deemed sufficiently safe, energy-efficient, and nonpolluting.

Moreover, to extract that quarter of the GNP that government spends, taxes must be high and comprehensive. This includes taxes on corporate income and property as well as others impinging directly on business decisions. Income taxes levied on employees also dampen businesses' ability to hire and retain workers. Entrepreneurs must motivate employees who, even after the federal reductions of 1981 and 1986, still lose 30 percent to 45 percent of each dollar earned to the government.

Entrepreneurial Styles for a Regulated Environment

The entrepreneur developing a contemporary company must cope with government regulations and the surprises such power can impose. Lee Iacocca illustrates such a quality admirably. He obviously drew upon such skills in asking Congress to guarantee the loans for Chrysler's revival. Being so bold in asking for public help used to be considered unseemly. But the rewards of either co-opting or deflecting the government have grown so large and commonplace that it is becoming a necessary part of business.

Modern CEOs spend much of their time placating such outside constituencies, government usually being the largest. Representatives of companies in petroleum, chemicals, and paper, for example, are repeatedly called to Washington, D.C., to account for the effect of their operations on the environment. Executives are constantly compelled to bargain with federal agencies to shape legislation as well as to negotiate specific rulings with regulatory commissions. Officers in any large banking, insurance, or brokerage business must cope with monetary regulations as well as deferring to pertinent congressional subcommittees and lobbyists.

Laws are made in a public forum, and, therefore, are shaped by public perceptions. Businesses must influence such opinions in order to advance their interests. Thus successful modern executives have taken on public relations. Increasingly companies provide training in communications, including speaking and fielding questions, for their officers. In the past, American businessmen often lacked, even disdained, such functions. Imagine Cornelius Vanderbilt giving a press conference, especially his responses to hostile questions! Henry Ford enjoyed provoking the press with unorthodox views, but these days his public relations staff would be whispering in his ear, "Tone it down and cut it short. You're undoing all the work we've done to convince people that we are a socially responsible business."

The environment of modern businesses virtually compels candidates for a top position to be effective in public arenas. This has progressed to include colleges. Most college presidents used to be former professors. In fact, some liked to picture themselves as scholars merely serving an obligatory term in the president's office. Anyone heading a major college or public university today, however, must continuously cope with outside constituencies. This strategy is both defensive and offensive. It ensures against surprises as well as elicits additional support. Most major, nonprofit organizations have developed such an external orientation. Unlike the nineteenth-century entrepreneur who was judged by the company's profits, today's entrepreneur is evaluated, to a significant degree, by his or her performance in the external environment. It has become common in business to divide the executive responsibilities into those performed by a chief executive officer and those appropriate to a president. While the CEO concentrates on running the internal organization, the president or the chairman of the board focuses on external constituencies such as government, the media, public relations, and stockholders.

Another index of the influence external forces have on business is the growth of lobbying organizations, particularly in Washington, D.C. The standard explanation by a constituency undertaking these functions is that it is protecting its interests in the legislative process. Every sizable group has come to recognize that it must watch out for its interests in this powerful arena. Influence and power are now applied there year-round, not just during elections. Government has become a huge, ongoing process where access influences results. The comprehensive interchange between government and business compels the latter to participate as well as to groom its executives to be proficient under such conditions.[1]

Andrew Carnegie would be frustrated operating among external forces such as those today. He maintained control over his companies through limited partnerships and tight restrictions on the sale of their stock. If he were operating a steel company today, it would not be long until he was confronted by some governmental agency, such as the Environmental Protection Agency. Or he would be surprised by IRS rulings denying his depreciation schedules on his blast furnaces, or other governmental dictates that to him would seem unfounded and outrageous. In contrast, modern American business has been forced to cope with such external forces, including developing managers who anticipate and manipulate them.

THINKING ABOUT GOVERNMENT'S ROLE

In the 1870s Americans' attitude toward the use of government regulation was: No doubt businesses collude when possible, which is not good, but incentives inevitably erode such combinations with time. Thus while trusts and monopolies will appear, they can't endure, so it is best to maintain a hands-off policy, rather than to impose additional, unpredictable costs from intervention. Accordingly, Americans judged that, over all, taking no action was better than the costs created by attempting to tidy up particular problems.

By the early twentieth century, however, perceptions had shifted so that the general attitude could be expressed as: We understand how competition should work such that we can remedy defective industries. The ideal model that people were employing was that of a competitive industry as it began to be expounded in economics in the 1930s and 1940s. Despite subsequent improvements in scholarship, this crude version is still often employed as a baseline for judging the competitiveness of industries. The instinctive appeal of its simplicity and policy implications has always seemed to smother doubts about its appropriateness. It assumes that a large number of small firms producing the same product will prevent anyone from controlling the market. The competitive environment forces each firm to sell at the lowest possible cost of production where consumer welfare is maximized.

The institution of antitrust was intended to force industries toward this ideal. Early antitrust cases, such as the 1911 action against the Standard Oil Company, divided large companies into smaller ones. While this admittedly stopped short of replicating what was seen as completely competitive, it was believed necessary to increase independent producers. Other tactics of antitrust policy such as forestalling mergers were also logical implications of the basic view that judicious intervention could improve the performance of the economy. This presumption gained wider acceptance in the twentieth century, until by the 1960s it was almost universally held.

The prevailing view was deficient, however, beginning with the premise that in order to compete firms must produce an identical product. Everyday experience suggests that many firms compete by offering products and services with distinct features rather than promoting the lowest possible price. Automobile producers, for example, direct much of their competitive energies into improving their products. While they advertise prices, they stress the advantages of particular features. The majority of contemporary consumer industries compete primarily through product differentiation. Thus traditional antitrust neglects one of the most important vehicles of competition, thereby underreporting its importance.[2]

The myopic view of competition further implied that product variety was wasteful because the resources employed did not create much of value. Most consumers, however, like to be able to choose among products and will pay extra for particular features that they— but not many others—appreciate. Nevertheless, antitrust authorities often interpreted advertising and the introduction of new styles as wasteful product differentiation. Failing to appreciate the value in such practices they scrutinized the competitiveness of firms employing them more skeptically.

Those advocating antitrust also assumed that substantial barriers blocked new competitors from many industries. Large firms that exploited economies of scales and heavily promoted the products were believed to make new competitors well-nigh impossible. Again, the prescription was breaking up giant firms. But in examining such situations one found much less in the way of barriers. The acid test occurs when it becomes profitable for new firms to enter the industry. If companies in an industry are making a relatively high return on their capital and other firms fail to enter, then barriers to entry become a plausible explanation. But that seldom happens. Usually potential competitors are repelled because earnings in the industry are unattractive. The American automobile industry appears to pose enormous barriers to a new firm, requiring billions of dollars to develop a product, to erect assembly plants and dealer networks, and then to work years to carve out a niche in the market. Since 1950, however, returns in the industry have not been high enough to interest domestic entrants, but foreign manufactures, with lower costs, have certainly not felt inhibited about entering.

A better measure of competition is *contestability*. The term was created to explain how competition worked among airlines in the wake of deregulation. There, too, it had been assumed that the traffic between most pairs of cities was insufficient to support more than two or three airlines and, therefore, real competition. But when deregulation allowed new entrants into any route, they responded vigorously, proving that virtually all routes were contestable. This struck another blow against the presumption that it required many firms to ensure competition and helped scholars conclude that competition should be viewed as active rivalry rather than a static condition.

Surely competition must mean that firms constantly try to improve products, expand their share of the market, and attract more consumers. The traditional model excluded such possibilities.

It is not surprising, therefore, that not only was antitrust policy missing its target but some of its tactics were counterproductive. In attempting to preserve "competitors" it frequently curtailed competitive behavior. Thus mergers of small, relatively inefficient firms into more productive units were discouraged by the tendency to focus on more firms rather than performance and behavior. Predictably this perverse policy was often seized by small firms using antitrust injunctions to shield themselves against competitors.

These distinctions are now appreciated to the degree that antitrust policies no longer target such simplistic villains as bigness and advertising. Now there is much less scrutiny of mergers through the presumption that they necessarily hamstring competition. This reappraisal has been occurring since the 1970s and seems likely to persist whichever party is in power. The intellectual reappraisal of the nature of competition, reinforced by disappointments with previous attempts at antitrust, have encouraged government to pull back from micromanaging the structures of industries.

The new view about competition has also affected the treatment of natural monopolies, cases where only one firm can feasibly serve an industry because its costs fall as output increases across an entire market. Natural monopolies are believed to characterize such services as electric utilities, natural gas systems, highways, telephones, and possibly airlines and railroads. It is presumed that the respective technologies of these industries dictate that only one supplier is feasible in a given locality. It follows that such a firm must be regulated to prevent it from exploiting its monopoly position. Regulation attempts to fix prices such that the firm makes a normal rate of return on its investment, a "fair profit." But this measure varies with the interest of the party, so that considerable effort is invested in studies and hearings all across the country in order to determine the "proper" rates.[3]

As in the case of antitrust, however, more competition develops within a natural monopoly than was believed possible. In telephones, for example, the local network of wires connecting users probably dictates one provider. Costs would be increased by installing parallel, mostly redundant systems. (New technologies might upset even that element of natural monopoly, however, much as television and VCRs bypassed the monopoly that local theaters held in showing movies.) A natural monopoly in one aspect does not dictate them in other parts of phone service. As the recent emergence of competition between long-distance services demonstrates, there are several means of connecting the local networks. This explains why long-distance rates have fallen while local rates have, at best, stabilized. Similarly, competition developed in phone equipment where suppliers have introduced progressively more productive, electronic models.

THE LOGIC OF REGULATION

While attempting to substitute for competition, regulation created new problems. Any organization naturally pursues activities according to their rewards, so that when a business is told that its prices will be set to recover costs, it loses much of the incentive to control the latter. Airline deregulation, beginning in 1978, made this point graphically. Previously airlines were almost automatically granted higher fares to cover their costs. But, of course, they still sought to attract customers, so while they were required to charge fixed fares, they competed by introducing other, costly services. (On North Atlantic flights, which were regulated similarly, limits had to be imposed on how much airlines could spend on each meal.) When deregulation forced airlines to compete in fares, it became apparent that large costs, which passengers did not find warranted, had been absorbed into operations. Between 1978 and 1985 average airline fares, adjusted for inflation, fell about 50 percent. Competition revealed that the previous system of regulation stymied, rather than encouraged, efficiency. From 1978 to 1985 deregulation is estimated to have saved consumers more than $10 billion. Deregulation also saved users of trucks and rail services about $25 billion. That is how important (mis)conceptions about economic operations can be when embedded in public policies. And that, therefore, is the difference that entrepreneurs can make altering political methods.

"Coping with Society's Concerns"

Entrepreneurs must operate within the larger context of social ground rules and conventions. Thus when society shifts its interests, businesses have to scramble to meet the new challenges. To compound the uncertainty, entrepreneurs can never reconstruct more than a small part of the total picture; that is, of the knowledge dispersed among society. A market system copes with this global complexity through prices, which provide distilled, decentralized information to individual businesses. When the public becomes more interested in safer products or less cholesterol in foods, for example, the price of such products increases. This prompts businessmen to work harder developing them. An individual entrepreneur need not understand all the forces behind such a development—the change in the price summarizes all relevant information as well as provides the incentive to implement it. Ironically, the narrowness of each individual's vantage becomes a strength when melded with others. Not bound by comprehensive guidelines, entrepreneurs pursue their own insights and inclinations, often turning up surprisingly idiosyncratic—and effective—solutions. When these individual solutions are pooled in the marketplace, the synergism can greatly enhance output.

Twentieth-century public policymakers have not placed much confidence in this self-acting solution, however. They believe that centralized, governmental direction is required to solve major social problems. A clear demonstration occurred during the 1970s when the price of oil shot up from $3 to $35 a barrel. The government decided its main effort should be a synthetic fuels program to convert low-grade coal into gasoline and other petroleum substitutes. But the project made sense only if the price of oil climbed above $75 a barrel. This, in turn, required the naïve assumption that people would go on using the same amount of oil at much higher prices because they lacked the capacity to devise substitutes. Not surprisingly, consumers found substitutes and suppliers found new supplies. The program never produced any oil and has been dismantled after wasting more than $10 billion.

Had the entrepreneurial procedures that the governmental program implied been understood, prospects would have appeared much less promising. For example, it began with too vague a goal—which was to produce more domestic energy. Entrepreneurs understand the importance of being very precise in identifying their targeted customers in order that their activity will zero in on a solution. They rehearse their business plan extensively, not only to clarify their plans, but also to assure potential supporters of the promise of the project. In contrast, the federal government failed to ensure such preparation. In large part, the energy program was crafted to win the support of several constituencies whose goals often contradicted. For example, domestic oil prices were held below the world level, encouraging consumption while tens of billions of dollars were being spent to create substitutes.

The federal government also neglected the vital step of following up on the original plan. Entrepreneurs recognize that the original conception requires continual refinements to achieve good results. They are willing to devote sustained effort because it is their own creation; that is, they expect to reap a good share of the rewards. But the incentives for bureaucrats are to pursue ends that often stymie improvements. They are rewarded by the amount of resources they employ—the bigger the better—and by publicizing problems that seem to require more resources.

Government also has difficulties managing risk. In contradiction to the prevailing stereotype, entrepreneurs do not enjoy assuming risks. Most eschew them by breaking goals into smaller, more manageable tasks. The federal program to build synthetic fuels, however, never received that constant reappraisal and modification. It continued on its initial path despite accumulating evidence that it was headed down the wrong path. Entrepreneurs employing their own resources would have made numerous midcourse corrections, thereby substantially reducing the risk that the completed effort would be so disastrous. But lacking such incentives the federal program plowed ahead using tens of billions of dollars.

The "energy crisis" was only one of many public initiatives with which business has had to cope. In the last half of the twentieth century American business faced numerous concerns under the heading of "social responsibility." This was not new, but it was sharply intensified as business decisions were inevitably drawn into the expanding public arena. The issue turns on how far business's responsibility extends beyond the obvious necessity of returning a competitive profit. Since World War II a sizable component of the public has come to believe that business does indeed have such a broad responsibility. It is obvious that business decisions in regard to location, product design, hiring, and prices affect parties other than the firm's stockholders. But, increasingly, the notion has taken hold that market solutions as evidenced in prices do not fully incorporate such concerns.

Some programs by businesses are intended to further both profits and social responsibility. For instance, large companies often invest in the neighborhoods of their enterprises, recognizing that the amenities of the locality affect their operations, especially in retaining employees. A business that supports local schools and retailers need not be slighting profit considerations nor be motivated solely by a social conscience. Usually social responsibility is understood to be sacrificing profits in order to obtain other forms of social gains. The central issue is whether a business should undertake efforts not benefiting itself, such as shouldering the extra cost of employing handicapped workers when adequate labor is available. Of course in some labor markets companies resort to busing in disadvantaged people from a considerable distance or providing extra training in order to obtain appropriate help. But such moves can be explained by the company's imperative to make profits. Only going beyond direct self-interest would be considered true social responsibility. Designing products that have extra safety features, reduced environmental impact, or other such features beyond what the market compensates or laws require are further examples.

The social role that is appropriate for business turns on how the criteria are specified. Discussions to date have drifted because an operational rule in lieu of maximizing profits has not been generally accepted. If business were to seek goals other than profits, these goals could be literally hundreds of different objectives. How should one choose among them? Is making a product safer more valuable than developing production processes that pollute less? Or is either increment more valuable, say, than the extra costs of hiring a handicapped worker? To complicate matters, what is commonly perceived to be important often changes dramatically. Concerns that were urgent a few years ago are largely forgotten today. The urgency to conserve fuel now is replaced by that of protecting jobs in mature industries and, in turn, by the provision of day-care centers. To the extent that meeting one concern requires investments not adaptable to other ends, costs linger beyond the shift in public concern.

The general uncertainty is a logical result of the manner by which "social responsibility" is shaped by government. Without public sanctions, the prospects of instituting most variants of it would vanish and its advocates would lose heart. As illustrated above, policies undertaken by government forums lack the vested interests to develop them to fruition. Agencies have little vested interest in increasing energy supplies. Succeeding therein, for example, often runs counter to expanding their bureau. Thus initial objectives—

usually vague themselves—are easily diverted and captured by entrenched interests.

Businesses generally exhibit more "social responsibility" as their vulnerability to government pressures increases. Historically AT&T has worked hard promoting the image that it serves the public. (The recent dissolution of the system weakened this incentive at the national level.) It has been subject to government regulation at several levels and, therefore, vulnerable to public perceptions, which influenced the regulatory bodies setting its rates. In other words, those businesses that are most vulnerable to extramarket pressures, usually meaning government, tend to emphasize public responsibility. When the regulators must approve a firm's basic parameters of operations, it understandably curries their favor. And their opinions, by and large, tend to reflect that of the general population. When people consider you a good citizen, you receive help— and conversely. Companies subject to less regulation are correspondingly less likely to employ such strategies.

Taxes with Representation

Taxes are a central influence on business. Modern government must extract a sizable share of resources from the private sector in order to finance its activities, and the manner of doing so significantly shapes business operations. For example, the 1981 tax cut substantially reduced the amortization time for depreciation of durable assets. Writing off investments faster postponed paying taxes, which prompted enormous ingenuity in creating new arrangements to maximize benefits from the faster schedules. New institutions were created, particularly in real estate financing, to leverage tax benefits, producing large credits in a short period. Investors in high marginal tax brackets could offset sizable amounts of taxes. This explains the resulting boom in qualifying real estate and the promotions of related limited partnerships until the law was changed in 1987.

Americans' manipulation of tax provisions illustrated their increased sensitivity to such influences since World War II. When during World War II the income tax was raised dramatically to its highest level, the rationale supplied was that people will do pretty much what they had planned anyway because they are not very responsive to taxes. In retrospect this sounds naïve, particularly as the highest rate was raised to 91 percent. When taxes take 91 cents out of every dollar earned, one could profitably spend 91 percent of his time devising means to avoid taxes rather than pursuing socially productive activities. Recent studies make clear that high marginal tax rates reduce and redirect work effort. Individuals will systematically avoid taxed activities, diverting their efforts to those assessed at lower rates. For instance, until 1986 the tax on capital gains was much lower than the corresponding income tax rate, commonly half. Thus the incentive was to shift income from regularly taxed sources into deferred income treated as capital gains. While the response of participants is understandable, the result is reduced productivity, lower national income, and resources shifted to less socially productive areas.

Americans' sensitivity to the effects of taxes has grown until politicians across the spectrum now recognize that high marginal taxes are self-defeating. During the early 1980s considerable attention was drawn to the "underground economy," which, by bypassing taxed activity, threatened to destroy the integrity of the entire tax system. The experience supported the logic of the "Laffer Curve," which predicted that taxes can be raised sufficiently to reduce rather than increase total tax revenue because the incentive to shield income outweighs the increased tax per dollar. Calculations suggest this occurs at about 30 percent.[4] And that's why Congress, while disagreeing about the distribution of tax changes, has worked to reduce marginal tax rates to about that level in recent years.

Americans have become more skeptical about the effect of government policies on the economy. Accordingly they have pulled back in antitrust policies, regulation of natural monopolies, and high marginal taxation. This trend seems likely to continue because it is being pushed along by a learning process. Americans turned to government because they perceived that problems were appearing in the operation of the private sector. Externalities prompted pollution. Natural monopolies allowed price exploitation. Significant disadvantages in access to resources necessitated bolstering the income of the poor. Each of these concerns was believed to require a compensatory government program. But not having tried such programs previously, Americans were naïve about how they actually would work. Since World War II the United States has, in effect, conducted a huge experiment in large-scale government. Americans have concluded that it yielded less than promised and that its programs required restructuring.

Previously the focus was on market failure—of which there were undeniable examples—with the unstated assumption that government would smoothly correct the problem. The latter would clearly identify the problem and apply a mechanism tailored to zero in on the solution. Now it has become evident that governments also misfire. Thus substituting a government program for private efforts is choosing between imperfect means. But while Americans have become more skeptical as to the value of government programs, they have stopped well short of returning to the common view in the middle of the nineteenth century. Compared with two decades ago they doubt the efficiency of government and are willing to consider some retrenching. Not infrequently they have asked whether it is worthwhile to pay additional taxes to support a program, and increasingly the answer has been no.

A corollary shift has occurred in the intellectual view as to government's appropriate role. In the 1930s and 1940s the Keynesian interpretation was adopted. It held that, left to itself, the economy would stagnate without government stimulation. This provided much of the rationale for a large government role in taxing and spending. In the last twenty years, however, much has been learned about the numerous barriers that make it difficult for government to offset recessions and inflations in a timely fashion. Again, the lesson is often that initiatives—no matter how well intended—can do as much damage as good.

If this intellectual trend continues, the next decade will see government pull back from business. Recent years have witnessed a marked slowdown in the introduction of new regulations. The 1960s was the era that "declared war" on poverty, launched major initiatives to deal with regional underdevelopment, and enacted major civil rights and affirmative-action legislation. Government attempted to correct all the perceived major problems in society. The resulting legislation became well embedded in society. This contrasted with the 1980s, during which contemporary proposals such as industrial policy and comparable worth did not go nearly as far. The types of initiatives believed crucial twenty years ago are commonly dismissed today. This reflects a significant change in judging government's role in society and, therefore, its role in business. This is evident in the federal register, which contains all existing laws and regulations. New regulations have slowed down significantly, and many are modifications of existing rulings rather than new initiatives. While an enormous number remain in effect, the change in tone is noticeable.

Entrepreneuring the New Doubts

The increased skepticism about government programs created opportunities for a new type of political entrepreneur. Of course, politicians often run "against Washington." Jimmy Carter, who derided the federal tax system, is a recent example. On taking office, however, he attempted actively to manage the entire federal system. The test of an entrepreneur is taking action to implement his vision.

Ronald Reagan clearly tapped antigovernmental sentiments in 1980 to become president. But probably the clearest example of implementing the new outlook is a former economics professor who achieved national attention primarily for devising one graphic vehicle to that end. As a modern scholar in economic behavior, both in markets and public institutions, Phil Gramm understood the environment that promoted special interests. He could retrace the FDR formula, in which groups with a concentrated interest created an advantage through information and access to win governmental support. The special interests could shift the collective costs of their program onto the less-organized and less-informed taxpayers, pushing the programs far beyond that which individuals would purchase if they had to buy them individually. In other words, the contemporary environment encouraged government spending well into the range where the social returns were negative. This explains Congress's consistent incentive to overspend as evidenced in the un-relieved deficits adding a trillion and a half dollars to the national debt in the last two decades.

Phil Gramm was elected to Congress in Texas in 1980 and soon became known as one of the "boll weevils," a group of mostly South-ern Democrats who worked for fiscal conservatism within the two-party structure. Having been stripped of his committee assignments for supporting the Republican initiatives to cut spending in 1981, Gramm resigned his Democratic post and ran for office and was reelected as a Republican. Then in 1984 he was elected senator from Texas.

Gramm understood that though much federal spending was producing a net loss overall, it might be repackaged to benefit the nation. If all programs could be lumped together and cut simulta-neously, the total benefits to the economy would exceed the cost. Along with Senator Rudman of New Hampshire he seized upon rising concern over the budget deficit to introduce the now-famous Gramm-Rudman Resolution, which required automatic across-the-board cuts in federal spending until the deficit was eliminated.

Congress has succeeded in sidestepping much of the intention of Gramm-Rudman, but the force of the idea lingers on, and even the most spendthrift representatives have been forced to acknowl-edge its influence. One indication of the generality of the idea is contained in the 1986 tax reform. The underlying idea was that total losses from concessions to special interests in taxation were greater than the public benefit derived. Thus general reductions in rates offset by eliminations of loopholes would produce a net gain. And when Congress was able to create such a package, much to the surprise of many in 1986, it demonstrated how political entrepreneurs can reform institutions to create net benefits.

Both the Gramm-Rudman Resolution and the 1986 tax reform demonstrate that repackaging the externalities of special interest behavior such that they are internalized can lead to net positive-sum behavior. In other words, just as economists have known that charg-ing people for behavior that formerly was borne by others would lead to better and more efficient behavior, so these new fiscal innovations have encouraged participants to use resources more efficiently. These appear to be models that other political entrepreneurs are likely to adopt and extend in the coming years. They build on the general conception that government needs to be reined in, and upon the rewards to those politicians who create net benefits for American citizens through government.

16

America's Advantage in Entrepreneurship

America emerged from World War II unchallenged, far and away the largest, most powerful economy in the world. In the intervening years other economies have gained ground, reducing that lead, but American business continued advancing across a wide frontier of goods and services, which the others have yet to reach. American productivity and per capita incomes have increased about two and a half times since 1945, creating enormous new opportunities for consumers and the entrepreneurs serving them. Even this impressive quantitative measure understates the improvement in economic well-being, however. Innovations such as television, polio vaccine, stereo sound systems, automatic transmissions, direct dialing, open-heart surgery, microwave ovens, plastic trash bags, satellite communications, jet travel, and computerized reservations give Americans opportunities that were not possible at any cost in 1945.

The United States became the wealthiest large economy in world history. This widespread affluence dictated much of the thrust of entrepreneurial efforts. Having met such basic needs as food and shelter, Americans turned their energies to improving their lives. Consumers put disproportionately large shares of added income into uses that extended and improved the quality of their lives.

Consider, for example, the gains to well-being through advances in medical care. By the eve of World War II the incidence of, and resulting deaths from, many diseases had already been severely reduced compared with most of human history. Improvements in public water supplies, insect control, vaccines, food, and housing accounted for most of the advance. If a severe case of pneumonia or tuberculosis developed, however, a doctor could do little more than isolate the patient, making him as comfortable as possible. In other words, improvements in health were primarily the result of higher incomes, not better medical techniques.

In the late 1930s scientists achieved modest success with antibiotics to attack bacterial infections, developing sulfa drugs. Then during World War II, penicillin, the basic "wonder drug," was created. Increasingly powerful derivatives as well as antibiotics with wider applications, such as streptomycin, followed. These proved effective not only against such basic ailments as pneumonia, rheumatic fever, tuberculosis, malaria, typhus, typhoid, and venereal disease but more than one hundred other assorted diseases as well. In addition, drugs were developed to counteract a wide range of nonbacterial ailments such as hypertension, hyperthyroidism, blood clotting, gout, muscle spasms, allergies, ulcers, epilepsy, and motion sickness.

Two other advances in pharmaceuticals were especially beneficial. Most individuals previous to World War II who became too mentally disoriented to function in society were institutionalized. This often meant a lifetime sentence, because only a small percentage of adults improved spontaneously. Beginning in the 1950s such psychotherapeutic drugs as chlorpromazine (Thorazine) and meprobamate (Miltown) allowed many of these "hopeless" patients to return to normal society. Even for severe cases still requiring confinement, the new medications reduced the necessity for harsh physical controls such as cells and shackles. Proportionately, three-quarters of the population in mental institutions had been freed by the 1970s. In addition, the general populace now accepted treatment of milder forms of anxiety and depression through tranquilizers and barbiturates. As a consequence of the new drugs Americans began to view emotional difficulties as treatable illnesses, something to take to a medical clinic, rather than as the horrifying, unspeakable disaster of years past when the family attempted to hide the victim in a back room.

Another major medicinal advance beginning in the early 1960s was the introduction of oral contraceptives, or what became commonly known as "the pill." For the first time it provided a highly effective, nonmechanical insurance against pregnancies. Combining this with the major reduction in childhood mortality that had been achieved by this time meant that couples could plan the size of their family very closely. An indication of how strongly they valued such control is that by the early 1980s half of American females of childbearing age were using oral contraceptives.

The rapidly rising costs of medical care in the postwar period originated outside of the prices of drugs. Their cost as a proportion of the GNP actually decreased despite the enormous expansion in services they were rendering. The explanation lies in the entrepreneurial gains in organizing drug research, which raised productivity and reduced prices. For example, the discovery of penicillin was spectacularly effective, but in retrospect employed an inefficient, ad hoc approach. It was first identified in a lab in London in 1928 by Alexander Fleming. But it was not until 1939 that techniques improved enough so that isolating and growing the culture was commercially effective.

The story is commonly repeated how a stray bit of penicillin mold landed on Fleming's slide of bacteria, killing everything around it. It is less noted that this serendipitous event had occurred in several other labs, but the researchers, not having their attention riveted on antibiotics, overlooked its significance. Basically Fleming tried substances randomly until discovering one that worked. This style of research is characteristic of a science in its early stage, when basic principles are insufficiently developed to pinpoint investigations. Advances since the 1930s have allowed research to isolate the cause of a malady more precisely and, therefore, specify drugs tailor-made to counteract it.

This systematic approach to drug research is best exemplified by P. Roy Vagelos, who became research director of Merck and Co. in 1976 and subsequently president. Being a medical researcher, Vagelos believed that understanding the basic molecular structure of human tissue was by far the most promising strategy for devising medical treatments. Therefore, at Merck he stressed basic research directed toward central concerns such as heart disease, high blood pressure, ulcers, and other applications employing new biotechnologies. He fostered a company culture that attracted top scientists, giving them the facilities and the support to elicit their creative interests. This organization has created path-breaking drugs for a wide variety of problems such that today Merck has an impressive array of commercial drugs, with further innovations emerging steadily from the development pipeline. This shift to systematic science, which identifies the specific source of the problem, earlier transformed industries such as metallurgy and electronics. It portends a continued high rate of productivity growth in the biological sector. It also exemplifies a managerial style that enlists the best from knowledgeable workers, a skill that is likely to become increasingly important as highly trained workers focusing on creative tasks loom larger in the economy.

From 1950 to 1980 medical expenditures other than drugs rose from $10 billion to $218 billion, more than doubling their share of the GNP. Hospital costs alone rose from less than $4 billion to almost $100 billion, a rate of compounded increase of more than 10 percent per year. There was considerable public grousing and resultant government initiatives to stem these cost increases. It is true that employer-paid medical plans helped by special tax treatment encouraged use of medical services, but spending could not have increased that dramatically without a robust demand by much of the population. Employees would not have tolerated the necessary large sacrifices in their take-home wages unless they believed the resulting medical care was valuable.

A short survey of the improvements in medical services since 1940 explains why people should want more of them despite rising costs. Certain operations such as appendectomies, hysterectomies, and gallbladder removal became nearly routine. Improvements in anesthesia, antibiotics, and surgical techniques eliminated most of the risk that previous to 1940 had caused people to dread and postpone surgery. Moreover, new forms of surgery began to be performed that were inconceivable before World War II. Heart surgery to repair damaged valves or arteries became possible with the introduction of the heart-lung machine. Microsurgical techniques were developed to restore hearing and severed nerves. And operations to repair the effects of congenital disabilities or accidents became more common as well as more sophisticated.

Surgical techniques were supplemented by a host of new diagnostic and treatment techniques. Some gave patients with a substantial likelihood of quick death a long extension of normal life. Others such as coronary monitoring equipment, artificial kidney machines, multicharacteristic automated blood testing, and computerized axial tomographs (CAT scanners) for three-dimensional X rays drastically reduced the necessity for surgery to diagnose internal malfunctions. Such devices were expensive, but given the dramatic improvements in well-being they provided, most people found them well worth the price. Since World War II, the average life span has grown by a decade and, despite considerable publicity about modern medicine being able to keep "vegetables" alive, the health of older Americans has also improved.[1]

Lifetime Learning

Education has also been a postwar growth sector. In 1950 Americans spent $8.8 billion or 3.3 percent of the GNP on it. By 1980 that expenditure had increased by more than eighteen times to $166 billion and almost doubled its share of the GNP to 6.3 percent. Underlying this surge was a large increase in the average amount of education. Before World War II a high school diploma was a significant accomplishment; less than 30 percent of the population twenty-five years and older had achieved one. In the postwar period it became a necessary entrée for all but the least desirable jobs. By 1980, 68 percent of the population twenty-five years and older had completed at least twelve years of schooling, and for persons aged twenty-five to twenty-nine the level was about 85 percent. Moreover, a larger fraction of the population was going on for a college degree, which was itself becoming a necessary prerequisite for entering more occupations. By 1980 almost one-quarter of the population aged twenty-five to twenty-nine held college degrees.

The demand for education reflected more than a quest for status. Calculations show that it was a profitable investment for most individuals. In fact, until the mid-1970s the return on resources spent for education was higher than that of most other kinds of investments. This accounted for its rapid growth up to that time. Education enhanced the productivity of labor, the resource responsible for two-thirds of the economy's output by enhancing general judgment as well as raising specific skills.

Education has also helped labor keep abreast of improvements in technology. Changes have come so fast that entire industries have been banished and new ones developed within a generation. This has made "retooling" and "second careers" common vocabulary. Much of the adjustment has been gradual and accomplished through less dramatic means, however. "Continuing education" became a growth industry after World War II. Some was initiated by adults seeking out evening classes, but much was sponsored by businesses either to keep their employees up to speed or, in the case of new hires, getting them to the starting gate.

Most of the short courses provided by businesses sought to enhance workplace skills. These were traditional offerings such as quality control, telephone skills, and typing (now word processing). These were increasingly joined by more general workplace skills such as time management, goal setting, and motivation. The last two programs tapped a strong, personal interest among employees to make more of their lives, of which working was obviously a major component. Such interests were given a major boost in the 1930s by two entrepreneurs of "success skills" who each wrote a seminal book. Dale Carnegie, who developed an education program in public speaking, wrote the still quoted *How to Win Friends and Influence People,* and Napoleon Hill, who interviewed and studied the lives of many successful Americans, wrote *Think and Grow Rich.* Although both obviously appealed to long-standing interests of mankind, the systematic study to achieve such goals was novel. In the last fifty years these pioneering works have expanded in a major outpouring of books, lectures, workshops, audiotapes, and videotapes. As in any maturing industry, individual efforts have grown into substantial firms. This has also meant that as part of the enhanced interest in entrepreneurship, individuals now believe they can consciously shape their careers and lives as well as a business.

For Fun and Profit

By 1985 Americans were spending more than 10 percent of their income on recreation and travel for recreational purposes. This growth had occurred despite the influence of television—the most significant innovation in this sector, which of itself drastically reduced spending. Television undoubtedly consumed most of the leisure time of Americans in the postwar period. Surveys indicated that by the mid-1960s the average American was watching television four to five hours a day. This was obvious to the operators of movie theaters, who had ridden out the depressed economy to become one of the most popular forms of entertainment in the 1930s. Now there were fewer such managers, with survivors scraping along on weekend showings, if not turning over their premises to branch banks or variety stores.

Television captured such a large share of the public's time by introducing a medium that was drastically cheaper as well as more convenient. The direct costs to viewers were only a few cents an hour, including the cost of the set and the electricity. (Less than one-half of 1 percent of the GNP was being spent on an activity that was occupying one-third of people's waking hours!) In addition it was right at hand in the living room or, as the number of families with two or more sets multiplied, in the den or bedroom or seaside cottage. There was no need to go to the trouble and expense of getting dressed and driving to a theater. But even including the indirect costs of programming, the medium was cheaper than virtually all other forms of entertainment. One billion viewing hours per day spread production costs very thin.

Most of the expense of television was paid indirectly by commercials. Sponsors saw the demand very clearly, however, particularly 100 million potential customers in prime viewing hours. And the advertisers understood the return from underwriting expensive programming to command their attention. Television created economies of scale in entertainment far beyond anything experienced to date. Performances that seldom had been seen live by more than 50,000 people could now reach national and even worldwide audiences. It is understandable, therefore, that attractions began to be shaped around the demands of television. To a large degree spectator sports such as professional football, basketball, and hockey—which expanded most in the postwar period—were those of predictable duration, rapid action, and compact courts; in short, conditions favorable for television coverage. This also favored increasing the salaries of performers who excelled in such forums. With millions of viewers at stake, producers found the contributions of a star fullback or a news anchorperson worth millions of dollars a year.[2]

About half of Americans' recreational expenditures were used for travel, 80 percent of which was within the United States. Innovations that lowered the cost of travel for a large portion of the population reinforced the effect of higher incomes. Previous to World War II most lengthy trips within the United States used railroads, and most trips overseas employed ocean liners. But since 1945 expressways and automobile ownership have become almost universal, national characteristics. Not only has the car become the predominant means of travel, but it substantially increased the amount of travel per person. The expansion was encouraged by the appearance of ubiquitous, dependable travel services such as motels, gas stations, and restaurants. In addition, forms of entertainment adapted to the automobile experienced an upsurge. One was the drive-in theater, the only segment of movie theaters to expand after 1945. Another was the revival of the amusement park, or theme park as it is now called in recognition of its larger size and more elaborate motif. Unlike the Coney Island–style amusement park, which was constructed from 1890 to

1920 at the end of a streetcar line designed to serve its city, the theme park drew almost exclusively on automobile traffic. This allowed the clientele to come from a much larger area—hundreds of miles was not unusual—and, therefore, come in much larger numbers.

For most travel across the oceans, jet planes replaced ocean liners. This also expanded travel possibilities for a large portion of the population. Not only was modern air travel cheaper, but it also reduced another major cost: that of the time required to reach a destination. Traveling coast-to-coast by train, for example, consumed three days each way. This was a large slice out of a two- or even three-week vacation. But with regular, frequent departures, air travel became practical for shorter vacations and even weekend trips. It also heightened competition for tourists among localities. Ski resorts in New England found themselves competing with those in the Rocky Mountains and the Alps, and Miami Beach frequently was passed over for sunny spots in the Caribbean or Mexico.

WALT DISNEY AND THE RISE OF MODERN ENTERTAINMENT

Walt Disney, born in 1901, grew up moving around the Midwest as his father tried various locales and occupations. From early on it was clear that he had a strong interest in commercial art. He took classes and sold cartoon slides that were shown between features at Kansas City movie theaters. In 1923 he moved to Hollywood to be near the best technical expertise and began a sustained effort to produce cartoons for the movies. His first notable contribution, appearing in 1928, was *Steamboat Willie,* which featured an early version of Mickey Mouse. It was also the first cartoon to employ its own sound. Another milestone was the production of *Snow White and the Seven Dwarfs* in 1937, marking the production of full-length cartoon films. Disney's main efforts in movies continued until about 1950, when the demand for such programs began to taper off. But he had acquired a valuable, irreproducible asset, which could be directed to other outlets. Ever since his arrival in Hollywood in 1923, Disney had been developing a large artistic staff, inspiring them to unequaled excellence.

Disney tried television programming in 1950, but it became clear that the demand for his style of films had peaked. Thus, he turned his creative energy to another of his dreams—Disneyland. Part of its success was achieved by updating the amusement park to the second half of the twentieth century and the pervasive influence of the automobile. This allowed a much larger facility and, therefore, the chance to develop extensive, elaborate features that placed it well beyond competitors. Disney also capitalized on his well-known cartoon characters, using them to embellish and advertise the park. Characteristically, Disney devoted much more attention to the design and the details of his park than proprietors of earlier models. The instincts of the cartoonist told him that everything had to be "picture perfect." It was successful from its opening in 1955.

Walt Disney World opened outside Orlando, Florida, in 1971, and incorporated much of what had been learned from Disneyland. From the beginning it was designed as the centerpiece of a much larger development, incorporating a wide range of accommodations and recreation facilities. EPCOT, an "adult version" of Disney World and a type of permanent world's fair, was opened in 1982. A large water-recreation area, an elaborate replica of a Hollywood studio tour, and a huge convention center are being added. It has become the world's largest tourist center, attracting more than 25 million people a year, more than 10 percent of America's total population.

Understandably, competitors sought to duplicate Disney's successes: the Six Flags amusement park expanded to a half-dozen parks; the excellent Marriott organization entered the industry with its Great America parks; the Kings organization produced Kings Dominion in Virginia and Kings Island in Ohio. But none were able to come close to the sustained excellence that Disney had put together or even reach 10 percent of its size. Disney also contradicted the presumption that Americans could not compete against foreign firms, especially those in Japan, by entering that market without challengers. Disney created the ultimate barrier to entry in an industry—a sustained organizational excellence that permeated its employees and innovations such that competitors were simply not able to approach its cumulative success. Thus Walt Disney personified the attractive qualities that made the new recreation, travel, and entertainment industry grow so rapidly in postwar America. His success in two of its major industries showed the strength and comprehensiveness of his skills.[3]

Growing Powerful by Thinking Small

The expansion of the service sector in the postwar period sometimes prompted the concern that the economy was doomed to stagnate. Services, it was assumed, used large amounts of labor, which, it was further assumed, could not be reorganized into more productive arrangements. The economy would cease growing, sliding into a stagnant cul-de-sac. One invention undercut much of the logic of that prediction, however, by showing how a new technology could provide many unanticipated means of extending labor. Electronics, particularly its most notable derivative, computers, suggests why growth can continue permeating well into the service sector.

Efforts to create computers began in the 1940s, prompted by applications where making complex calculations rapidly was critical, such as artillery and missile trajectories. By current standards the first machines were slow, expensive, enormous, and consumed a large amount of electricity, which they converted into a correspondingly large amount of troublesome heat. A key to much of the subsequent progress was the development of the transistor in 1948. By utilizing a few electrons passing through thin wafers of material, it duplicated the sorting functions of bulky, costly vacuum tubes. The next four decades progressed toward the ultimate implementation of that ideal as techniques were developed to make transistors smaller and able to stack more together on a single chip, thereby reducing the time, material, and electricity per calculation. Compared with the first ENIAC computer developed at the University of Pennsylvania in 1946, models in the 1980s were more than 100,000 times faster, sold at less than 1 percent of the initial cost, and used less than .1 percent of the electricity.

Predictably, the enormous reduction in the cost of calculating spurred entrepreneurs to find a broad array of applications. They also expanded the potential by developing numerous devices to transform information into more usable formats. These were reflected in a new group of common terms in the modern vocabularies. *Memories* stored data between applications. *Programming* provided the detailed instructions to process crude numbers into usable answers. Printers and plotters turned out *hard copy*. The new technology's impact has been far-reaching, and undoubtedly far from assimilated yet. The applications have spread well beyond the initial objective of speeding calculations. A far from complete list includes engine controls on automobiles, high-quality music recordings, factory automation, three-dimensional X rays, advanced telephone switching, electronic mail, word-processing equipment, and, of course, video games. This versatility resulted because the new technology is much more fundamental than simply a better adding machine. Essentially it is a general means that very economically processes signals and can automatically execute or issue commands. Hence it can duplicate many mechanical, electrical, management, and communication processes. By this index, future applications will be limited only by human ingenuity.

ENTREPRENEURING COMPUTERS

Arguably the entrepreneur who best exemplifies the development of modern electronics is Thomas Watson, Sr. Born in 1874 Watson spent his early career at National Cash Register under John Patterson, who is often credited as being the father of modern salesmanship. In 1911 Watson moved to the forerunner of IBM, which then produced office machines such as time clocks and accounting machinery. When Watson assumed its presidency he began instilling the company culture for which IBM has since become famous. It was built around a respect for individuals, encouraging their personal contribution while demanding high personal commitment. Employees were given extensive orientation and their skills were honed and encouraged by a company policy of lifetime employment.

In the 1930s and 1940s Watson's policy was well ahead of its time and was often demeaned as paternal and dictatorial. But its ultimate vindication was its adoption by most of America's best large enterprises after World War II. It was also widely adopted in Japan, forming a good part of the "Japanese style of management" that Americans found so attractive in the 1970s.

Watson's other major contribution was the *conceptual* basis of the computer. While others were developing a super adding machine, he visualized the advantages of a machine that could be shifted among tasks—in other words, reprogrammed—and repeat routine functions; that is, had a memory. Though this design was just beginning in 1956 when Watson died and IBM was only a small fraction of what it has since become, it is the basic design for the modern computer.

IBM was not the first company to sell computers commercially. But consistent with its traditional strategy, it promoted the sales and service aspects that were to prove critical in their use. Without skilled operators the computer is simply a large, intimidating calculator. It requires considerable programming and hands-on development to become effective for the typical businessperson. Watson's strategy of stressing customer service was tailor-made for that environment. As the price of computers fell, widening feasible applications, IBM's comprehensive support eased new groups of uninitiated operators into use. One measure of the value of such services to customers was that IBM was typically able to charge premiums of 20 to 40 percent for their equipment over competitive models. They were providing relevant, complementary services. Much like Cyrus McCormick, who discovered the essential combination of services his customers required, Thomas Watson demonstrated that helping customers use his product was the central component of his product.[4]

PRODUCTIVE SERVICE

One of the more dramatic examples of how the productivity of services can be bolstered is evident in a firm that has been in the entrepreneurial limelight in recent years. Fred Smith founded Federal Express in 1971, moving it to Memphis in 1973. An oft-repeated story tells how Smith introduced the concept in a paper at Yale. (It is also commonly reported that he received only a *C* for the paper—a feature that students particularly enjoy citing. But because most concepts improve through review the grade may well reflect Smith's progress to that date rather than an instructor's myopia.) Smith sought a system to assure overnight delivery of packets and small packages throughout the United States. He judged correctly that the urgency of business documents, replacement parts, and out-of-stock items would grow much faster than the economy.

In order to succeed, however, this type of environment had to be tackled in a big way. Comprehensive service requires a big commitment to facilities before consumers can see that the service is so usefully comprehensive. In fact, in its early years Smith's venture came close to failure when receipts failed to cover the overhead of a large system. Now volume is working for Federal Express. Sixty-five large planes deliver some 600,000 items to Memphis early each morning to be sorted on forty-five miles of conveyer belts and loaded back into the planes for delivery. Extensive use of computers down to individual delivery trucks allows each package to be closely monitored, assuring the "absolutely, positively" on-time delivery by which the company has made its hallmark. As this assurance has become commonplace, businesses have reorganized procedures to make the most of it. Some firms have stocked supplies in Memphis in order to provide almost immediate service on rush items.

Overnight delivery is clearly a service business; no tangible product results, just speeding up the movement of parcels from one location to another. It also seems to demand an irreducible amount of labor, picking up, sorting, and delivering items. In other words, it matches the prescription for stagnation of productivity that is so widely anticipated. Yet Federal Express exemplifies just the opposite. The company uses large amounts of capital—trucks, sorting warehouses, computers, and jet transports (the latter at about $25 million each)—yet the average output of its workers is very high. Federal Express is an instructive example of how American services are developing. In contrast to the overblown portrayal of service jobs being dead-end positions in fast-food outlets, more than half of new openings require extensive skills and pay well above average. As at Federal Express, many are leveraged by extensive computer services to produce large amounts of output per worker. It only stands to reason that in an economy where labor continues to grow more expensive, employers would show concentrated ingenuity raising its return.

The Rise of Self-Conscious Entrepreneurship

The growth of service sectors in the postwar period encouraged managers to enlist workers to raise quality in their offerings. Since the beginning of the twentieth century, scholars of business organizations have been examining how the structure and the policies of organizations are correlated with their performances. It has long been recognized that firms facing similar markets and employing comparable equipment achieve markedly different levels of productivity. It recalls the guide conducting a tour of a factory who was asked, "How many people work here?" His answer was, "About half." Most organizations operate well below their full potential, as indicated by what other firms in those circumstances can accomplish. Thus separable, powerful forces must account for such large differences.

About the turn of the twentieth century scholars began studying the employment of workers in the same way that industrial engineers approached the design and the placement of machines. This "scientific management," which is often associated with Frederick W. Taylor, marked the beginning of the modern discipline of management. But the early theories got off on the wrong foot by treating individuals as if they were machines, attempting, for example, to find the most efficient motions to shovel material. This overlooked the fact that individuals have a creative will, which affects how much material they want to move. It also makes a big difference as to how much energy employees devote to detecting better techniques to move materials.

Management scholars began to recognize the importance of employee motivation in the 1930s and 1940s by distinguishing between what became known as Theory X and Theory Y. The former was the traditional and then still-dominant view of management, which said that employees disliked to work, were likely to shirk, and thus had to be supervised closely in order to remain productive. Theory Y, in contrast, assumed that individuals welcomed responsibility, would make innovative contributions, and wished to be recognized for doing a good job. Of course, the roots of the difference between these two views is more than a difference between the personal styles of managers. Older organizations, which typically used less-skilled workers and more routinized production techniques, were more likely to find Theory X appropriate. Modern services whose employees were more likely to exercise judgment would find Theory Y a better guide.

In the postwar period management theory has embodied the spirit of Theory Y, emphasizing that the attitude of employees plays a critical role. Studies of well-managed companies show they consciously place people at the heart of their philosophies and expend considerable effort encouraging, training, exhorting, and generally developing their employees.

The traditional management style might be termed *mechanical* because it views a business organization to be much like a machine. It assumes that if all parts of the organization are properly organized and behaving as directed, success follows. It is also top-down management, such that bosses give orders and underlings carry them out. The alternative style, which Thomas J. Peters and Robert H. Waterman, Jr., publicized in *In Search of Excellence,* builds on an *organic* model of organization, recognizing that each employee is a self-interested and self-directing individual.[5] The success of such an organization depends crucially on enlisting the interests and aspirations of every (independent) employee. Ignoring such aspirations by treating individuals as passive cogs in a machine often prompts them to work against the organization's interests.

Successful organizations publicize the contributions of their employees in order to encourage efforts toward the goals of the organization. They seek to foster a company culture, a style and set of shared beliefs with which employees can identify. In the most successful cultures the employees often support the company much like an extended family. Such a culture not only embodies the company's aspirations but, by contributing to employees' interests, focuses their energy on those objectives. Company cultures vary but most emphasize qualitative rather than quantitative goals. Few excellently managed companies state their primary goal as making profits. Of course it's silly to run a company intending *not* to make profits. But treating that as the foremost objective, as many companies tried in the 1960s, so diffuses the essential priority of serving customers that the company actually earns less.

Good companies emphasize quality in delivering and servicing their product. Caterpillar Tractor, for instance, has dominated major lines of heavy earth-moving equipment worldwide. In addition to building machinery to stand up under very adverse working conditions, Caterpillar prides itself on a service network that will deliver a part anywhere in the world within forty-eight hours. Considering the remote locations in which some of their machinery is used, this is an extraordinary promise. On the face of it, it is an expensive and wasteful commitment. It is costly to maintain dispersed depots of parts and/or purchase express transportation. But that forthright goal focuses the efforts of employees, making their efforts meaningful by emphasizing their achievement of exceptional standards.

McDonald's motto is QSCV, which stands for quality, service, cleanliness, and value. This handy acronym, kept in front of every employee, reminds them of what they are seeking to achieve. Other well-run companies have comparable themes. Delta Air Lines, for instance, proudly broadcasts that their organization is essentially people. Delta's ads stress that their individual employees all the way down to the baggage handlers have made a lifelong commitment to the organization and go to extraordinary lengths to assure excellent service.

These examples are drawn from very disparate markets: industrial equipment, fast food, and transportation, to which could be added the seemingly unlikely candidate of commodity automobile parts. Dana Corporation seeks the active participation of its employees in decisions at each level of the organization. It requires such contributions, because, as the company states it, no one has a routine job at Dana. General Electric, widely regarded as one of the best incubators of good managers in the United States, summed up its approach in the section on "Company Culture" on page five in their *1983 Annual Report*:

> Successfully implementing a strategy to become the world's most competitive enterprise demands a special company culture—one that's strongly cohesive, fostering a high

level of understanding of what General Electric is trying to do and be. We are advancing a culture that has a sense of urgency, that demands the very best and that emphasizes how crucial an individual's contribution can be to the success of our enterprise.

But while we challenge and shrink the non-essentials in our Company, our main goal is to expand—expand the climate for *excellence,* to get more and more people to do what even *they* thought they couldn't do.

Excellence means rewarding those who win—*and* rewarding those who try.

Note the boldness of the last sentence. Traditional management assumed that a mistake indicated an employee was not following orders and should be punished. Theory Y organizations, however, encourage employees to risk mistakes in searching for improvements. The *Report* continues:

> . . . the fuel for *entrepreneurship* is in a large company. Nurturing entrepreneurship at GE means expunging the punitive aspects of failure from the good try and, instead, focusing on rewards for those who will to dream, to reach, to dare.

This contrasts with the traditional Theory X view, but it also contrasts with what might be termed the logical approach. Logic suggests that large companies must follow certain procedures to remain competitively efficient. But better companies frequently violate some of these guidelines. Consider the classic concept of economies of scale where unit costs fall with increasing production runs. Most people, including those not in business, instinctively believe that relation is important. But the flip side is that large, specialized facilities can lose their adaptability as well as quality. Outstanding companies are seldom their industry's lowest-cost producer. They typically trade away competitiveness in cost to emphasize service and quality, which they perceive are more crucial to consumers. Entrepreneurial companies also avoid complicated and inflexible structures in order to encourage employees to innovate.

The logical mind-set also suggests careful planning in order to avoid mistakes. Proposals should be carefully cross-examined to screen out errors. But logic has limits in that no matter how meticulous the planning, the relative size of forces and influences can be discovered only in practice. Good organizations quickly move beyond formal planning to try out ideas. They have "a bias for action," eagerly testing concepts in prototypes or on sample customers. Innovation is seldom an exact science. It produces continual surprises, some of which suggest improvements along with the disappointments. Even the best-formulated products from the most careful companies prove disappointing. Du Pont, for example, spent enormous effort developing Corfam, a substitute for leather. It was cheaper, its quality more uniform, and it was less vulnerable to disruptions in natural materials. But consumers simply didn't like Corfam's appearance and texture, so, despite enormous investment, it had to be abandoned.

Procter and Gamble is widely considered one of the world's best marketers. It tests products extensively, samples consumers continuously, and quizzes buyers in focus groups. Thus when it commits a product to national sales, it expects a sizable share of the market. It expected its reconstituted potato chips, Pringles, to have important advantages over competitors. They were judged for quality, texture, taste, and convenience in thousands of experiments. But sales proved disappointing. No amount of testing can replace the test of the market. Good companies appreciate that, which explains why they strive to please their customers by constantly asking, "Is that what you seek? How can we improve it?" and, "What other features would you value?"

This qualification does not discredit the logical approach—to be successful every enterprise must be organized and focused on its primary objectives. But American businesses must be dynamic organisms that balance innovation against the advantages of statically efficient structures. Good entrepreneurs instinctively recognize that the optimal balance promotes both planning and ad hoc inspiration. Entrepreneurs endlessly analyze and project, but they also encourage the serendipitous discoveries that customers and alert employees invite.

The Continuing American Miracle

While societies sometimes lose heart, entrepreneurs instinctively look to the future. They have a good dose of faith, believing that somehow hard work will find a way, even when others are intimidated by current disappointments. Usually the entrepreneurs are proved correct. Those problems that cannot be turned into opportunities often fade into obscurity as emerging sectors leave them behind. Currently Americans are very concerned about foreign competitors, especially Japan. The Japanese seem to be beating Americans at their own game, producing quality goods for a large, affluent market. But this is much less surprising or threatening than widely perceived. Japan is the second-largest economy in the free world, so many of its products and technologies have followed paths similar to those in the United States. Given cost advantages in producing some goods, it is not surprising that Japan cultivated American sales into its largest foreign customer.

But American entrepreneurs are not immobilized by the prospects of competing with Japanese imports, because their prime function is opening *new* areas of competition. When Americans withdrew from serious competition in oceanshipping at the beginning of the nineteenth century, better opportunities were also bidding away its resources. The current American advantage in international trade is the entrepreneurial function of creating new enterprises or equity. Not only are Americans unchallenged in creating the new systems of participatory management, but they are the world's leader in creating new businesses as well. No other society prompts so many of its members to take the plunge to fashion their own ventures.

Along with the concern about foreign competition there has been much moaning about foreigners "buying up America." This is a gross misjudgment based on a few publicized incidents. It also overlooks that growing enterprises are one of America's best products, attractive to foreigners because their abundance makes them relatively cheap. Americans have a comparative advantage in entrepreneurship. It is one of their best products and contributions to the world. Foreign investors recognize this, trading their products to obtain it.

American entrepreneurship is irrepressible. It emerges in seemingly unlikely places under adverse circumstances. Consider, for example, Cleveland, which just a few years ago was considered the very epitome of the hopeless rust bowl. And consider plastics, which has relinquished the reputation it held for high tech right after World War II to other sectors. Furthermore, look to the automobile industry, another seeming loser, as your major customer. But Dan Moore was not intimidated by prevailing perceptions. He visualized a market for plastic parts with noise-suppression qualities and set to work creating them. Future automobile drivers will thank him for the quiet as well as reward his ingenuity. When entrepreneurship flourishes in such an environment, the economy is assured of an abundant, continuing supply.

Notes

1: FOUNDING THE COLONIES

1. The seminal discoveries are Moses Abromowitz, "Resource and Output Trends in the United States Since 1790," *American Economic Review* (May 1956), and Robert Solow, "Technical Change and the Aggregate Production Function," *Review of Economics and Statistics* (1957). Subsequent research has reinforced their discovery that increases in the productivity of resources rather than their quantity is the primary cause of growth.

2. Consider, for example, that long-standing staple, Samuel Eliot Morison and Henry Steele Commager, *The Growth of the American Republic* (New York: Oxford University Press, 1930, et cetera), which places primary emphasis on government decisions even before the federal government became large.

3. Peter Drucker, *Innovation and Entrepreneurship* (New York: Harper & Row, 1985), pp. 1–17.

4. An early example of management by objective (MBO), a tactic used to set clear goals while allowing employees to devise the best means to reach them. The difficulty was that at this stage of the venture—in effect, a feasibility study—the proper goals themselves were not yet clear.

5. Mark Casson, *The Entrepreneur: An Economics Theory* (Totowa, N.J.: Barnes & Noble, 1982).

2: INNOVATING WITHIN THE COLONIAL ENVIRONMENT

1. Still the best account after many years is Percy W. Bidwell and John I. Falconer, *History of Agriculture in the Northern United States, 1620–1860* (Washington, D.C.: The Carnegie Institution, 1925).

2. Ivan T. Sanderson, *Follow the Whale* (Boston: Little, Brown, 1936), chapters 9 and 10.

3. William T. Baxter, *The House of Hancock: Business in Boston, 1724–1775* (Cambridge, Mass.: Harvard University Press, 1945).

4. Simon Kuznets, *Economic Growth and Structure, Selected Essays* (New York: W. W. Norton, 1965).

5. Edwin J. Perkins, *The Economy of Colonial America* (New York: Columbia University Press, 1988).

6. Nathan Rosenberg and L. E. Birdzell, Jr., *How the West Grew Rich: The Economic Transformation of the Industrial World* (New York: Basic Books, 1986).

7. Jonathan R. T. Hughes, *Social Control in the Colonial Economy* (Charlottesville: University Press of Virginia, 1976).

8. U.S. Department of Commerce, Bureau of the Census, *Historical Statistics of the United States, Colonial Times to 1970* (Washington, D.C.: U.S. Government Printing Office, 1975), chapter 2.

9. Gary M. Walton and James F. Shepard, *The Economic Rise of Early America* (Cambridge: Cambridge University Press, 1979).

3: ENTREPRENEURING PERMANENT OPPORTUNITIES DURING REVOLUTIONARY TIMES

1. Piers MacKesy, *The War for America, 1775–1783* (Cambridge, Mass.: Harvard University Press, 1964).

2. Curtis P. Nettels, *The Emergence of a National Economy, 1775–1815* (New York: Harper & Row, 1962), pp. 8–13.

3. Clarence L. Ver Steeg, *Robert Morris, Revolutionary Financier* (Philadelphia: University of Pennsylvania Press, 1954).
4. Gordon S. Wood, *The Creation of the American Republic, 1776–1787* (New York: W. W. Norton, 1972).
5. James Madison is often credited as the "Father of the Constitution," but much of his influence was at the tangible level of direct application. Mason was more the architect of basic concepts.

4: BUILDING VALUE AS GROUND RULES SHIFT

1. Douglass C. North, *The Economic Growth of the United States, 1790–1860* (Englewood Cliffs, N.J.: Prentice-Hall, 1961).
2. James D. Phillips, *Salem and the Indies* (Boston: Houghton Mifflin, 1947). Samuel Eliot Morison, *The Maritime History of Massachusetts, 1783–1860* (Boston: Houghton Mifflin, 1941).
3. Don R. Adams, Jr. *Finance and Enterprise in Early America: A Study of Stephen Girard's Bank, 1812–1831* (Philadelphia: University of Pennsylvania Press, 1978).
4. Kenneth W. Porter, *John Jacob Astor, Businessman,* 2 vols. (Cambridge, Mass.: Harvard University Press, 1931).
5. George Rogers Taylor, *The Transportation Revolution, 1815–1860* (Harper & Row: New York, 1951).
6. Cynthia O. Philip, *Robert Fulton, a Biography* (New York: Franklin Watts, 1985).
7. Robert L. Thompson, *Wiring a Continent, the History of the Telegraph Industry in the United States, 1832–1866* (Princeton: Princeton University Press, 1947).

5: EXPLOITING THE NEW NATIONAL MARKET

1. Ronald M. Hartwell, *The Causes of the Industrial Revolution in England* (London: Methuen, 1967).
2. Barbara M. Tucker, *Samuel Slater and the Origins of the American Textile Industry* (Ithaca, N.Y.: Cornell University Press, 1984).
3. Robert F. Dalzell, *Enterprising Elite: The Boston Associates and the World They Made* (Cambridge, Mass.: Harvard University Press, 1987).
4. Constance Green, *Eli Whitney and the Birth of American Technology* (Boston: Little, Brown, 1956).

5. Simeon N. D. North, *Simeon North, First Official Pistol Maker of the United States; a Memoir* (Concord, N.H.: Rumford Press, 1913).
6. Jack Rohan, *Yankee Arms Maker: The Incredible Career of Samuel Colt* (New York: Harper & Brothers, 1935).

6: BUILDING LATE-NINETEENTH-CENTURY COMPLEX ENTERPRISES

1. The classic study is Alfred D. Chandler, Jr., *The Visible Hand, The Managerial Revolution in American Business* (Cambridge, Mass.: The Belknap Press of Harvard University Press, 1977).
2. William T. Hutchinson, *Cyrus Hall McCormick,* 2 vols. (New York: Appleton-Century, 1930, 1935).
3. Alfred D. Chandler, Jr., *The Visible Hand, The Managerial Revolution in American Business* (Cambridge, Mass.: The Belknap Press of Harvard University Press, 1977), chapter 9.
4. Oliver E. Williamson, *The Economic Institutions of Capitalism* (New York: Free Press, 1985).

7: ENTREPRENEURS ADJUST TO THE EXPANSIVE ECONOMY

1. Joseph F. Wall, *Andrew Carnegie* (New York: Oxford University Press, 1970). For Carnegie's managerial contributions, Harold C. Livesay, *Andrew Carnegie and the Rise of Big Business* (Boston: Little, Brown, 1975).
2. Allan Nevins, *Study in Power: John D. Rockefeller, Industrialist and Philanthropist* (New York: Scribner's, 1953).
3. Alfred D. Chandler, Jr., *The Visible Hand, The Managerial Revolution in American Business* (Cambridge, Mass.: The Belknap Press of Harvard University Press, 1977), chapter 13.
4. Ford was not so rigid as the legend suggests, but his policy of vehicle design made it very difficult to change. Ford attempted an enclosed cab on the Model T, for example, but the frame was too light to carry an adequate structure.

8: PUBLIC PERCEPTIONS OF ENTREPRENEURS

1. Note the parallel to the international specialization and integration that national economies are undergoing today, commonly called *globalization.*
2. Despite widely publicized instances of foreign advances, the United States still maintains a sizable lead across the board, creating and applying new technology.

3. A zero-sum view is described in Lester Thurow, *The Zero-Sum Society, Distribution and the Possibilities for Economic Change* (New York: Basic Books, 1980). But events suggest it is more a reflection of the author's thinking than the nature of economic conditions.
4. Alfred D. Chandler, Jr., *The Visible Hand, The Managerial Revolution in American Business* (Cambridge, Mass.: The Belknap Press of Harvard University Press, 1977), chapter 10.

9: CREATING OPPORTUNITIES AND CONTROLLING CHOICES

1. Maury Klein, *The Life and Legend of Jay Gould* (Baltimore, Md.: Johns Hopkins University Press, 1986).
2. Lloyd J. Mercer, *E. H. Harriman, Master Railroader* (Boston: Twayne Publications, 1985).

10: DEVELOPING TWENTIETH-CENTURY FINANCIAL MECHANISMS

1. Vincent P. Carosso, *The Morgans: Private International Bankers, 1854–1913* (Cambridge, Mass.: Harvard University Press, 1987).
2. While the United States ran a deficit in foreign trade for 310 years, this was not seen as a weakness in the economy, as recent deficits have been interpreted. The higher productivity of capital in the United States made both American and European investors eager to swap American equities for European goods.

11: MECHANDISING TO A LARGE, AFFLUENT SOCIETY

1. Glenn Porter and Harold C. Livesay, *Merchants and Manufacturers* (Baltimore: Johns Hopkins University Press, 1971).
2. Harold F. Williamson, ed., *The Growth of the American Economy* (New York: Prentice-Hall, 1951), chapter 26.
3. Alfred D. Chandler, Jr., *The Visible Hand, The Managerial Revolution in American Business* (Cambridge, Mass.: The Belknap Press of Harvard University Press, 1977), chapter 7.
4. Boris Emmet, *Catalogues and Counters; a History of Sears, Roebuck and Company* (Chicago: University of Chicago Press, 1950). Gordon L. Weil,

Sears, Roebuck, U.S.A.: The Great American Catalog Store and How It Grew (Briarcliff Manor, N.Y.: Stein & Day, 1977).

5. John F. Love, *McDonald's: Behind the Arches* (Toronto: Bantam Books, 1986). Ray Kroc, *Grinding It Out: The Making of McDonald's* (Chicago: Henry Regnery, 1977).

12: CONSTRUCTING INSTITUTIONS FOR MODERN SCIENCE

1. Ronald W. Clark, *Edison: The Man Who Made the Future* (New York: G. P. Putnam's Sons, 1977). Matthew Josephson, *Edison* (New York: McGraw-Hill, 1959).

2. Leonard S. Reich, *The Making of American Industrial Research: Science and Business at GE and Bell, 1876-1926* (New York: Cambridge University Press, 1985).

3. Alfred D. Chandler, Jr., *The Visible Hand, The Managerial Revolution in American Business* (Cambridge, Mass.: The Belknap Press of Harvard University Press, 1977), pp. 426–433.

4. A now-dated account of the old Du Pont is William S. Dutton, *Du Pont: One Hundred and Forty Years* (New York: Charles Scribner's Sons, 1942).

5. Alfred D. Chandler, Jr., and Stephen Salsbury, *Pierre S. Du Pont and the Making of the Modern Corporation* (New York: Harper & Row, 1971).

13: CREATING TWENTIETH-CENTURY MOBILITY

1. There are, of course, numerous accounts of Henry Ford. The classic treatment is Allan Nevins et al., *Ford,* 3 vols. (New York: Charles Scribner's Sons, 1954, 1957, 1963).

2. Alfred P. Sloan, *My Years with General Motors* (Garden City, N.Y.: Doubleday & Co., 1964), is a fundamental book in management. See also Alfred D. Chandler, Jr., *Giant Enterprise; Ford, General Motors, and the Automobile Industry* (New York: Harcourt, Brace & World, 1964).

14: THE ENTREPRENEURS OF GROWING GOVERNMENT

1. Robert Higgs, *Crisis and Leviathan* (New York: Oxford University Press, 1987).

2. Thomas K. McCraw, *Prophets of Regulation* (Cambridge, Mass.: The Belknap Press, 1984), chapter 1.

3. Ibid., chapter 3.
4. George Soule, *Prosperity Decade, from War to Depression, 1917–1929* (New York: Harper & Row, 1968), chapters 1, 2.
5. Milton Friedman and Anna Schwartz, *The Great Contraction, 1929–1933* (Princeton: Princeton University Press, 1965).
6. James MacGregor Burns, *Roosevelt: The Lion and the Fox* (New York: Harcourt, Brace & Co., 1956).

15: WORKING WITH MATURE GOVERNMENTS

1. Hedrick Smith, *The Power Game: How Washington Works* (New York: Random House, 1988).
2. Dominick T. Armentano, *Antitrust Policy: The Case for Repeal* (Washington, D.C.: Cato Institute, 1986).
3. Thomas J. DiLorenzo, "Classroom Struggle, the Free Market Takeover of Economics Textbooks," *Policy Review* 40 (Spring 1987), pp. 44–49.
4. James Gwartney and Richard Stroup, *Economics: Private and Public Choice* (New York: Academic Press, 1983).

16: AMERICA'S ADVANTAGE IN ENTREPRENEURSHIP

1. Erwin H. Ackerknecht, *A Short History of Medicine* (Baltimore, Md.: Johns Hopkins University Press, 1982).
2. George N. Gordon, *The Communications Revolution: A History of Mass Media in the United States* (New York: Hastings House, 1977).
3. Bob Thomas, *Walt Disney, An American Original* (New York: Simon & Schuster, 1976).
4. Robert Sobel, *I.B.M.: Colossus in Transition* (New York: Times Books, 1981).
5. Thomas J. Peters and Robert H. Waterman, Jr., *In Search of Excellence* (New York: Harper & Row, 1982).

Annotated Bibliography

CASSON, MARK. *The Entrepreneur: An Economic Theory* (Totowa, N.J.: Barnes and Noble, 1982). The best explanation of entrepreneurial behavior that has been built from economic theory.

CHANDLER, ALFRED D., JR. *The Visible Hand, The Managerial Revolution in American Business* (Cambridge, Mass.: The Belknap Press of Harvard University Press, 1977). The classic study of the emergence of large, vertically integrated firms in America. Extensive examples.

DRUCKER, PETER F. *Innovation and Entrepreneurship* (New York: Harper & Row, 1985). Probably the best statement of entrepreneurship as a practice.

GILDER, GEORGE. *The Spirit of Enterprise* (Princeton: Princeton University Press, 1981). A spirited effort to capture the heart and soul of entrepreneurship.

HIGGS, ROBERT. *Crisis & Leviathan* (New York: Oxford University Press, 1987). A standard reference for a serious study of the growth of government.

HUGHES, JONATHAN. *The Vital Few* (New York: Oxford University Press, 1986). Detailed biographies of eight entrepreneurs, including several making important contributions outside the economic sector.

KLEIN, MAURY. *The Life and Legend of Jay Gould* (Baltimore, Md.: Johns Hopkins University Press, 1986). A superb work of history, detailing Gould's contribution as well as the persisting distortions of his record.

LIVESAY, HAROLD C. *American Made* (Boston: Little, Brown, 1979). A spritely account of eight important entrepreneurs in manufacturing.

MC CRAW, THOMAS K. *Prophets of Regulation* (Cambridge, Mass.: The Belknap Press of Harvard University Press, 1984). Four entrepreneurs central to bringing government regulation to America.

MERCER, LLOYD J. *E. H. Harriman, Master Railroader* (Boston: Twayne Publishers, 1985). A clear, quantitative demonstration of Harriman's productive role in railroads.

PETERS, THOMAS J., and ROBERT H. WATERMAN, JR. *In Search of Excellence* (New York: Harper & Row, 1982). The best-selling business book. Extensive, lively examples.

PUSATERI, C. JOSEPH. *A History of American Business* (Arlington Heights, Ill.: Harlan Davidson, Inc., 1984). A good survey of the history of American business.

RONSTADT, ROBERT D. *Entrepreneurship: Text, Cases, and Notes* (Dover, Mass.: Lord Publishing, 1984). An encyclopedic compilation of research and case studies of entrepreneurship.

SLOAN, ALFRED P., JR. *My Years with General Motors* (Garden City, N.Y.: Doubleday & Co., 1964). A classic book in management describing the creation of the General Motors model.

TAYLOR, GEORGE ROGERS. *The Transportation Revolution, 1815–1860* (New York: Harper & Row, 1951). Still an enlightening, detailed account of how transportation opened up the interior of America.

WILLIAMSON, OLIVER E. *The Economic Institutions of Capitalism* (New York: The Free Press, 1985). The best of current research into why businesses adopt particular structures.

Acknowledgments

There is no shortage of books about entrepreneurs these days, so the obvious question is "Why another one?" This volume grew out of frustrations in preparing an earlier effort. That book sought to explain economic growth and the central role it has played in the development of the Western world. Such a study has yet to be adequately reported, which is a costly omission. Not far into my project, I discovered that the critical catalyst for economic growth, which was, of course, the entrepreneur, wasn't itself sufficiently understood. Most recent coverage of entrepreneurs has either misrepresented their role or condemned it to misleading obscurity.

This book attacks the deficiency on parallel fronts. First, it explores entrepreneurship, incorporating the recent major gains of our understanding of that human activity. Second, it applies that understanding in one of the broadest possible workouts, the history of the American economy. Serendipitously, we uncover some insights about the American character and American institutions.

This book really got under way with a grant from the Institute for Educational Affairs to continue my work on economic growth. Arthur Kaufman and Philip Marcus were central to arranging that support. I appreciate their understanding that the focus on entrepreneurship in this volume is an integral step in what proved to be a major, long-term undertaking. This volume has also benefited from the support of the Manhattan Institute, particularly Larry Mone, vice president of research at the Institute, and Robert Higgs, William E. Simon Professor at Lafayette College, who served as an acquiring editor. David Theroux of The Independent Institute of San Francisco has also been helpful.

Here at Trinity College the innumerable drafts, corrections, and modifications of this book have been helped along by the good patience of Susan Sass, Sandra Magee, and Sandra Andrews. I also owe a special thanks to students in Business and Entrepreneurial History at Trinity who offered suggestions that often were implicit in the form of puzzled looks, suggesting ideas that needed further qualification. Finally, I should like to thank Truman Talley, my editor and publisher, who recognized the broader significance of my discussion of nineteenth-century turnpikes in *The Wall Street Journal.*

All major efforts in scholarship of this kind owe a debt to a large number of collaborative scholars, which is impossible to detail. So, those who are not specifically mentioned here will understand that that's the nature of scholarly rewards.

Index